DESIGNING CRIMINAL TRIBUNALS

For our mothers, Sharon and Erika,
whose strength and spirit are a source of inspiration

Designing Criminal Tribunals

Sovereignty and International Concerns in the Protection of Human Rights

STEVEN D. ROPER
Eastern Illinois University
Charleston, IL, USA

LILIAN A. BARRIA
Eastern Illinois University
Charleston, IL, USA

Routledge
Taylor & Francis Group
LONDON AND NEW YORK

First published 2006 by Ashgate Publishing

Reissued 2018 by Routledge
2 Park Square, Milton Park, Abingdon, Oxon, OX14 4RN
711 Third Avenue, New York, NY 10017, USA

Routledge is an imprint of the Taylor & Francis Group, an informa business

First issued in paperback 2018

A Library of Congress record exists under LC control number: 2006003911

ISBN 13: 978-0-815-38849-4 (hbk)
ISBN 13: 978-1-138-61933-3 (pbk)
ISBN 13: 978-1-351-16012-4 (ebk)

Contents

List of Tables

Preface

The genesis of this book began in spring 2002 in an international law and human rights course. While searching for appropriate readings for the course, we noticed that no volume explored the origins, the structure and the influence of all the newly created international and hybrid criminal tribunals. While there had been much written about the International Criminal Tribunal for the former Yugoslavia (ICTY), and to a lesser extent the International Criminal Tribunal for Rwanda (ICTR), far less of the literature focused on the Special Court for Sierra Leone (SCSL), the Serious Crimes Panel for East Timor (SCPET) and the Extraordinary Chambers for Cambodia (ECC). Indeed, no single volume attempted to analyze and compare all the tribunals in order to draw more general lessons concerning their effectiveness in delivering justice and providing reconciliation. The lack of comparative literature forced us to think about what lessons were important to understand in order to place these tribunals within a historical context.

As political scientists and not legal scholars, we saw these institutions as essentially political in nature and as an outcome of nation-state consensus building following the end of the Cold War. However to truly appreciate these institutions and their broader influence requires an understanding of how international humanitarian law has developed as well as the complexity of the crimes which were committed. Therefore over the course of the last three years, we have endeavored to educate ourselves in international law in order to better understand the tribunals and the importance of cases such as *Tadić* and *Akayesu*. As individuals trained as comparativists, this has been a rewarding intellectual experience which has provided much food for thought and allowed us to venture far outside our intellectual comfort zone.

While all the *ad hoc* tribunals are scheduled to cease operations by 2010 (some much sooner than this), the entry into force of the International Criminal Court (ICC) in 2002 will provide scholars, practitioners and organizations ample opportunity to continue to explore issues of justice, sovereignty and reconciliation. The *ad hoc* tribunals are more than a research project – for many they represent the best hope for justice and societal reconciliation. The tribunals have been established in countries in which a total of over one million individuals have perished, and we hope that our account does justice to the memory of those that have died. While examining the legal reasoning of a specific case or the political debate which occurred in the United Nations Security Council, it is sometimes all too easy to forget that thousands upon thousands who lost loved ones are still awaiting justice.

Numerous individuals have assisted us in our journey to understand the tribunals and the memory of those that are gone. We were fortunate to be able to visit The Hague, Cambodia and Indonesia for vital fieldwork, and we want to acknowledge the financial assistance of Dean Mary Anne Hanner of the College of Sciences at Eastern Illinois University as well as the Council for Faculty Research which provided a 2005 Fall and Summer Research Award which allowed Dr. Barria to return to Cambodia in March 2005. In addition, we are grateful to the United States-Indonesia Society for providing a grant which allowed us to travel to Indonesia and the US Embassy in Cambodia for a 2004 Target-of-Opportunity Grant during May 2004. Dr. Roper was on leave during the academic year 2004–2005 at the US Air War College which provided a wonderful environment in which to write and to travel. He wants to thank his colleagues for their support and encouragement. It should be noted that the opinions, conclusions and recommendations expressed or implied within are solely those of the authors and do not necessarily represent the views of Air University, the US Air Force, the Department of Defense or any other US government agency.

Over the last three years, portions of the book have been presented at various conferences and workshops, and we want to thank all those that provided essential comments at the American Political Science Association Annual Meeting in 2004 and 2005, the Midwest Political Science Association Annual Meeting in 2003, 2004 and 2005 as well as the Judging Transitional Justice Workshop in 2004. In addition, portions of the research for this book have appeared in different forms in articles, and we want to thank the editors of the *International Journal of Human Rights*, *Human Rights Review* and the *Journal of Human Rights* for allowing us to use ideas from these publications.

We have greatly benefited from discussions and insights with numerous individuals including US Ambassador Pierre-Richard Prosper, Chief Prosecutor Carla Del Ponte and ICTY President Claude Jorda. In Indonesia we benefited from the assistance of the staff at the Indonesian Legal Aid and Human Rights Association, Ifdhal Kasim, Executive Director of the Institute for Policy Research and Advocacy (ELSAM) and IHRC Judge Roki Panjaitan. In Cambodia, we want to thank Dr. Helen Jarvis, Dr. Kek Galabru, Dina Nay and Sok Sam Oeun, as well as Kevin Doyle and the faculty at the Royal University of Law and Economics. Danilo Carlos at the ICTR and Peter Anderson at the SCSL provided invaluable assistance with data collection. We have also benefited from the assistance of outstanding graduate assistants over the years including Chad Cross, Emin Nabiyev and Arne Romanowski. Finally, we have received encouragement for this project over the years from many colleagues and friends, and we especially want to thank our good friend Joe Profaizer for his advice as well as Dave Wight for always picking our brain and making insightful comments. Discussions always seem more productive over a bottle of Lewelling wine.

About the Authors

Steven D. Roper, (Ph. D. University of Missouri) is an Associate Professor of Political Science and International Studies Coordinator at Eastern Illinois University. He has published widely on post-communist human rights, conflict resolution and party development. He is the author of *Romania: The Unfinished Revolution* (2000).

Lilian A. Barria, (Ph. D. University of Missouri) is an Assistant Professor of Political Science at Eastern Illinois University. She is a member of the Steering Committee of the Human Rights Section of the American Political Science Association. Her research has appeared in various journals including *Human Rights Review* and the *International Journal of Human Rights*.

About the authors

List of Abbreviations

AFRC	Armed Forces Revolutionary Council
ASEAN	Association of Southeast Asian Nations
BiH	Bosnia and Herzegovina
CDF	Civilian Defense Forces
CPK	Communist Party of Kampuchea
CSCE	Conference on Security and Co-operation in Europe
DAC	Development Assistance Committee
DK	Democratic Kampuchea
ECOMOG	Economic Community of West African States Ceasefire Monitoring Group
ECC	Extraordinary Chambers for Cambodia
EU	European Union
Fretilin	*Frente Revolucionaria do Timor-Leste Independente*
ICI	International Commission of Inquiry
ICRC	International Committee of the Red Cross
ICC	International Criminal Court
ICTR	International Criminal Tribunal for Rwanda
ICTY	International Criminal Tribunal for the former Yugoslavia
IHL	International Humanitarian Law
IHRC	Indonesian Human Rights Court
IMT	International Military Tribunal
IMTFE	International Military Tribunal for the Far East
INTERFET	International Force for East Timor
KLA	Kosovo Liberation Army
KOMNAS HAM	National Human Rights Commission
KPP HAM	Commission of Inquiry
NCC	National Consultative Council
NGO	Non-governmental Organization
NPFL	National Patriotic Front of Liberia
OHR	Office of the High Representative
OSCE	Organization for Security and Co-operation in Europe
OTP	Office of the Prosecutor
RoR	Rules of the Road
RS	*Republika Srpska*
RUF	Revolutionary United Front
RPF	Rwandan Patriotic Front
SCPET	Serious Crimes Panel for East Timor
SCSL	Special Court for Sierra Leone

SCU	Serious Crimes Unit
SFOR	Stabilization Force
TNI	Indonesian Military
TRC	Truth and Reconciliation Commission
TRCSL	Truth and Reconciliation Commission for Sierra Leone
UDT	Timorese Democratic Union
UN	United Nations
UNAMIR	United Nations Assistance Mission for Rwanda
UNAMSIL	United Nations Mission in Sierra Leone
UNCHR	United Nations Commission on Human Rights
UNTAC	United Nations Transitional Authority in Cambodia
UNTAET	United Nations Transitional Administration in East Timor
WCC	War Crimes Chamber

Chapter 1

From Impunity to Imprisonment: Individual Accountability under International Law

> Before there could be crimes of war there had to be laws of war. Before there could be laws of war there had to be customs of war. Before there could be customs of war there needed to be some sense that war had limits (Well, 1991, p. 91).

It is difficult today to open a newspaper or watch television without some discussion of international law. The genocide in Darfur marks one of the first test cases for the International Criminal Court (ICC) while coverage of the trials of Slobodan Milošević and Saddam Hussein highlight a new era in which heads of state are held accountable for crimes committed under their watch, many of them against their own citizens. The reporting might leave the impression that international law in regards to human rights and humanitarian issues has developed in a linear fashion with ever increasing codification of the law as well as crafting of institutions of justice. The reality is much more complex—the creation of the ICC occurred more than fifty years after Nuremberg, and while the elements of the crime of genocide are well-defined, other criminal acts have just recently been incorporated into notions of crimes against humanity and war crimes. Even with increased codification, the creation of international tribunals has proven problematic. Indeed for some, the trials of Milošević and Hussein represent flawed justice in which either the defendant has been able to prolong and subvert the process or is a victim of "victor's justice" (Meernik, 2003). International law, tribunals and law enforcement mechanisms have developed unevenly in the 20th century as a reflection of political realities.[1]

The struggle to provide justice for individuals who have been the victims of violations of international humanitarian and human rights law has often been a struggle against nation-state sovereignty (Chopra and Weiss, 1992). Historically, international law regulated the conduct and relationship of states and ignored the individual as a subject of the law. The only area of international law that systematically addressed violations of individual rights by states concerned actions by governments against citizens of other states, and it was mostly silent on mandating specific consequences for perpetrators.[2] During the Cold War, heads of state could act with impunity against their own citizens because of the lack of consensus among United Nations (UN) Security Council members (Mingst and Karns, 2000). During this period, heads of state, as individuals, could use state sovereignty to justify actions and as a shield against criminal charges. It is not surprising that the first of the post-Nuremberg war crimes tribunals to deal with human rights violations and humanitarian atrocities was formed only after the end of the Cold War. However, the end of the Cold War has not created a consensus for a "New World Order." While there have been several war crimes tribunals established since 1993, only two have been created under UN Chapter VII authority which provides guaranteed financing as well as a requirement for state cooperation. In addition while the ICC has been overwhelmingly supported by the international community, states such as the US, China and India remain outside of the system (Mayerfeld, 2003). Finally, the "war on terror" has led to a bitter debate over the protection of rights and definitions of citizenship and soldier. The use of the term "enemy combatant" by the Bush administration in order to avoid obligations under the Geneva Conventions is just one of many examples in which the precepts of international law are being undermined by often legitimate fears of terrorism. In this book, we argue that legal concerns are embedded within a political process (either domestic or international) in which rights and obligations are re-defined based on political necessity.

To hold individuals accountable for their crimes under international law in a meaningful way requires the creation and the implementation of mechanisms designed to provide justice. Despite sporadic efforts to establish a permanent international tribunal, the ICC did not emerge until the late 1990s. Instead, states have established *ad hoc* international criminal tribunals, with the Nuremberg Tribunal the most historically significant until the International Criminal Tribunal for the former Yugoslavia (ICTY). This book examines all the *ad hoc* tribunals created since the early 1990s, including the ICTY, the International Criminal Tribunal for Rwanda (ICTR), the Special Court for Sierra Leone (SCSL), the Extraordinary Chambers for Cambodia (ECC) and the Special Crimes Panel for East Timor (SCPET) as well as the Indonesian Human Rights Court (IHRC) which was a purely domestic response to the human rights violations in East Timor. All these tribunals have been created in order to provide mechanisms to address accusations of war crimes, crimes against humanity and genocide under international law.

The institutions of justice that we discuss in this book have provided the greatest impetus for the development and clarification of international law since World War II. The statutes of the ICTY and the ICTR have advanced the codification of international law, and the early decisions of the ICTY and the ICTR have played an authoritative role in clarifying international legal principles. Each *ad hoc* tribunal has influenced the jurisprudence and practice of others as well as national courts, the ICC[3] and even the International Court of Justice (ICJ). In addition, establishing tribunals for Sierra Leone, East Timor and Cambodia also demonstrated the international community's commitment to end impunity beyond the former Yugoslavia and Rwanda.

However, these tribunals represent a political compromise within the international community concerning issues of sovereignty, finance and authority and reflect a changing political consensus. States have to cooperate in order to carry out a successful prosecution before an international tribunal. Cooperation has to be secured from the state where the atrocities took place as well as other states with custody of potential defendants and evidence. Where the offenders have been defeated unconditionally, as in Nazi Germany after World War II, these considerations may not pose a significant problem. However, where the offenders retain some degree of political power or remain outside the government's reach, prosecutions before an international tribunal become considerably more problematic.

The four international and one purely domestic tribunal that we analyze were established within a decade of each other; however, there are a number of organizational, legal and financial differences among them. These variations in institutional design were not necessarily based on considerations of how to improve the delivery of justice but often on political and financial concerns. This is not surprising as the history of the Nuremberg and the Tokyo tribunals also reflected prevailing political alignments in which notions of justice were often a secondary concern of states. In this book, we examine both the political realities of these institutions as well as their legal and judicial underpinnings. One of the issues that we frequently explore is how the political compromise which established these tribunals impacted the delivery of justice for victims and the rights of the accused. In short, this book is about the international community, states, victims and defendants. In order to understand the prosecutions discussed in subsequent chapters, we first provide some core definitions of the various subfields of international law in order to place the tribunals within a general legal framework.

The Rationale and Fields of International Law

The focus of this book is on crimes that were committed under international humanitarian law, previously known as the laws of war. The four Geneva Conventions and their Additional Protocols, as well as the Hague Conventions, are the most well-known treaties which cover humanitarian law. These laws define the conduct and the responsibilities of belligerent and neutral states as well as individuals engaged in warfare in relation to each other and to protected persons (*e.g.*, civilians). There are also other customary, unwritten rules of war many of which were explored at the Nuremberg trials. Humanitarian law applies during a period of armed conflict and seeks to limit the suffering caused by war and protect those who have fallen into the hands of an adversary. The law's primary focus is to safeguard the rights of combatants, prisoners of war and civilians. Unfortunately, the historical evolution of international humanitarian law has been characterized by two contradictory trends. While there has been enormous progress in the codification of the law, gross violations continue to occur, particularly in recent armed conflicts where there has been an alarming increase in the types of atrocities and the number of victims.

International human rights law codifies legal provisions governing general human rights in various instruments including the UN Declaration of Human Rights. Human rights law begins to be codified after World War II and can apply either during a time of war or peace, but is primarily concerned with protecting citizens against government violations of their UN-recognized civil, political and social rights.

While the two forms of international law are distinct, the core crimes contained in the fourth Geneva Convention regarding civilians as well as in the UN Declaration are often the same as both laws begin to intersect after World War II. Both forms of law seek to protect individuals from harm and maintain human dignity. Crimes such as rape and genocide are elements found in both humanitarian and human rights law, and therefore the difference between these forms of international law has less to do with the criminal element than the circumstances in which the crime occurred (*i.e.*, whether during war or peace).

While there is a consensus regarding the use of the terms humanitarian and human rights law, the use of "international criminal law" is subject to controversy. Ratner and Abrams (2001) argue that international criminal law deals with international crimes and the tribunals established to adjudicate cases in which persons have incurred international criminal responsibility. While some refuse to use the term, most legal scholars agree that a recognizable body of international criminal law does exist, but the boundaries of this body of law are often unclear. In this book, we use the term international criminal law to refer to those international humanitarian law crimes which are being prosecuted by the tribunals. We also use the more common and less specific term "war crimes" to cover a broad range of crimes committed under humanitarian law including rape, torture and genocide.

There are a number of reasons given as to why under international humanitarian law individuals should be held accountable. First, the pursuit of accountability serves to provide victims with a sense of justice and closure. Second in transitional regimes, accountability can help promote national reconciliation and help society come to terms with the reasons why the law was violated. Third, accountability may deter future violations either by demonstrating to those contemplating such violations the prospect of punishment or more generally by promoting justice, government reform and the rule of law. Finally, the rehabilitation of the offender is regarded as an essential result of accountability and reconciliation. What follows is an overview of the historical evolution of international law and more specifically humanitarian law including the establishment of the Nuremberg and Tokyo tribunals. This historical discussion serves to highlight issues that have not only influenced the evolution of the law but also the institutions created to adjudicate the law including the post-Cold War tribunals which have been constrained by some of the political considerations outlined below.

The Development of International Humanitarian Law before World War II

The regulation of the conduct of war has been a product of domestic and international concerns for centuries but was only codified in the past 150 years. The first major attempt to codify the laws of war was the Lieber Code[4] which was prepared during the US Civil War and promulgated by President Abraham Lincoln in 1863 (Schindler, 2003). Although it was binding only on US forces, the Lieber Code influenced the further codification of the laws of war and the adoption of similar regulations by other nation-states. The Code ultimately formed the basis for the International

Declaration Concerning Laws and Customs of War agreed to at the Brussels Conference of 1874 which led to the adoption of the Hague Conventions on land warfare of 1899 and 1907. At the same time that the Lieber Code was passed in the US, the first International Red Cross Conference was held to address the treatment of prisoners of war, leading to the first Geneva Convention of 1864. These early treaties covered issues concerning the conduct of war such as appropriate weaponry and targets as well as the status of neutrality. They also prohibited the attack of undefended towns, arms which would cause unnecessary suffering, poisonous weapons and included various protections for hospitals, religious and cultural sites as well as family honor. In general, the Hague Conventions regulate the conduct of hostilities while the Geneva Conventions regulate the protection of victims of war. While the codification of international humanitarian law began to advance in the 19th and early 20th centuries, the treaties on the laws of war unfortunately failed to provide protection to civilians during World War I.

At the close of the War in 1919, the Allies appointed a Commission on the Responsibility of the Authors of the War and on Enforcement of Penalties. The Commission was directed to investigate war crimes and to recommend appropriate action against Germany and its allies (Blakesley, 1994). As part of the recommendations of the Commission, the Treaty of Versailles had three articles providing for the creation of an Allied military tribunal for individuals accused of violating the laws and customs of war. While a majority endorsed the recommendations of the Commission, the US representatives objected to the tribunal on the grounds that such a court had no precedent in international law and that international custom prescribed that the soldiers be tried by courts in their own country. Furthermore, the US refused to accept the application of the doctrine of superior responsibility to high officials in government whereby an individual could be prosecuted for having failed to prevent a criminal action. The idea behind the doctrine of superior responsibility was that a leader is responsible for the acts of subordinates if they knew or should have known that a subordinate had committed or was about to commit the acts and that they did not take necessary and reasonable measures to prevent the acts or punish the subordinate. Therefore, this first attempt at an international tribunal to enforce the laws of war was not successful.

Eventually as a political compromise, the Allies consented to allow the Supreme Court of the Reich of Leipzig to try the war crimes cases. The Court only tried twelve individuals out of a list of 900 which was submitted by the Allies. Even with the small number of defendants before the Court, several obstacles hindered the Leipzig trials. In the first place, many Allies, including the US, doubted that anyone could be tried for a war crime unless the defendant's country first criminalized the act. Second, custom dictated that soldiers be tried under the military code of their country rather than under the precepts of the laws of war. Finally, it was asserted that the Geneva Convention of 1864 and the Hague Conventions of 1899 and 1907 did not cover the crimes for which the defendants were charged. While the German defendants were charged for criminal acts drawn from various state legal codes, they were ultimately given light sentences which further demonstrated the inability of states to hold individuals accountable for their actions. The failure to create an Allied military tribunal as well as the sentences delivered during the Leipzig trials demonstrated that state sovereignty still superseded international humanitarian law and thwarted the creation of an effective mechanism for adjudication (Bass, 2000).

The interwar years did not lead to major developments in the laws of war. While the 1928 Kellogg-Briand Pact outlawed war, the Pact only regulated state behavior by criminalizing aggression and specifically excluded the actions of individuals. Under the leadership of the International Committee of the Red Cross (ICRC), a new Geneva Convention was drafted in 1929 dealing with the treatment of prisoners of war, but efforts to revise the Hague Conventions met with resistance by states. Success proved elusive with respect to the most important problem, namely the protection of civilians against the effects of war, especially aerial warfare. Several proposals were drafted, but none led to the adoption of a binding convention, and thus no treaty for the protection of civilians existed during World War II. However, the horrific abuses of the Holocaust finally forced states to end impunity for individual actions under the laws of war.

The Aftermath of World War II: The Nuremberg Tribunal

In October 1943, a War Crimes Commission was established to begin gathering evidence on war crimes committed by Germany and other states during World War II. On 8 August 1945, an agreement was reached among the Allies for the prosecution and punishment of major war criminals (Meltzer, 2002). In order to avoid a repetition of what had occurred at Leipzig whereby states asserted the right of sovereignty in regards to the prosecution of criminal acts, changes were enacted regarding who could conduct the Nuremberg trials. The Allies took the position that at the close of the war, no German or Japanese government existed and that they constituted the official German and Japanese governments. Thus, the Allies could, in accordance with international custom, organize the proceedings and conduct the trials (ultimately, an assertion of sovereignty). Based on the Leipzig experience, one of the important issues that was addressed before the trials was to identify the appropriate elements of international law which the Axis powers violated. The laws claimed to have been violated needed to have preceded the crimes in question in order to avoid a possible claim of the application of *ex post facto* laws (Tusa and Tusa, 1986).

Article VI of the Charter of the International Military Tribunal (IMT, also known as the Nuremberg Charter) listed the charges under which the accused were to be tried. The charges incorporated under the term "war crimes" included violations of the laws of war, such as the maltreatment of prisoners of war, civilians in occupied countries and devastation not justified by military necessity. In addition, the charges included what was called "crimes against humanity" which addressed the treatment of civilians, especially the attempt to exterminate a group on religious, political or racial grounds. Finally, "crimes against the peace" were also included which involved the planning and waging of an "aggressive war."[5] The Nuremberg Charter relied on the Hague Conventions, the Geneva Conventions and the Kellogg-Briand Pact as sources of recognition of the illegality and criminality of aggressive war.

Article VI of the IMT Charter provided for prosecution of war crimes and crimes against humanity defined as:

> [V]iolations of the laws or customs of war. Such violations shall include, but not be limited to, murder, ill-treatment or deportation of slave labour or for any other purpose of civilian population of or in occupied territory, murder or ill-treatment of prisoners of war or persons on the seas; killing of hostages, plunder of public or private property, wanton destruction of cities, town or village, or devastation not justified by military necessity. [M]urder, extermination, enslavement, deportation, and other inhumane acts committed against any civilian population, before or during the war, or persecution on political racial or religious grounds in execution of or in connection with any crime within the jurisdiction of the Tribunal, whether or not in violation of the domestic law of the country where perpetuated.

The conception of crimes against humanity was that government leaders who authorized torture or genocide against their own population were criminally responsible under international law and could be punished. For the first time, it could be said that individuals had a "right" to be treated humanely by their own governments—heads of state could not hide behind sovereignty as an excuse for state action or inaction in regards to citizens. In addition, other governments now also had a duty to uphold these individual rights by trying the perpetuators who were under their jurisdiction (Taylor, 1992). For the US, crimes against the peace were the chief offense of the Nazis, and the criminality of aggressive war needed to be enshrined in international law.[6] The IMT Charter also eliminated the defense of act of state immunity, superior orders and re-asserted the notion of superior responsibility. Article VII of the IMT affirmed that the leaders of the state were not exempt from criminal liability even when acting in their official capacity. Article VIII stated that obedience to superior orders did not constitute a basis for defense.

The Nuremberg Tribunal was composed of four judges, and conviction required a majority vote. The mandate of the Tribunal was for one year, and during this period, it conducted the trial of twenty-four German defendants. Nineteen were found guilty, and twelve were sentenced to death. Wasserstrom (1974) argues that in some respects, there were really two Nurembergs: The Nuremberg *Charter* and the judgments of the Nuremberg *Tribunal*. While the Charter rejected the defense of superior orders, the Tribunal allowed defendants to plead duress, and it also created a separate crime of conspiracy (only for the commission of crimes against the peace).

The Aftermath of World War II: The Tokyo Tribunal

The International Military Tribunal for the Far East (IMTFE) was established by proclamation of General Douglas MacArthur on 16 January 1946 to try Japanese accused of various atrocities committed during World War II (Brackman, 1987). The Charter of the IMTFE defined the jurisdiction of the Tribunal as well as its legal procedures. During the war, both the US and the UK had expected the Japanese government to abide by the provisions of the 1929 Geneva Convention on the treatment of prisoners of war. The first formal warning to Japan that the government was not abiding by the Convention followed the signing of the Inter-Allied Declaration on Punishment of War Crimes in January 1942. Indeed, evidence presented at the IMTFE showed that the Allies had repeatedly filed complaints with the Japanese authorities during the war concerning gross violations of the laws of war.

The Potsdam Declaration in July 1945 established the statute for the trial and punishment of Japanese war criminals. Article V of the IMTFE Charter empowered the Tribunal to try and punish Japanese charged with war crimes, including "crimes against peace: namely, the planning preparation, initiation or waging of a declared or undeclared war of aggression, or a war in violation of international law, treaties, agreements or assurances, or participation in a common plan or conspiracy for the accomplishment of any of the foregoing." The IMTFE also exercised jurisdiction over violations of the laws or customs of war and crimes against humanity or inhumane acts committed before or during the war mainly against non-Japanese civilian populations. The IMTFE, however, insisted that it would only hear cases in which the defendant was charged with offenses including crimes against the peace. All other defendants were to be tried by other courts. The Nuremberg Charter contained no such provision; however, like the Nuremberg Charter, the IMTFE Charter relied on the Hague Conventions, the Geneva Conventions and the Kellogg-Briand Pact as sources of recognition of the illegality and criminality of aggressive war. Article XIII of the IMTFE Charter dealt at length with the question of evidence. The Allies recognized the unique character of these war crimes trials and the need to modify the normal strict rules of evidence. Therefore, the IMTFE extended its scope beyond the boundaries set by the technical rules of evidence and adopted instead an evidentiary standard which admitted any evidence which the Tribunal deemed to have probative value (Lee, 2003).

The Tribunal consisted of eleven judges, and all decisions, including conviction and sentencing, required a majority vote of those members present.[7] A total of twenty-eight Japanese were indicted,[8] and defendants were selected based on whether they could be charged with crimes against peace, were representatives of the Japanese government, and whether they had a position of leadership and had primary responsibility for the violations charged. All of the defendants were convicted with seven receiving a death sentence.[9] Allied prosecutors excluded from indictment representatives of the Japanese industrial group or *zaibatsu* as well as Emperor Hirohito. The decision to exclude these individuals was not a judicial decision but rather a political and an economic decision as the *zaibatsu* and Emperor Hirohito were deemed vital to the post-war re-building efforts.

The Aftermath of the Nuremberg and Tokyo Tribunals

How should history judge the role of the Nuremberg and the Tokyo tribunals in codifying international humanitarian law and providing a judicial mechanism for justice? Many legal scholars argue that the trials had no actual basis in international law and that they did not establish a long-term human rights precedent. The offenses for which the Germans and the Japanese were tried did not exist in law. Tradition had required soldiers to obey the order of their superiors, and it was customary to exonerate individual soldiers from actions taken while following orders. In addition, there was no clear definition which distinguished between an aggressive versus a defensive war, one of the major charges by the Allies against the defeated German and Japanese forces. Ultimately, the Nuremberg and Tokyo tribunals were viewed by politicians as unique institutions established for a specific set of circumstances rather than as precedent-setting (Hodosa *et. al.*, 1986).

That being said, the Nuremberg and Tokyo tribunals contributed to the expansion of the definition and application of the term "war crimes" and the further codification of international law. The Allies chose not to restrict the term to violations of the laws of war or offenses against civilians. Instead, after some initial disagreement, the definition was expanded to include what they considered to be the greatest crime against civilization: The plotting and waging of an aggressive war which was indiscriminate and ignored the normal protections afforded to civilians. The Nuremberg trials also altered the legal landscape of the laws of war by establishing individual responsibility for violations of the laws or customs of war. In addition, the Nuremberg and Tokyo tribunals represented a first effort by the international community to create a judicial mechanism for addressing the atrocities that can be committed during war.

The further codification of international humanitarian law continued throughout the post-World War II period and overlapped with the newly emerging precepts of human rights law. However, the immediate post-World War II period saw little desire on the part of states to create an international legal infrastructure which would be authorized to deal with individual culpability. The UN and the ICJ created a legal structure which regulated the behavior of states *vis-à-vis* other states and non-citizens; however, no international court was established which regulated the conduct of states *vis-à-vis* their own citizens and which held heads of state accountable for actions committed during a time of war or peace. While judicial institutions were not crafted to deal with abuses, the further codification of international law helped develop a broader state consensus which ultimately was necessary for the creation of the ICTY and other international tribunals at the end of the 20th century (Robertson, 2000).

Emerging from the Holocaust, governments and human rights organizations have generally viewed genocide as the most heinous "international criminal crime." Genocide has been typically regarded as an element of crimes against humanity, but unlike the other crimes against humanity, it has been authoritatively codified in a single widely accepted international instrument, the Genocide Convention of 1948. Article I declares genocide to be a crime under international law whether committed in time of war or peace. This distinguishes genocide from war crimes or crimes against peace as discussed at Nuremberg. Article II of the Convention defines genocide to include a number of acts committed with the intention of destroying a national, ethnic, racial or religious group. The Genocide Convention's definition of genocide enjoys the status of custom or universal acceptance (Baehr, 2001). However until the 1990s, there were few actual prosecutions of this crime. The creation of international tribunals has generally lagged behind the codification of international law. While the post-World War II period witnessed important advances in international humanitarian law, there was no accompanying legal infrastructure in which to try cases.

For example, when the UN's International Law Commission selected topics for codification at its first session in 1949, the majority of the Commission declared their opposition to the further codification and development of sanctions associated with the Hague Conventions. They were, however, receptive to further defining the Geneva Conventions. In 1949, the Geneva Conventions were revised at the initiative of the ICRC. To the three Conventions on wounded, sick, shipwrecked and prisoners of war was added a fourth Convention on the protection of civilian persons in time of war.

The Conventions were adopted a few months after the proclamation of the 1948 UN Declaration of Human Rights. Ultimately, the attention paid to human rights and protections granted to individuals both in time of war and peace has led to the gradual transformation of the laws of war into a human rights-oriented law. This can already be seen in the 1949 Conventions which speak of the rights of protected persons instead of only imposing obligations on belligerents. Furthermore, Common Article 3 discussed the protections and rights that individuals have in the event of an internal armed conflict, an issue which was traditionally regulated by human rights provisions. Ultimately, the previously unknown term "international humanitarian law" was introduced by the ICRC in the early 1950s largely replacing the term "laws of war."

While numerous treaties were signed over the next four decades, including the Covenants on Civil and Political Rights and on Economic and Social Rights, the major problem with these and other human rights accords was the absence in the text of any specific obligation for states to prosecute and punish human rights violators. Instead, these two covenants, as well as other international documents, contain less precise obligations to "respect and ensure to all individuals within its territory and subject jurisdiction the rights recognized [therein], and to provide an effective remedy for violations thereof." By the mid-1950s, Cold War politics and the assertion of state sovereignty undermined attempts of enforcing obligations on states and political leaders.

In the 1960s, the process of de-colonization brought new attention to international humanitarian and human rights law. During wars of "national liberation," there was an alarming increase in the number of civilian victims (Ishay, 2004). The UN General Assembly adopted several resolutions demanding that wars of national liberation be regarded as international armed conflicts in which the Geneva Conventions were fully applicable and that freedom fighters be treated as prisoners of war. However, it would take another decade before two additional protocols were added to the Geneva Conventions. The 1977 Additional Protocols improved the protection afforded civilian populations against the effects of war. They confirmed the customary principle that the parties to armed conflicts have to distinguish at all times between civilians and combatants and between civilian objects and military objectives. Protocol I set out a new definition of armed forces and combatants to minimize the distinction between regular and irregular forces, and Protocol II elaborated rules on non-international conflicts.

The Additional Protocols were an important development in international humanitarian law as most conflicts were internal and either a product of de-colonization or due to the instability of post-colonial state-building. Indeed in many new states, tribal, ethnic and religious divisions erupted after the withdrawal of colonial powers. Therefore by the late 1970s, there was a legal basis for dealing with internal armed conflict and the resultant humanitarian problems. However, while the Security Council under Chapter VII authority had the right and the responsibility to protect international peace and security, Cold War politics limited the application of its authority in situations which were deemed essentially internal. The Security Council proved an ineffective enforcement mechanism of international humanitarian and human rights law precisely because Cold War politics was based on "spheres of influence" in which state sovereignty was more important than individual rights. This is not to say that there were no attempts to deal with human rights abuses during the Cold War. The use of truth and reconciliation commissions (TRCs) in Latin America and the economic blockade of Apartheid South Africa in the 1980s are just two examples. However, these were state-based solutions for human rights abuses not an international effort that supported the enforcement of international humanitarian and human rights law.

The Post-Cold War Period

The end of the Cold War allowed both states and the Security Council to become a more effective mechanism for the enforcement of international law. Perhaps the most important development in the post-Cold War period was the decision of the Security Council that large-scale violations of human rights and the resulting human suffering constituted a threat to international peace and security and required measures under Chapter VII of the UN Charter. This recognition was unfortunately all too necessary as the end of the Cold War did not usher in a "New World Order" but instead a "New World Disorder" in which internal conflicts that had previously been kept under control by totalitarian regimes or outside powers erupted into some of the worse human rights violations witnessed since the Holocaust. Atrocities such as genocide, ethnic cleansing, forced displacement, starvation of civilians, denial of humanitarian assistance as well as deliberate attacks against civilians and humanitarian personnel led to worldwide concern, and it was quickly realized that such situations could not be brought under control without action by the international community.

On the basis of this realization, the Security Council not only authorized the use of force to assist with humanitarian disasters but also established two *ad hoc* international criminal tribunals for the former Yugoslavia and for Rwanda. In establishing these two *ad hoc* tribunals, the Security Council went beyond purely military measures, convinced that judicial bodies to address the violations of humanitarian and human rights law would contribute to the restoration and maintenance of peace. These tribunals gave a renewed impetus to further defining and elaborating international criminal law. The entry into force of the ICC in 2002 as a permanent criminal court overcomes many, but certainly not all, of the enforcement and logistical problems that have plagued the *ad hoc* tribunals.

In the post-Cold War period, many states have also enacted legislation for the prosecution of persons having committed violations of international humanitarian and human rights law. The efforts by Spain to arrest and extradite former Chilean dictator General Augusto Pinochet from Great Britain was the first time since Nuremberg that a former head of state faced prosecution for human rights violations. In the last decade, we have seen the progressive assimilation of the law of internal conflicts and the law of international armed conflicts. The legal distinction between the two types of conflict has gradually lost its importance and all humanitarian law treaties adopted since 1995 have been made applicable to both forms of conflict.

While the acceptance of international humanitarian law has evolved over time with more states adhering to its principles, the reality is that over the last twenty years we have seen widespread violations of the law with often horrendous consequences for victims. One of the main causes of the present-day non-observance of international humanitarian law is that most armed conflicts are internal conflicts which create a problem in distinguishing between combatants and civilians. A further reason for the non-observance lies in the inclination of parties to armed conflicts to consider their war as a *just war* directed against a party violating the law. These parties believe that they have accordingly more rights and fewer duties than their opponents. Therefore, the codification of international humanitarian law must be accompanied by the creation of judicial institutions in order to try cases of non-observance and hopefully prevent further acts.

The Logic of this Book

This chapter has provided a legal and political examination of the development of international humanitarian and human rights law in order to be able to understand the institutional, the legal and the historical basis of the post-Cold War international criminal tribunals. We argue throughout this book that these tribunals are legal institutions embedded within a political environment in which the need for nation-state consensus can undermine their judicial effectiveness and ultimately the quest for justice under international humanitarian and human rights law. One theme that we examine in this book is how the demands of state sovereignty and finance have contributed to the constant innovation of these tribunals. Indeed within a period of less than a decade, we have witnessed three periods in the evolution of tribunals in which tribunals transformed from purely international to hybrid and finally into purely domestic institutions. These developments have often not been based on considerations of how to best provide justice to victims but rather have been based on the need to forge a political consensus.

In Chapter 2, we discuss the issues surrounding the creation of the ICTY and the ICTR. Of all the tribunals examined in this book, these are the only two that are authorized as subsidiary organs of the UN through Chapter VII authority. These tribunals were established to deal with some of the worse human rights abuses seen since World War II. The number of individuals that were murdered in the former Yugoslavia and Rwanda exceeds one million, and the genocidal intentions of the perpetrators recalls the horrors of the Holocaust. While these tribunals were initially ineffective in apprehending and trying the most important suspects, the ICTR and especially the ICTY have become much more effective legal institutions. For many, however, the costs of these two tribunals, in excess of $4.5 billion, reflects gross administrative waste, incompetence and a subversion of state sovereignty.

As a result of these issues, the international community by 2000 established a new form of tribunal called a "mixed" or "hybrid" in which the state collaborates with the international community in establishing the legal guidelines, chooses judges and prosecutors and shares in the financial burdens. Significantly, none of the tribunals established for Sierra Leone, East Timor and Cambodia are based on Chapter VII authority. As discussed in Chapter 3 and 4, these tribunals represent a compromise within the international community and between the states and the community in regards to legal codes and organizational structure. Finally, the establishment of the IHRC in Jakarta to try individuals for human rights violations in East Timor represents a return to state sovereignty.

East Timor represents an interesting case in which individuals have been charged with the same crimes by both a hybrid as well as purely domestic tribunal. The criticisms of the IHRC that we note in Chapter 4 are hardly surprising given the political environment in which the trials were conducted. In the three case study chapters, we explore the nature of the conflict, the political debate and negotiations concerning the establishment of the tribunal, the tribunal's organizational and legal statutes and finally examine the overall record of the tribunal in ending impunity as well as providing reconciliation to the society. We are particularly concerned with what role these tribunals play in the efforts to enforce international humanitarian and human rights law. While this is a book concerning primarily international tribunals, we also address the role of TRCs as a concomitant process in Sierra Leone as well as the use of national courts in the former Yugoslavia and Rwanda. We organize the three case study chapters by examining the tribunals comparatively based on certain issues rather than as a singular instance. We believe that a comparison of the conflicts, actions by the international community and the legal organization and cases of the institutions allows us to draw similarities and differences among tribunals.

The last three chapters explore the tribunals thematically and focus on issues of finance, termination and justice. In Chapter 5, we explore in greater detail the financing of international justice. We examine the factors that are associated with funding the tribunals and address why countries voluntarily contribute to the tribunals, especially in the case of those which have guaranteed funding through Chapter VII such as the ICTY and the ICTR. While we argue that the funding of tribunals can be viewed as a form of foreign assistance, we find that voluntary contributions for these tribunals do not accord with traditional motivations of donor countries and might be better explain by political calculations. Undoubtedly, funding is a major consideration when establishing and continuing these judicial bodies.

Chapter 6 explores the Completion Strategies of the ICTY and the ICTR. Both tribunals are scheduled to complete their activities by 2010. In order to accomplish this goal, the international community has urged the tribunals to transfer cases to the national court system as well as use plea bargaining in order to reduce the case backlog. Some argue that returning cases to the national court system serves to strengthen the system by requiring judicial training as well as more clear legal procedures. Especially in post-conflict societies, national courts can continue the process of incorporating and enforcing the precepts of international law. Others argue, however, that the Completion Strategies are motivated primarily by a desire on the part of the international community to reduce its financial obligation to the tribunals and that the Completion Strategies create "junk justice" (Zoglin, 2005).

Chapter 7 concludes our discussion by examining the critical issue of how effective the tribunals have been in providing justice. This is a very contentious issue among scholars, states and the non-governmental community. Using the "black letter law" tradition, we analyze the key resolutions of the ICTY and the ICTR and the number of actual indictments, trials and convictions in order to assess the effectiveness of the tribunals. In addition, we explore whether hybrid tribunals might actually be a more preferred form, and whether the SCSL, the ECC and the SCPET serve a judicial capacity-building function which is more cost effective and superior to purely international tribunals. We also look at the purely domestic process in Indonesia and its strengths and weaknesses. We conclude the chapter by considering the role that the tribunals have played in the creation of the ICC, and whether this institution provides a superior mechanism to achieve justice. We include appendices which cover the resolutions referred to in the chapters and an appendix which summarizes the structure, jurisdiction and composition of the various tribunals.

As *political* as well as *legal* institutions, tribunals in all their forms have a number of limitations. However, there can be little doubt that the emerging international consensus which resulted in the creation of the ICTY in 1993 further consolidated and led to the adoption of the ICC by 1998. While the *ad hoc* tribunals have often been criticized for not fulfilling their broad-ranging mandates, they have made an important contribution to the development of international law and institutions. History will look back on the decade of the 1990s as a milestone in the protection of human rights and the elimination of a culture of state and individual impunity.

Notes

1. Generally speaking, international tribunals are part of the larger notion of the legal enforcement of human rights. However in this book, we use the term enforcement in a more narrow sense to apply only to law enforcement agencies that are charged with the apprehension of defendants. We dedifferentiate between international tribunals as judicial bodies and law enforcement agencies in order to emphasize the difficulty of enforcement even with an international tribunal (a particular problem which plagued the ICTY until the early 2000s).
2. These laws include the law of state responsibility for injury to aliens and the laws and customs of war.
3. The broad geographic jurisdiction of the ICC will allow it to play an even more important role in advancing the implementation and elaboration of international law.
4. The Lieber Code is also known as the Lieber Instructions as well as General Orders No. 100.
5. The British maintained that only war crimes were proper charges and that crimes against the peace and crimes against humanity had no precedent in law.
6. The only internationally accepted definition of crimes against the peace is in the IMT Charter. It incorporates two notions: Direct planning and waging of aggressive war as well as the conspiracy to do so.
7. In order for proceedings to occur, a quorum of six was required.
8. Of the twenty-eight defendants charged, two died before judgment, and one was released due to insanity.
9. For a detailed critique of the Tokyo Tribunal see, Minear (1971).

Chapter 2

History in the Making: The International Criminal Tribunal for the former Yugoslavia and the International Criminal Tribunal for Rwanda

The 1990s witnessed the greatest developments in international humanitarian law[1] in fifty years. The creation of the International Criminal Tribunal for the former Yugoslavia (ICTY) and the International Criminal Tribunal for Rwanda (ICTR) represented significant advancements in the interpretation and implementation of international law. The ICTY and the ICTR are the first post-Cold War institutions established based on a new international consensus regarding individual accountability for crimes committed during war and peace. With the creation of additional tribunals in the early 2000s, it is easy to forget how the ICTY and the ICTR are truly historic institutions which represent the best intentions of the international community. However as institutions established by states, these tribunals exist within a political environment in which sovereignty and concerns over cooperation and financing often conflict with the delivery of justice.

This chapter is organized into three sections. First, we outline the nature of the conflict in the former Yugoslavia and Rwanda and the international response to these conflicts. Next, we analyze the debate over the creation of the tribunals, and conclude by examining the structure of the tribunals and their initial problems in organizing the rules of procedure. The comparison of the conflicts, actions by the international community and the legal organization and cases of the institutions allows us to draw similarities and differences between the two tribunals. Because of the importance of these ribunals as the first post-Cold War institutions to address gross violations of human rights, we further examine their institutional and their judicial characteristics in the three concluding thematic chapters of the book. In Chapter 5, we analyze the ongoing debate concerning the financing of the tribunals. The international community through the United Nations (UN) has spent $4.5 billion on these tribunals, and this has become a source of political conflict among UN member-states. In Chapter 6, we examine the Completion Strategy for the ICTY and the ICTR and the development of national courts as venues for trying war crimes. While strengthening the national court system in post-conflict states is an important goal in the continued effort to protect human rights, it is questionable whether the national courts in the former Yugoslavia and Rwanda have sufficient ability to try complex war crimes cases. Finally in Chapter 7, we turn to the important issue concerning the effectiveness of these tribunals. While the ICTY and the ICTR were initially unsuccessful in apprehending high-ranking suspects, pressure from the European Union (EU), the US and the UN has led to most indictees being captured or voluntarily surrendering with the trials of Slobodan Milošević and Biljana Plavšić and the pending trial of Ante Gotovina the most important since Nuremburg and Tokyo.

The Conflict in the former Yugoslavia

The conflict in the former Yugoslavia between Serbia, Croatia and Bosnia-Herzegovina (BiH) was an international war between the former republics of Yugoslavia.[2] However, it was also a civil war in BiH, as Bosnian Croats, Bosnian Serbs and Bosnian Muslims (also known as Bosniacs) fought each other.[3] Before the disintegration of Yugoslavia in 1991, the country displayed a significant ethnic diversity. The ethnic situation was complicated by the fact that most nationalities were not confined within the borders of a specific republic, province or even district.[4] Croatia had a substantial Serbian minority of about 12 per cent. Macedonia contained Turks, Vlachs and an ever increasing Albanian population. While Bosniacs, Serbs and Croats comprise the population of BiH, no single ethnic group formed a majority. Only Serbia proper,[5] Slovenia and Montenegro were largely homogeneous.

Between 1945 and 1980, Josip Tito was able to contain religious and ethnic rivalries among the various groups within Yugoslavia; however, no real effort was made by the political or religious leaders to settle the historical differences between the ethnic groups. As the power of the constituent republics began to increase at the expense of the federal government after the adoption of the 1974 constitution, there was a concomitant expansion of Croatian, Slovenian, Muslim and Albanian ethnic autonomy. It was only after Tito's death in May 1980 that long-standing differences were finally expressed within the communist parties of the country's republics and provinces. Throughout the 1980s, ethnic conflict was channeled through the Communist Party which served to mediate ethnic claims.

The deepest and oldest ethnic rivalry in Yugoslavia was between the Serbs and the Croats who, despite their shared language, possessed different political cultures and religious beliefs. When the Kingdom of Serbs, Croats and Slovenes was created after World War I,[6] Serbs dominated the government.[7] This gave rise to an anti-Serb sentiment, particularly in Croatia, which preferred outright independence. In April 1941, Yugoslavia was occupied by the Axis powers. The Croatian extreme right, the *Ustaše*, with the assistance of Nazi Germany, formed the "Independent State of Croatia." The power of the *Ustaše* also extended into BiH. Extermination camps were established in both Croatia and BiH where Serbs, Jews and Roma were killed. The *Cheniks* (Serbian forces) attacked those living in Croatia and BiH. It is estimated that more than 1,500,000 people died in Yugoslavia during World War II (Neier, 1998). The historical animosity among these ethnic groups in Yugoslavia was never properly addressed and these events established the political backdrop for the war that broke out fifty years later in Croatia and BiH in 1991.

Croatia and Slovenia were the first to declare independence in 1991,[8] followed by Macedonia and BiH in 1992.[9] The secession of Slovenia and Macedonia was relatively peacefully. However in the newly independent Croatia, Serbs became classified as a minority by the new government which dismissed most Serb bureaucrats from government positions and replaced them with Croats. President Franjo Tudjman also encouraged nationalist sentiments which were associated with the rule of the *Ustaše* provoking fear among Serbs in Croatia.[10] In order to protect the Serb minority, the Yugoslav army (composed of Serbian and Montenegrin forces) started a war immediately after Croatia's declaration of independence in June 1991. By December, the Yugoslav army and Serb separatists within Croatia had taken nearly a third of Croatia's territory.[11] A ceasefire was agreed to between Serbia and Croatia in January 1992 under the auspices of the UN. It is estimated that 20,000 people died and 400,000 became refugees during this period of the Croatian war.

By April 1992, another conflict began in BiH. As in Croatia, the Serbian population in BiH went from being the dominant plurality in Yugoslavia to being a minority in the new state. In BiH, however, Serbs were still a significant minority (approximately 30 per cent of the population). The Serbs who lived there were determined to remain within a united Yugoslavia and to build a "Greater Serbia." They received strong support from the central government in Belgrade. The war in BiH quickly surpassed the conflict in Croatia in the number of killings and forms of violence, including ethnic cleansing and mass deportation of civilians. By 1993, the Bosnian Muslim government was besieged in the capital Sarajevo. They were surrounded by Bosnian Serb forces which controlled approximately 70 per cent of the territory. In central BiH, the mainly Muslim army was fighting a separate war against Bosnian Croats who wanted to be part of a "Greater Croatia." The UN finally became involved in the conflict and deployed the UN Protection Force to monitor a ceasefire agreement and to establish "safe zones" which included Sarajevo and Srebrenica.[12] The UN efforts were generally a failure, and in July 1995, Srebrenica became the site of one of the worst massacres in the conflict when an estimated 7,500 Muslim men and boys were killed by Bosnian Serbs.[13] It is estimated that between 1992 and 1995, 200,000 died and two million became refugees in the war in BiH.[14]

Eventually, conflict also erupted between the central government of the Federal Republic of Yugoslavia[15] and the province of Kosovo.[16] In 1989, President Milošević made changes to the Yugoslav constitution that ended the autonomous status of the provinces of Vojvodina and Kosovo.[17] In Kosovo, he established direct Serbian rule over the province, expelled Albanians from the Kosovo parliament, the state bureaucracy, state-owned enterprises and closed the state-run school system. In response, Kosovar Albanians pressed for independence, and in 1992 elected a nominal parliament and boycotted Serbian elections. Finally by 1998, the Kosovo Liberation Army (KLA) began to actively target Serbians and Serbian institutions with the support of the ethnic Albanian majority.

The international community, while supporting greater autonomy, opposed the Kosovar Albanians' demand for independence. The Serbian government then escalated the conflict by sending armed forces into the region. It is estimated that more than 11,000 individuals died during this period and approximately 1.5 million were driven from their homes due to the conflict. In February 1999, the two parties where forced to the negotiating table in Rambouillet, France to create a peace agreement. With air strikes by the North Atlantic Treaty Organization in March 1999, the Serbian army was forced to leave Kosovo, leading to the return of a large numbers of ethnic Albanians to Kosovo.

The Conflict in Rwanda

Unlike the human rights abuses in the former Yugoslavia, the genocide in Rwanda was essentially an internal conflict between the two major tribes; however, the conflict between the tribes was used by other states in the region to de-stabilize Rwanda and gain economic and political advantage. Violence between the majority Hutu and minority Tutsi tribes had occurred sporadically even before the period of de-colonization in 1962. For much of the colonial period, the German and later the Belgian government relied upon the Tutsi minority for local administration. While the Hutus constituted approximately 85 per cent of the population, they held less than 4 per cent of the chieftain positions (Magnarella, 2000). In the 1920s, the Belgians introduced identity cards to differentiate between the tribes (Beigbeder, 1999). Prunier (1995) argues that these cards were essential to establishing the two different tribes because they had "none of the characteristics of tribes, which are micro-nations. They shared the same Bantu language, lived side by side with each other without any 'Hutuland' or 'Tutsiland' and often intermarried" (1995, p. 5). In addition to sharing the same language, the tribes also shared a dominant Roman Catholic faith. Therefore unlike the war in the former Yugoslavia, the basis of the 1994 genocide was more political in nature.

While the Belgians promoted the minority Tutsis, eventually in 1959 the Tutsis began to advocate independence. The Belgian government quickly withdrew support for the Tutsi minority. Haile-Mariam goes so far as to argue that the break between the Belgian authorities and the Tutsi elite constituted a "starting point for the germination of the genocide in Rwanda" (1999, p. 680). Following the demands of the Tutsis, the Belgian government organized elections in 1960 in which the Hutus received the vast majority of mayoral posts. Within two years, the Hutus had completely supplanted the Tutsis as the local elites. During this transition, there were numerous reports of widespread Tutsi massacres that led to a mass exodus of the Tutsi minority to neighboring countries (Morris, 1997).

Systematic killings of Tutsis continued after the country became independent in 1962 and were well-documented in 1963, 1966 and 1973 (Shraga and Zacklin, 1996). By the time of the 1973 coup lead by a Hutu military officer, Juvénal Habyarimana, it was estimated that some 700,000 Tutsi refugees lived in Burundi, Uganda, Tanzania and Zaire (Prunier, 1995). Although there was still sporadic violence under the

Habyarimana regime, Kuperman argues that "large-scale violence against domestic Tutsi largely disappeared for 15 years" (2000, p. 95).[18] However during this time, the Rwandan government prevented the return of Tutsi refugees which by now had organized into a paramilitary force known as the Rwandan Patriotic Front (RPF) which launched military operations into Rwanda from bases in Uganda. From 1990 through 1993, there were various RPF incursions into Rwanda which eventually led to the signing of the Arusha Peace Accords between the Rwandan government and the RPF in August 1993. The Accords mandated power-sharing between Hutu elites and the RPF in a transitional government monitored by the UN Assistance Mission for Rwanda (UNAMIR) peacekeeping mission.

The uneasy peace between the Hutus and the Tutsis ended on 6 April 1994 when President Habyarimana's plane was shot down. To this day, it is unknown whether the plane was fired upon by RPF insurgents or by conservative elements of the Hutu elite that were displeased with the Arusha Accords. What is well-documented is that starting that same day, the Hutu elite, including the elite Presidential Guard, began to round-up and kill Tutsi opposition leaders.[19] Contingents of UNAMIR forces were quickly withdrawn so that the international community had an insignificant presence and was unable to prevent the genocide (Magnarella, 2000).[20] The perpetrators of the genocide quickly moved to eliminate not only the Tutsi elite which were part of the transitional government but also villagers including women and children. While Tutsis are lighter-skinned than Hutus, there is no obvious basis for differentiating the two tribes, and therefore the Rwandan-issued identity cards created during the Belgian colonial government were used during the initial roadblocks to capture Tutsi politicians and activists (Vassall-Adams, 1994).

What is so amazing about the Rwandan genocide is the speed by which it occurred. Within two weeks after the genocide started, some 250,000 Tutsis were massacred. Those not killed at Tutsi gathering sites, fled to neighboring countries, especially Uganda. As Tutsi refugees in Uganda reported the atrocities, the RPF launched a northern offensive; however, the RPF's offensive "simply could not match the pace at which the militiamen and soldiers were massacring civilians" (Vassall-Adams, 1994, p. 37). Indeed, the extent of the genocide is beyond comprehension. By the time the RPF had captured Kigali in July 1994, some 500,000 to 1,000,000 Tutsis had been systematically killed while between 10,000 and 100,000 Hutus were killed as the RPF re-took the country.[21] In addition to those that were killed, over two million Hutus fled the country to Zaire and many Tutsis and Hutus were internally displaced within Rwanda (Morris, 1997).

The International Response: Creating the International Criminal Tribunal for the former Yugoslavia

The UN and the EU observed with growing concern the developments in the former Yugoslavia. Two ceasefire agreements were negotiated in September 1991 between Croatia and Serbia, but they were quickly broken. Security Council Resolution 713 adopted in September 1991 acknowledged the efforts of the EU and the Conference on Security and Co-operation in Europe (CSCE) for encouraging a dialog between the warring parties. Over twenty countries had provided information to the UN about the violations of international humanitarian law which were taking place in the former Yugoslavia (O'Brien, 1993). In response to the failure of the cease fires, the UN Security Council imposed an arms embargo on all parties to the conflict. Ironically, this particularly harmed the Croats and the Bosnian Muslims because the Yugoslavian army was mainly composed of Serbs.

On 6 October 1992, the Security Council adopted resolution 780 establishing a Commission of Experts to investigate and collect evidence on "grave breaches of the Geneva Conventions and other violations of international humanitarian law" in the conflict in the former Yugoslavia (Bassiouni, 1996). By this time, war was raging in BiH, and the UN was particularly concerned about the ethnic cleansing taking place. The Commission issued its first Interim Report on 22 February 1993 stating that the establishment of an *ad hoc* international tribunal was necessary. The experts were skeptical of the potential use of national courts to deal with the conflicts. With the disintegration of Yugoslavia, there was no faith in the capacity of the national judicial system to provide justice (O'Brien, 1993).[22] The governments of Croatia and BiH expressed support for the creation of the international tribunal through the CSCE while the Federal Republic of Yugoslavia completely opposed its establishment (O'Brien, 1993).

For the first time since Nuremburg, the international community established an *ad hoc* process for trying war criminals and those responsible for committing human rights atrocities. Based on the Commission's first Interim Report, the 3 May 1993 report by the Secretary-General outlined the structure of the ICTY. The Security Council established the ICTY through Resolution 827 on 25 May 1993. The Resolution states that the ICTY was created "for the sole purpose of prosecuting persons responsible for serious violations of international humanitarian law committed in the territory of the former Yugoslavia between 1 January 1991 and a date determined by the Security Council upon the restoration of peace." The temporal mandate of the Tribunal was not specified since the conflict had not yet ended. In addition, The Hague was selected as the seat of the Tribunal. Unlike other tribunals discussed in the book, there was unanimous support within the Security Council for the creation of the ICTY (Burns, 1996). Some argue that states in the Security Council found the creation of the Tribunal appealing because it provided an economically and politically inexpensive means of responding to demands for international action.[23]

Using its authority under Chapter VII, the Security Council passed the Resolution creating the ICTY for the purpose of prosecuting four types of offenses: Grave breaches of the 1949 Geneva Conventions, violations of the laws or customs of war, genocide and crimes against humanity (Yacoubian, 1998). To indict on charges of grave breaches, violations of the laws or customs of war or crimes against humanity, the prosecutor was expected to show the existence of a state of war while this was not required for the charge of genocide.[24] Article 7(1) of the Resolution provides that a person who "planned, instigated, ordered, committed, or otherwise aided and abetted in the planning, preparation or execution of a crime" shall be individually responsible for the crime. However, the Resolution does not specify the level of participation in criminal act necessary for indictment.

The International Response: Creating the International Criminal Tribunal for Rwanda

Similar to the situation regarding the ICTY, the UN Security Council requested that the Secretary-General empanel a Commission of Experts to investigate and report on the evidence of Hutu violations of international humanitarian law. In October 1994, the Commission reported to the Security Council that there was undeniable and overwhelming evidence that the actions taken against the Tutsis constituted genocide and that a tribunal should be established. Unlike the government of the Federal Republic of Yugoslavia, the Rwandan government strongly urged the Security Council to establish a tribunal and offered its full cooperation (Shraga and Zacklin, 1996).

Resolution 955 authorized the creation of the ICTR and was adopted in November 1994. Like the ICTY, the ICTR was created under Chapter VII authority which specifies that the Security Council has the right to take actions to maintain peace and security.[25] The Tribunal's competencies extend to violations of international humanitarian law including specifically genocide, crimes against humanity and violations of Common Article III to the Geneva Conventions and Additional Protocol II.[26] While the basic logic, competencies and organization of the ICTR were very similar to the ICTY, there were some significant differences. First, Resolution 955 only provided the ICTR temporal jurisdiction over crimes that were committed between 1 January and 31 December 1994. Any violations of international humanitarian law that were committed prior to January 1994 were beyond the jurisdiction of the ITCR. Second, the trial chambers for the ICTR were not specified in the resolution. UN member-states were later asked to submit a request to host the ICTR. Ultimately Arusha, Tanzania was chosen because of its proximity to Rwanda. These differences between the tribunals reflect the different nature of the conflicts. While the ICTR was established in essentially a post-conflict environment, the ICTY was created while war was still raging.[27]

While Rwanda had initially made a request to the Security Council to create a tribunal, the country ultimately voted against Resolution 955. There were a number of objections that Rwanda raised concerning the jurisdiction, competency and location of the ICTR. First, the Rwandan government objected to the temporal jurisdiction. The government argued that the Tribunal's jurisdiction should have covered crimes committed since 1990 and that the jurisdiction should be limited to July rather than December 1994 (Magnarella, 2000). The government wanted earlier crimes committed before the Arusha Accords to be under the jurisdiction of the ICTR, and the government did not want to extend temporal jurisdiction to December so that retribution crimes that occurred against Hutus would not be covered.

Second, the government objected to the penalties prescribed in Resolution 955. While the Rwandan penal code provides for the death penalty, Resolution 955 limits penalties to imprisonment. The more limited penalty combined with stratified concurrent jurisdiction with domestic courts and *non bis in idem* meant that those indicted by the ICTR would not face the possibility of the death penalty.[28] This was an important issue because most individuals believed that the ICTR would be responsible for prosecuting those in the former regime and the principal planners of the genocide. This meant that those who were most culpable would not face the possibility of the death penalty while lower level offenders going through the national court system would confront the death penalty (an issue that we explore in Chapter 6).

Third, the Rwandan government wanted to limit the scope of crimes solely to the act of genocide (Shraga and Zacklin, 1996). By limiting the scope to genocide, acts perpetrated by Tutsis after July would not be subject to ICTR jurisdiction. While Resolution 955 places genocide first on the list of crimes, it also includes crimes against humanity and violations of the Geneva Conventions. Fourth, the Rwandan government objected to the location of the ICTR in Arusha. The government argued that the "deterrent effect of the trial and punishment will be lost if the trials were to be held hundreds of miles away from the scene of the crime" (Haile-Mariam, 1999, p. 698). While the government voted against the Resolution, Rwandan President Bizimungu later promised to fully cooperate with the Tribunal.

The Structure and Initial Growing Pains of the International Criminal Tribunal for the former Yugoslavia

Initially, the ICTY was composed of eleven judges (three judges for each of two trial chambers and five appellate judges). The appellate chamber of the ICTY is shared with the ICTR. The first judges of the ICTY were elected in September 1993, and the Tribunal held its inaugural session at The Hague in mid-November of that year. Initially, the Secretary-General's report proposed the establishment of three court rooms with a staff of around 400 assisting the Tribunal's work. The General Assembly, however, reduced the budget allocation, allowing for a single courtroom and a staff of approximately 100. By May 1998, the Security Council expanded the number of ICTY judges from eleven to fourteen, and in 2000, the number of judges was further expanded to sixteen, with the addition of nine *ad litum* judges to assist with the increased workload of the Tribunal. By 2000, three trial chambers were operational.[29]

For most of its first two years, the ICTY had no defendants in custody even though it already had issued thirty-four public indictments (Murphy, 1999). The ICTY's greatest difficulty early on was securing the apprehension of indictees. This problem began to be overcome at the end of 1994, when some of the indictees were transferred to The Hague. However, these initial arrests and transfers were of low-ranking officials. The ICTY continued to have difficulty in arresting high-ranking suspects for a number of years. Starting in mid-1995, the ICTY shifted from simply issuing indictments towards trials of the accused. The first trial began in April 1995, and the *Tadić* case established the rules and procedures that would serve as the basis for future cases. In the *Tadić* case, one of the first issues ruled on was the legality of the Tribunal, and whether the Security Council had exceeded its Chapter VII authority when it created this institution. The appeals chamber ruled that the ICTY's establishment under Chapter VII was legal and that the Tribunal had the legal authority to try defendants.

Later, the authority of the Tribunal was expanded in 1999. As war broke out between Albanians and the Serbian army in the province of Kosovo, it was announced that the ICTY's jurisdiction under its original statute would be extended to Kosovo. Interestingly, many of those accused in this conflict had already been accused of committing crimes during the conflict in BiH. The ICTY announced in June 2000 that it would also begin investigating alleged KLA atrocities against Serbs.

The Structure and Initial Growing Pains of the International Criminal Tribunal for Rwanda

The ICTR was also composed of eleven judges (three judges for each of the two trial chambers and five appellate judges). Significantly, the appeals chamber is shared with the ICTY and therefore located at The Hague rather than Arusha. While many have criticized the appellate structure, Morris argues that "the importance of developing a coherent body of international criminal law may weigh against having separate appellate courts potentially rendering conflicting statements of international law" (1997, p. 55).[30] The ICTR became operational in July 1995 and issued its first indictment of eight Rwandan officials suspected of genocide in November 1995.

Within a year of the first ICTR indictments, the Rwandan Organic Law authorizing the prosecution of the crime of genocide was passed by the Rwandan legislature. Unlike the temporal jurisdiction of the ICTR, the Organic Law covers the period of 1 October 1990 through 1 December 1994 (Sarkin, 1999). The passage of this law came at a time in which approximately 90,000 defendants were being held in Rwandan jails (Morris, 1997). Unlike Resolution 955, the Organic Law contains four categories of suspects, and those prosecuted under category one can receive the death penalty. Because of the large number of defendants, the law provides the other three categories a fixed sentence reduction as part of a guilty plea agreement. However by 1999, a number of those who had been convicted received the death sentence and less than 10 per cent had been acquitted (Sarkin, 1999).

Perhaps because of the imposition of the death penalty, there has often been a conflict between the ICTR and the Rwandan national courts over the custody of defendants. Because of stratified concurrent jurisdiction, the national courts must hand over any defendant in custody to the ICTR when it serves the interests of justice. In addition if both the ICTR and the Rwandan government seek the transfer of a suspect from another country, the transfer order of the ICTR takes precedence. As noted however in Chapter 6, as the ICTR transfers cases back to the national courts as part of the Tribunal's Completion Strategy, there is the possibility that these defendants may receive the death penalty.

Conclusions

The creation by the international community of the ICTY and the ICTR represented a unique moment in history which has greatly assisted in the development of international humanitarian law. Not since Nuremberg and Tokyo had an international effort been made to apply war crimes, crimes against humanity and genocide to state leaders. The procedures and rulings by the two tribunals have served to further clarify and codify international law. However, the structure, the jurisdiction and the success in prosecuting cases are an outcome of political considerations and constraints by states where sovereignty claims remain an important consideration.

While the ICTY and the ICTR have been criticized for not fulfilling their mandates, perhaps their greatest contribution will be that we may never again witness the creation of *ad hoc* justice. The ultimate expression of this new international consensus regarding individual accountability is found in the creation of the International Criminal Court (ICC). However, this may be of little comfort to the hundreds of thousands of family members who lost loved ones in the former Yugoslavia and Rwanda. For them, justice is not defined in terms of historical precedent and international consensus but in brining to justice those responsible for some of the worse atrocities ever seen.

Throughout this book, we discuss the constant struggle between justice for individuals, society and the international community of states. As we note in Chapter 7, tribunals are a poor instrument to provide reconciliation for post-conflict societies. The relatively small number of individuals that will stand trial in The Hague and Arusha cannot begin to provide individual justice and social reconciliation. Ultimately, national systems of justice need to be strengthened in order to process suspects, to provide a fair trial and to encourage a rule of law culture. However as we discuss in Chapter 6, it is unclear whether the decision to end these two tribunals by 2010 and remand cases back to the national judiciaries will strengthen or overwhelm the justice system in these fragile states.

Notes

1. As discussed in Chapter 1, international humanitarian law governs the conduct of the state and individuals during armed conflict. Roberts argues that while international humanitarian law provides a set of internationally approved standards, the laws should not be viewed as a "system of international criminal justice" (1998a, p. 277).
2. Yugoslavia was composed of six republics including Bosnia-Herzegovina (BiH), Croatia, Macedonia, Montenegro, Serbia and Slovenia.

3. The Bosnian Croats received support from Croatia while the Bosnian Serbs received assistance from the Federal Republic of Yugoslavia.
4. While approximately 98 per cent of all Yugoslavia's Slovenes lived in Slovenia and about 96 per cent of Macedonians lived in Macedonia, only 60 per cent of the Serbs lived in Serbia proper and only 70 per cent of Montenegrins lived in Montenegro.
5. Serbia contains two autonomous provinces (Kosovo and Vojvodina) that had significant ethnic minorities. Serbia proper (in other words Serbia without the inclusion of the two autonomous provinces) was almost completely homogeneous.
6. It was re-named Yugoslavia in 1929.
7. Serbs also dominated the military which gave them an advantage over the other ethnic groups once Yugoslavia collapsed in 1991.
8. In May 1991, Croatian voters supported a referendum calling for independence which was passed by the parliament in June. A similar referendum in Slovenia passed in December after the parliament had already declared independence.
9. In January 1992, Macedonia declared independence. Bosnian Serb leaders also declared independence in January, and at the beginning of March, the non-Serb population voted for independence.
10. Franjo Tudjman was the leader of the Croat Democratic Union which was formed in 1989. A former partisan general, he was imprisoned in the 1970s for upholding Croatian rights.
11. The territory included western Slavonia and Krajina until the Croats recaptured most of the territory in 1995.
12. The "safe zones" were established in 1992 and included Tuzla, Gorazde, Zepa, Sarajevo, Bihac and Srebrenica.
13. Srebrenica was supposedly protected by Dutch peacekeepers, but they proved ineffective in preventing the massacre.
14. The Dayton Accords signed in November 1995 established the legal entity of BiH with a Bosnian Serb republic (*Republika Srpska*) and a Bosniac and Croatian Federation.
15. The Federal Republic of Yugoslavia was created in 1992 between the Republic of Serbia and Montenegro.
16. The Kosovo region was considered the homeland of Serbs which were defeated by the Ottoman Turks in the Battle of Kosovo of 1389. After the Serbian defeat, Albanians settled into the region becoming the overwhelming majority with Serbs constituting only about 10 per cent of the population.
17. Slobodan Milošević was the leader of the Communist Party and became President of Serbia in 1989. He was elected President of the Federal Republic of Yugoslavia in 1997.
18. According to Haile-Mariam (1999), the Habyarimana government imposed a severe quota system which limited Tutsis to 9 per cent of school enrollment and civil service positions and prohibited them from entering the military.
19. This period began the so-called "*interahamwe*" (a Rwandan term meaning those who kill together).
20. One of the major issues that emerged from the genocide was the culpability of the international community. Numerous scholars have argued that the international community could have taken steps to either prevent or at least reduce the number of causalities. However, Kuperman (2000) argues that any form of international intervention would have still resulted in the deaths of hundreds of thousands of Tutsis.
21. The exact number of deaths is difficult to determine. Prunier (1995) argues that as

many as 800,000 Tutsis were killed. Kuperman (2000) argues that that the total Tutsi population of Rwanda was estimated at 650,000 and based on aid agency reports, approximately 500,000 Tutsis were killed. Others claim that the 1991 census data severely under-reported the Tutsi population. While the exact number will never be known, the fact is that at least 500,000 persons were systematically killed within a span of three months.

22. However in 2002, ICTY President Claude Jorda and Chief Prosecutor Carla Del Ponte traveled to BiH to explore the possibility of holding trials for mid-level indictees. This has lead to the devolution of cases to domestic courts as part of the Completion Strategy of the ICTY as discussed in Chapter 6.
23. By 2000, the costs of the ICTY and the ICTR were a major concern of the international community. We discuss this issue in greater detail in Chapter 5.
24. Violations of the laws or customs of war have been viewed quite broadly by the Tribunal and have been often invoked when the other three offenses did not appear to be justified.
25. Similar to the *Tadić* case at the ICTY, the authority of the Security Council under Chapter VII to create a tribunal was the subject of one of the first cases at the ICTR. The ICTR trial chamber in the *Kanyabashi* case addressed this issue and affirmed the legality of the ICTR.
26. Article III of the Geneva Conventions specifically deals with "armed conflict not of an international character." While Rudolph (2001) argues that the creation of the ICTR is an unprecedented expansion of international law, Common Article III specifically deals with domestic conflicts among contracting parties.
27. This is an important distinction that we return to when examining the effectiveness of international tribunals in Chapter 7.
28. Article 8, Section 2 of Resolution 955 provides that the ICTR "shall have the primacy over the national courts of all States." Therefore, the ITCR has stratified concurrent jurisdiction with Rwandan national courts. In addition, the concept of *non bis in idem* is similar to the American legal notion of double jeopardy. Therefore, the Rwandan courts could not prosecute those that were found innocent by the ICTR.
29. The US and the Netherlands funded the construction of the two additional chambers.
30. However as noted in Chapter 6, sharing the appeals chamber makes completing all appeals by 2010 much more difficult to accomplish.

Chapter 3

The Creation of Hybrid Tribunals: The Special Court for Sierra Leone and the Extraordinary Chambers for Cambodia

The year 2000 marked a turning point in the development of international tribunals. Up to that point, *ad hoc* tribunals had been established by the international community, composed of international judges and located in international venues. The International Criminal Tribunal for the former Yugoslavia (ICTY) and the International Criminal Tribunal for Rwanda (ICTR) were established as auxiliary organs of the United Nations (UN) under Chapter VII authority to deal with a range of crimes committed under international law. The ICTY was established in 1993 as the conflict raged in the former Yugoslavia while the ICTR was established in 1994 in a post-conflict environment. While there are important differences between these two tribunals, they were both established as international institutions to try individuals in countries in which the legal system was unable or unwilling to cope with the legacy of human rights violations.

As these tribunals were authorized under Chapter VII authority, financing was provided as an assessed share of the UN budget. As noted in Chapter 2, the two tribunals have received over $4.5 billion through Chapter VII financing. Ultimately, the financing of these tribunals became a concern for the international community. This concern coupled with the resistance of some states to relinquish sovereignty over individuals to an international process led to the innovation of "hybrid" or "mixed" tribunals.

Within the span of eights months in 2000, three tribunals had either been established through a memorandum of understanding or had begun functioning. These tribunals included the Serious Crimes Panel for East Timor (SCPET)[1] in March, the Extraordinary Chambers for Cambodia (ECC)[2] in July and the Special Court for Sierra Leone (SCSL) in August. While these tribunals vary considerably in their jurisdiction, composition and financing, all of them are a movement away from an ICTY and an ICTR international tribunal model to a hybrid model involving both international and domestic components.

In this chapter, we examine the SCSL and the ECC.[3] Because Security Council members are suffering donor fatigue, they did not wish to establish tribunals that drew upon the UN's general budget. In addition states, as in the case of Cambodia, wanted to have more influence in the crafting of the institution as well as the legal processes that would be used as the basis for trials. Another important difference with these tribunals is that they were established after the founding of the International Criminal Court (ICC), and the definition of crimes including war crimes and crimes against humanity for these tribunals reflect the legal framework established by the ICC.

The SCSL and the ECC have both significant domestic and international components which is why they are referred to as hybrid tribunals. As we discuss below, the tribunals include a combination of domestic and international judges, utilize domestic and international laws and are administered by a domestic and an international prosecutorial team. In many respects, these institutional changes have been brought about because of criticisms of the ICTY and the ICTR. As in the case of the SCPET (discussed in Chapter 4), these newer tribunals reflect a significant departure from the institutions created in the early to mid 1990s. The tribunals for Sierra Leone, Cambodia and East Timor represent an attempt by states to re-insert themselves into the post-conflict legal process and reassert their sovereignty.[4] The question remains whether states such as Sierra Leone, which has just recently emerged out of a decade-long conflict, can provide the necessary rule of law and integrate within their domestic legal framework the rules that have been developed in international law regarding war crimes, crimes against humanity and genocide. In both Sierra Leone and Cambodia, legal institutions were under-institutionalized before the outbreak of conflict and especially in the case of Cambodia, the legal system itself came under attack during the conflict and was virtually destroyed.

However, it is a mistake to view these tribunals simply as a mixture of domestic and international law and judges. In certain areas, these tribunals have had to deal with new issues and establish new institutions which create important precedents and innovations in international law. In the case of both the SCSL and the ECC, lawyers have had to address the legality of amnesties that have been provided to individuals that are prime suspects. In terms of the SCSL, it is the first tribunal to establish a separate procedure for juvenile suspects (so-called "child soldiers"), and the SCSL is one of the first tribunals to function alongside a truth and reconciliation commission. The ECC is unique because it is the only tribunal discussed in this book in which the temporal jurisdiction covers crimes committed during the Cold War and is the only tribunal that will be established after the entry into force of the ICC in 2002. Therefore, the SCSL and the ECC offer interesting innovations that go beyond the debate over the combination of domestic and international legal processes.

This chapter is divided into four sections. First, we analyze the nature of the conflict in Sierra Leone and Cambodia as well as the types of crimes that were committed. Second, we examine the debate on the creation of these tribunals and some of the limitations brought about by the negotiations. Third, we present the structure of both tribunals and finally conclude by examining the current status of each tribunal and its ability to fulfill its mandate. In Chapter 7, we turn our attention to the fundamental question of whether these hybrid tribunals are a more effective mechanism for providing justice and reconciliation than purely international solutions.

The Nature of Conflict in Sierra Leone

The conflict in Sierra Leone has a number of characteristics that differentiates it from the conflict in the former Yugoslavia, Rwanda and Cambodia. In the case of Sierra Leone, the atrocities committed against individuals and the society did not have an ethnic component. Attacks by the rebels were not aimed specifically at the Temne, Mende or Krio communities. This is an important aspect of the conflict which influences the tribunal. Because the ethnic dimension was absent during the conflict, the crime of genocide has not been included in the statute of the Court. Another important difference is that the Khmer Rouge's atrocities were committed based upon a well-developed albeit perverse ideology. In Sierra Leone, the rebels that committed most of the crimes were not driven by an ideology but by a quest for personal enrichment (Hirsch, 2001).

The civil war in Sierra Leone was part of a larger regional African security crisis in which Liberia and Charles Taylor figured prominently. So in trying to understand Sierra Leone, or for that matter Cambodia, the conflict should be viewed as having both a national and an international component.[5] It is clear that since independence in 1961, Sierra Leone has suffered from corrupt and authoritarian governments. In the post-independence period, there has been a blurring of civilian and military authority. The first military coup that occurred in 1967 (the military government itself was overthrown by another coup of junior officers a year later) established a pattern that continued throughout the 1990s. From 1967 to 1985, President Siaka Stevens established a one-party state in which his nepotism and cronyism was financed through the illicit smuggling of diamonds from the eastern province of the country (especially the mineral-rich Kono region). In 1985, Stevens retired and handed power to his military chief, Major General Joseph Momoh. Gallagher (2000) argues that under Momoh two important trends emerged: First, the level of unemployment, particularly of youth, dramatically increased which increased the criminality of the society. Second, there was growing student militancy at universities.

During the 1980s, Libya became a refuge for student activists and a military training ground for those from all over Africa. Foday Sankoh, the leader of the Revolutionary United Front (RUF), was trained in Libya alongside Charles Taylor. The two established a close personal relationship that continued once Taylor returned to Liberia and Sankoh took-up arms against the government of Sierra Leone. While Sankoh and the RUF borrowed ideological phrases from Qaddafi's Green Book, the RUF did not manifest any coherent ideology or political objectives (Fritz and Smith, 2001). When the RUF invaded eastern Sierra Leone in 1991, it entered the country via Liberia which provided arms, troops and a safe haven. For Taylor, supporting the RUF and de-stabilizing Sierra Leone provided two essential advantages. First and foremost, Taylor provided arms and supplies to the RUF in exchange for "conflict diamonds" which were smuggled out of the eastern Kono region into Liberia and the Ivory Coast. Second, Taylor used the RUF to undermine the Momoh government which had provided the Economic Community of West African States Ceasefire Monitoring Group (ECOMOG) an airbase from which to launch attacks against Taylor and his National Patriotic Front of Liberia (NPFL) (Hirsch, 2001).

Taylor's NPFL and the RUF used similar tactics and strategies. Both groups practiced amputations on victims irrespective of their age, and both engaged in the practice of child abduction, forcing boys to become soldiers and girls to become wives or concubines. Boys were often drugged to make them more vicious when fighting, and girls suffered rape and were sold in Sierra Leone and throughout West Africa. Boys and girls were employed in some of the most dangerous work as they were viewed as expendable. As many as 10,000 children are estimated to have fought in the civil war which began in 1991 (Amann, 2001). Bald (2002) argues that the situation in Sierra Leone is not isolated and reports that as many as 300,000 children under the age of eighteen are fighting in armed conflicts globally. This is why the trial of child soldiers and the creation of a juvenile chamber within the SCSL have drawn so much interest from human rights groups and the international community.

The major RUF offensive began in the eastern region of Sierra Leone in 1991. When the rebels invaded in 1991, they "allegedly began in order to fight against government corruption" and maintained this *façade* throughout the civil war (Macaluso, 2001, p. 347). While the RUF's motivation can be questioned, there is no doubt that government corruption had undermined the legitimacy of the Momoh government. Shortly after the invasion, Momoh was overthrown by a group of young junior officers represented by Captain Valentine Strasser. By the mid-1990s, Sierra Leone's state apparatus had completely collapsed. The RUF controlled the lucrative mining areas in the east, and the state was unable to engage in any significant economic activities. Customs duties and taxes were not collected, and the military continued to complain about low salaries which discouraged them from attacking the RUF (Hirsch, 2001). Indeed, the Sierra Leone army was further marginalized as the government employed a private security force, Executive Outcomes, which provided security to Freetown and the surrounding areas. Aside from the private security force, civilian militias were formed throughout the country based on the traditional hunter-gather culture which supported the government (the best known of these was the Civilian Defense Forces or CDF). Like the RUF, these civilian militias also recruited child soldiers and were involved in committing atrocities in the name of the community. Because of the chaos and the collapse of the formal economy, the country existed primarily through grants and loans from the international community.

Therefore when the international donor community urged the government to hold democratic elections in 1996, it had no choice but to comply. President Ahmad Tejan Kabbah was elected on a peace platform and soon after began to negotiate with the RUF. Executive Outcomes had earlier stopped an RUF advance on Freetown, and therefore the rebels were more disposed to an agreement, particularly one that would legalize and solidify their control of the eastern mining region as well as eliminate the presence of foreign security forces. The Abidjan Accord was signed in November 1996 and called for an immediate ceasefire, disarmament and demobilization. It also provided the RUF and all other combatants an amnesty. By early 1997, Executive Outcomes departed and soon after, the rebels sensed their advantage and renewed their attacks.

In May 1997, President Kabbah was overthrown by the Armed Forces Revolutionary Council (AFRC) lead by Johnny Paul Koroma. The actions of the AFRC were based on the military's lingering resentment that mercenary forces had been employed and paid better than the under-paid military.[6] Within a matter of days, the AFRC invited the RUF to form a new government. Gallagher argues that this is not surprising given that "[g]overnment troops had also long been suspected of colluding with the RUF and exploiting the country's diamond resources" (2000, p. 157). These troops have come to be known as "sobels" or soldiers who wore a uniform by day and like rebels looted and attacked at night. In June, Nigerian troops arrived to reinforce the ECOMOG force that was still in Sierra Leone. By February 1998, ECOMOG troops had restored President Kabbah to office. Sankoh, the leader of the RUF, was captured in Nigeria and returned to Sierra Leone where he was sentenced to death. However by 1998, the Sierra Leone government was barely functioning and relied almost exclusively on ECOMOG and civilian militias for support. Even with Sankoh in jail by the end of the year, the rebels controlled over half of the country and extended their control to the northern province.

In January 1999, the RUF launched a massive attack on Freetown. After fierce fighting in which the rebels abducted some 4,000 children, the ECOMOG troops were able to recapture the capital (Amann, 2001). By 1999, it was clear that neither side would ever gain a complete victory. The stalemate and mounting pressure from the UN and the international community forced the two sides back to the negotiating table. In July 1999, the recently released Sankoh and President Kabbah signed the Lomé Agreement which included many of the same elements as the previous Abidjan Accord. Sankoh was specifically granted a pardon and provided the chairmanship of the newly created Commission for the Management of Strategic Resources, National Reconstruction and Development. A provision of the agreement established a Truth and Reconciliation Commission for Sierra Leone (TRCSL), and significantly, the Lomé Agreement included an amnesty provision for all combatants. Francis Okelo, the UN Secretary-General's Special Representative, added a last minute reservation to the provision stating that the amnesty would not apply to "international crimes of genocide, crimes against humanity, war crimes, and other serious violations of international humanitarian law" (Fritz and Smith, 2001, p. 397).

Unlike after the Abidjan Accord, the UN committed a peacekeeping force to carry out the provisions of this agreement. In October, the United Nations Mission in Sierra Leone (UNAMSIL) arrived in Freetown with 6,000 peacekeepers. Even with the UN presence, the RUF failed to disarm and began to attack the UNAMSIL forces. In May 2000, several hundred UNAMSIL peacekeepers were taken hostage by the RUF and in the same month Sankoh was re-arrested. The Lomé Agreement had completely collapsed, but with Sankoh in jail, mounting international pressure on Liberian President Taylor and a sizeable commitment of peacekeepers, Sierra Leone was able to stabilize the security situation and in June 2000 requested the assistance of the UN to establish a court to try those that had committed civil war atrocities. By early 2002, the de-militarization and de-mobilization of ex-combatants had been completed and presidential and parliamentary elections took place in which President Kabbah was re-elected. By December 2005, the Sierra Leone security forces assumed full responsibility for security of the country as the UNAMSIL's mandate expired. Thus since 2002, the relative calm in Sierra Leone has allowed the SCSL and the TRCSL to operate without interruption.

The Nature of Conflict in Cambodia

After five years of civil war, the forces of the Khmer Rouge entered Phnom Penh in April 1975, and the state of Democratic Kampuchea (DK) was established, headed by Saloth Sar, who became known as Pol Pot or "Brother Number One." Ideologically, the Khmer Rouge sought to create a utopian society in which Cambodia would become a completely agrarian state. In order to eliminate dependence on foreign powers, the Khmer Rouge advocated self-reliance through food production. Surpluses were exported in order to increase state revenues, and in order to increase agricultural production, the regime created massive rural communes while emphasizing the virtues of the countryside and peasant life. The regime also abolished all social classes (everyone became a peasant) as well as money, education and religion.

Politically, the regime eliminated all those who were perceived to be opposed to the new state, including domestic and foreign enemies. Within Cambodia, the Khmer Rouge focused on individuals associated with the deposed government of former Prime Minister Lol Nol, the middle class and the educated who did not support the goals of the regime. In addition, ethnic Chinese, Vietnamese and Laotians were targets, facing elimination or expulsion from Cambodia (Kamm, 1998). The Khmer Rouge distrusted the Vietnamese who had advised other communist groups in Cambodia in the 1960s and early 1970s against the Khmer Rouge. Members of the Khmer Rouge party, the Communist Party of Kampuchea (CPK), had very few connections with the homegrown communist groups in Cambodia which had been sponsored by the Vietnamese. A number of the leaders of the Khmer Rouge were teachers who had gone to France in the 1950s and 1960s and had been exposed to leftist ideas there. By 1967, the CPK had begun its armed struggle within Cambodia and was suspicious of Vietnamese motives.

The major event that would lead to the ascendancy of the Khmer Rouge occurred in 1970, when Prince Sihanouk was deposed through a coup carried out by Nol. Sihanouk had been the leader of Cambodia since 1941, first under French colonial power and later after independence in 1953. In the 1960s, he expressed sympathy for the left and tacitly accepted the presence of Vietnamese troops on Cambodian soil as part of the expanding theater of the Vietnam War. After the 1970 coup, China advised Sihanouk to form an alliance with the CPK in order to fight Nol and regain power. The civil war that ensued during 1970–1975 left over half a million people dead. In addition, over two million refugees fled to Phnom Penh escaping the countryside. By 1973, large parts of the country were under CPK control. During this period, the Khmer Rouge instituted a policy of eliminating communist allies, Khmer communists returning from Hanoi and ethnic minority members within the CPK. In April 1975, Nol resigned and left the country as the Khmer Rouge forces advanced towards Phnom Penh (Chandler, 1992).

Beginning on 17 April 1975, over two million people were re-located from the cities to the countryside in the span of a week. The "new people" or "17 April people" were re-settled among rural people in agricultural labor camps where they were deprived of wages and rights. Much of the migration took place from the southwest area to the more fertile northwest which was an excellent place in which to grow rice. While the Khmer Rouge relied on agricultural production to feed the army and gain export revenues, the population did not have enough to eat. By early 1976, food became scarce and the country faced famines during 1977 and 1978 (Kiernan, 1996).

Between April 1975 and January 1979, approximately two million people died as a direct result of Khmer Rouge policies. In the countryside, these policies involved overworking people, neglecting or mistreating the sick and giving everyone less food than was needed to survive. Nearly one million people died of starvation and disease while another million were executed. This represents about one fourth of the population of Cambodia at that time. In addition by September 1976, a split within the CPK precipitated a series of purges within the party. Approximately 25,000 high ranking party members, military commanders and officials overseeing the eastern zone of Cambodia immediately became targets. Most of them were sent to the interrogation center at Tuol Sleng in Phnom Penh to face torture and death.

In 1976, the regime began to mount attacks on Vietnam as the CPK was interested in the possibility of creating a "Greater Cambodia" which would include Cambodian ethnic minorities in the southern region of Vietnam. The CPK had the support of China against Vietnam; however, the forces of the Khmer Rouge were over-run by the Vietnamese army. In December 1977, the Vietnamese launched a counter-offensive, and by April 1978, over 100,000 Vietnamese troops were amassed near the Cambodian border. On Christmas Day 1978, Vietnamese troops invaded Cambodia, and by January 1979 they had entered the capital, forcing the government to retreat into the countryside and ending the Khmer Rouge regime. Cambodians who had gone into exile in Vietnam during the Khmer Rouge regime took power in January 1979 with Vietnamese support. Having lost power, the Khmer Rouge retreated to the Thai border and established itself as a guerilla force. Vietnam occupied Cambodia from 1979 to 1989, supporting the regime of Prime Minister Hun Sen. It would take almost fifteen years after the withdrawal of the Vietnamese before a legal process would begin in Cambodia to address the atrocities of the Khmer Rouge (Kiernan, 2002).

Negotiating the Special Court for Sierra Leone

The ICTY and the ICTR were created by the Security Council under Chapter VII authority which made these tribunals auxiliary UN institutions. Security Council members were unwilling to establish the SCSL and the ECC under Chapter VII authority because any UN administrative organ is financed based on an assessed share of the general budget (this is an issue that we deal with extensively in Chapter 5). While the Sierra Leonean government was open to the idea of a Chapter VII-based tribunal, the Cambodian government, as discussed below, did not want a tribunal that was essentially controlled by the international community. The legal basis of the SCSL and the ECC provided the governments much more involvement and control over the final institution.

When negotiations began between the UN and Sierra Leone, there was never any serious discussion within the Security Council that the SCSL would have the same legal and ultimately financial status as the other two *ad hoc* tribunals. Indeed, the name of the tribunal referring to it as a "special court" (or in the case of Cambodia an "extraordinary chamber") indicates that these are not the same type of international institutions as the ICTY and the ICTR and that they are grounded within the domestic legal process. McDonald concludes that "it is thus a *sui generis* Special Court, not so much because this was necessarily the best or most effective approach to take in the particular circumstances of Sierra Leone, but because it was the only politically acceptable option" (2002, p. 124).

In August 2000, the Security Council passed Resolution 1315 which mandated that the Secretary-General begin negotiations with the Sierra Leonean government over the creation of the SCSL. The resolution stipulated that the Court would try those individuals "who bear the greatest responsibility" for human rights violations. Amann argues that "because of the narrow language, the Security Council's action was dubbed the 'Sankoh resolution'" (2001, p. 172). In October, the Secretary-General submitted a draft statute and agreement to the Security Council. The statute envisioned the SCSL based on a treaty between the government of Sierra Leone and the UN. Most of the provisions outlined by the Secretary-General were retained in the final draft. However, the Security Council rejected several elements of the draft statute and agreement. The Secretary-General substituted "greatest responsibility" with the phrase "most responsible." Ultimately, the Council rejected this language as too broad. The Secretary-General also recommended granting Chapter VII powers for the specific purpose of requesting the surrender of an accused suspect as well as using the UN general budget to finance the tribunal. He was concerned that the voluntary contributions called for in Resolution 1315 would not be sustainable.[7] These recommendations were also rejected by the Security Council.

One of the major issues of discussion concerned the recommendation by the Secretary-General to authorize charges against juveniles between the age of fifteen and eighteen. While much of the draft statute reflects legal reasoning found within the statute of the ICC, this provision was a significant departure from the ICC norm. The ICC statute expressly forbids the prosecution of individuals under the age of eighteen when they are alleged to have committed a crime. The Secretary-General's proposal was unique in that for the first time in a tribunal, children would be specified as both victims and defendants.[8]

The UN was harshly criticized by human rights and child advocacy groups for allowing the possibility of children, who were subject to some of the worst atrocities, being prosecuted; however, there was strong support within Sierra Leone that children should be part of the legal process and accountable for their actions. The Secretary-General recognized the unique problem of trying child soldiers. On the one hand, there is the question of whether children at this age could have the *mens rea* to be found guilty. On the other hand, he had to balance consideration for children with the evidence that indicated that many child soldiers were involved in committing atrocities. He tried to find a middle ground by establishing a special Juvenile Chamber with at least one judge on the panel experienced in juvenile justice. The Security Council rejected this provision and instead encouraged the referral of juvenile cases to the TRCSL rather than using a trial process.

The other contentious issue that the Secretary-General had to confront was the temporal jurisdiction of the SCSL. Similar to the ICTR, there was disagreement over the start date of the Court's jurisdiction. Before the Secretary-General could establish the temporal jurisdiction, he first had to decide on the legality of the amnesty provided in the Lomé Agreement. The position of the UN at the signing of the agreement as well as in Resolution 1315 had consistently been that the amnesty did not extend to international crimes. However, the Secretary-General's report did not address the issue of whether the amnesty should be revoked in cases tried under Sierra Leonean domestic law. This ultimately created a bifurcated temporal jurisdiction in which the jurisdiction for international crimes starts on 30 November 1996 while only those domestic crimes that were committed after 7 July 1999 are prosecuted.

While the date of 7 July 1999 was established for domestic crimes because of the amnesty provisions of the Lomé Agreement, there was a debate as to when temporal jurisdiction should begin for international crimes.[9] An argument can be made that the conflict in Sierra Leone began on 23 March 1991 when RUF forces invaded the eastern part of the country. The Secretary-General used the 30 November 1996 signing of the Abidjan Accord because he was concerned that "the Prosecutor and the Court should not be overloaded. It was necessary to avoid a date with political connotations, but it should be such as to encompass the most serious crimes" (McDonald, 2002, p. 128). The end date of the temporal jurisdiction was left open as the discussions at the UN occurred while the civil war was still taking place. One of the criticisms of the temporal jurisdiction was that many of the crimes which were committed in the provinces occurred before 1996. Many sectors of Sierra Leonean society felt that the temporal jurisdiction restricted the crimes to those that were committed during the sieges of Freetown.[10] In other words, some perceived that there would be justice for those in the capital but not for those in the provinces.

While there were disagreements on specific issues, much of Resolution 1315 and the Secretary-General's draft statute and report are part of the final statute adopted by the Security Council. Moreover, the SCSL was established with the full participation of the Sierra Leonean government. In fact, the involvement of the government was crucial in order to incorporate elements of the domestic criminal code. The draft statute contained provisions based on the Sierra Leone 1926 Prevention of Cruelty to Children Act as well as the 1861 Malicious Damage Act. While there were issues of contention among the participants, there was much more widespread agreement in these negotiations than in the previous discussions concerning the ICTY and the ICTR. This is one of the benefits of the state being a full partner in the creation of the tribunal. In the case of the ICTY, however, there was no possibility that the state could have participated in the crafting of the Tribunal. Indeed, the lack of judicial independence and political will are some of the major reasons why the ICTY was necessary.

Negotiating the Extraordinary Chambers for Cambodia

The negotiations surrounding the ECC were unusual because unlike other tribunals, the negotiations began eighteen years after the Khmer Rouge regime was defeated by Vietnamese forces in 1979. The US and the Chinese supported the Khmer Rouge in exile even as information about atrocities began to be made public. The Khmer Rogue was seen as a preferable alternative to the Vietnamese-sponsored Sen government as both China and the US feared Vietnam's expansionist designs in Southeast Asia (Mayall, 1996).

It was the Vietnamese who first exerted pressure on the Sen government to try Pol Pot and other members of the regime for genocide (De Nike, Quigley and Robinson, 2000). In August of 1979, a special court, the People's Revolutionary Tribunal, was created to try Pol Pot and Ieng Sary, but the prosecution was conducted *in absentia* and amounted to nothing more than a show trial (Heder and Tittemore, 2001). The Khmer Rouge, with the backing of members of the international community, continued to fight against the Sen government and the Vietnamese for most of the 1980s without success.[11] However by 1989 as Soviet aid diminished, the Vietnamese withdrew their military forces from Cambodia. In an effort to minimize the power of Sen, members of the Security Council and other interested states convened the Paris Conference on Cambodia. The Khmer Rouge was one of four delegations representing Cambodia.[12] It took two more years of negotiations before the signing of the Paris Agreement in October 1991. The agreement called for the creation of the United Nations Transitional Authority in Cambodia (UNTAC) to organize elections with full Khmer Rouge participation (Ratner and Abrams, 2001).

However by June 1992, the Khmer Rouge refused to continue to abide by the Paris Agreement and ended its cooperation with the UN. It boycotted the election process in May 1993 and continued to target Vietnamese in Cambodia while also attacking members of the UNTAC. The US changed its position regarding the Khmer Rouge in April 1994 when Congress passed the Cambodian Genocide Act which committed the US to support efforts to bring the Khmer Rouge to justice. The Cambodian parliament also passed a law in July 1994 outlawing the Khmer Rouge.

While the new Cambodian government engaged in military campaigns against the Khmer Rouge, it also offered amnesties to those who agreed to defect from the organization. In August 1996, Ieng Sary, Deputy Prime Minister in charge of foreign affairs in the Khmer Rouge regime, negotiated an amnesty for those who defected from the CPK. This amnesty created another split within the Khmer Rouge in 1997 which further focused international attention on accountability for the actions of the regime.[13]

It was the Secretary-General's Special Representative for Human Rights in Cambodia who began the process that led to negotiations for a tribunal. In July 1997, the two Cambodian prime ministers, Sen and Norodom Ranariddh (son of King Sihanouk) were persuaded by the Special Representative to request the creation of an international tribunal to try members of the Khmer Rouge.[14] The Special Representative marshaled Resolution 52/135 through the General Assembly condemning the Khmer Rouge genocide and requesting that the Secretary-General provide assistance to Cambodia. Interestingly, the Security Council was not involved in this effort as there were concerns over the potential use of China's veto.

At the request of the Cambodian government, the Secretary-General convened a group of experts to examine the available evidence and in March 1999, the experts' report found that the Khmer Rouge had committed not only war crimes and crimes against humanity but also genocide and other violations of the 1949 Geneva Conventions. The report also recommended the creation of an international tribunal modeled on the ICTY and the ICTR due to concerns regarding the level of independence and transparency of the judicial system in Cambodia.[15] The Cambodian government rejected this recommendation arguing that it had the obligation to prosecute violators of human rights and would do so within its domestic court system (Jarvis, 2002). Part of the reason for this change by the Cambodian government was the result of a coup staged by Sen which removed Ranariddh from the coalition government. Ranariddh appeared to favor an international tribunal while Sen favored a Cambodian-managed tribunal. During this period, two more senior members of the Khmer Rouge (Nuon Chea and Khieu Samphan) where granted amnesty.[16]

International pressure to hold elections and delayed membership in the Association of Southeast Asian Nations (ASEAN) forced Sen to reconsider his position. In September 1999, he presented two alternatives for UN involvement in the Cambodian tribunal: The UN could provide a legal team which would participate in the tribunal (established within the existing Cambodian legal system), or the UN could provide a legal team that would only serve in an advisory capacity. Otherwise, Sen suggested that the UN withdraw completely from the process (Cook, 2001). The Cambodian government created a taskforce to negotiate with the UN over its role and the structure of the ECC. The negotiations focused on creating a mixed tribunal, including international and domestic judges. In 1999, the Cambodian government drafted the tribunal statute, and in July 2000, the UN and the Cambodian government finalized details in a Memorandum of Understanding on the Chamber's structure.

In January 2001, Cambodia's parliament enacted the Law on the Establishment of Extraordinary Chambers in the Courts of Cambodia for the Prosecution of Crimes

Committed during the Period of Democratic Kampuchea. However, the legislation that the Cambodian government referred to the parliament did not abide by the agreement in the Memorandum of Understanding. Thus, the UN Office of Legal Affairs decided to end the negotiations in February 2002 (Jarvis, 2002). The UN argued that the Cambodian government wanted UN assistance but under Cambodia's terms without considering any recommendations (United Nations Legal Council, 2002).

However, members of the UN did not support this decision by the Office of Legal Affairs. The General Assembly passed Resolution 57/228A and Resolution 57/228B in December 2002 calling for further negotiations. On 6 January 2003, the negotiations resumed and on 17 March, the Cambodian government and UN officials agreed on a draft framework to prosecute the surviving leaders of the Khmer Rouge. This draft resolution was approved by the Cambodian government and the UN General Assembly. The agreement established that the ECC would have temporal jurisdiction from 17 April 1975 through 6 January 1979. This decision has been controversial as some in Cambodia believe that the period of 1970–1975 should also be included.[17] The issue of the 1996 amnesty for Ieng Sary and other members of the Khmer Rouge was addressed by the agreement between the UN and Cambodia. It was determined that the ECC would take up the issue, and the agreement also stipulated that the Cambodian government would not request additional amnesties or pardons for individuals under investigation or convicted. It remains to be seen how the ECC deals with the amnesties.

Regarding the financing of the ECC, the Cambodian government agreed to cover the costs of the premises as well as those associated with Cambodian personnel while the UN would finance the international personnel, witness and defense expenses, safety and security and other areas agreed to with the Cambodian government. The estimate of $56 million over three years has been viewed by many donor governments as excessive, but this amount is similar to the SCSL (see Chapter 5 for a further discussion regarding the financing of the ECC). The agreement required the ratification by the Cambodian parliament which was delayed by the 2003 election in which no political party received a 2/3rds majority to form a government as required by the constitution. This prevented a government from being formed until negotiations were brokered between the Sen and the Ranariddh parties in June 2004. The legislation was finally approved by parliament in October 2004.

The Structure and Jurisdictions of the Special Court for Sierra Leone

The agreement formally establishing the SCSL was signed in January 2002, and the Court began operating in July of that year. As a mixed court, the SCSL is composed of international and domestic judges and adjudicates cases based on international and domestic law. The SCSL is composed of one trial and one appeals chamber.[18] The trial chamber consists of three judges, one appointed by the Sierra Leonean government and two appointed by the Secretary-General. The appeals chamber consists of five judges, two appointed by the government and three appointed by the Secretary-General. The presiding judge of the appeals chamber is the president of the Court. All judges are appointed for a three-year term. Unlike the ICTY and the ICTR which are located outside of the countries where the conflict took place, the SCSL is located in Freetown. While the prosecutor is appointed by the Secretary-General, the deputy prosecutor is appointed by the government.[19] The SCSL has concurrent and primary jurisdiction with domestic courts and can request that a case be transferred to it.

While the statute describes the structure of the Court and its relationship to other domestic institutions, it is silent on the relationship of the SCSL to the TRCSL. There were concerns raised that statements and testimony provided to the TRCSL could be used as evidence in SCSL proceedings. While this is legally possible, SCSL Prosecutor David Crane has stated in radio and newspaper interviews that TRCSL statements will not be used by the Court. However, it is unclear whether there is any prohibition to defense attorneys using TRCSL testimony and compelling witnesses to appear before the SCSL.[20]

The SCSL has material jurisdiction over three sets of crimes (two international and one domestic). The definition of crimes against humanity draws most heavily upon the language of Article 3 in the ICTR statute.[21] The second set of crimes involves violations of humanitarian law as found in Common Article III of the Geneva Conventions and Additional Protocol II. The third set of crimes involves violation of Sierra Leonean law including offenses found in the 1926 Prevention of Cruelty to Children Act as well as the 1861 Malicious Damage Act. Fritz and Smith argue that the application of domestic laws involves significant hardships as "to ensure consistency in application of these laws, judges on the Special Court would need to have reference to court decisions by Sierra Leone domestic courts, but publication of Sierra Leone court decisions ceased in the 1970s" (2001, p. 410).

As Cerone (2002) notes unlike the ICTY and the ICTR, the SCSL statute does not contain a provision regarding the territorial jurisdiction of the Court. While the statute provides that those that commit crimes on Sierra Leonean soil can be held responsible, there is nothing to preclude prosecuting individuals outside of Sierra Leone for ordering crimes or complicity. Indeed, the indictment against Charles Taylor is not based on any actions that he personally undertook while on the territory of Sierra Leone. While the SCSL can indict individuals for crimes that they have committed while outside of the territory of Sierra Leone, the problem confronting the prosecution is extraditing defendants. As previously noted, the SCSL was not established under Chapter VII so a country such as Nigeria, which harbored Taylor, had no obligation to surrender him to Sierra Leone.[22] While this is an obvious impediment, states have repeatedly refused to abide by their Chapter VII obligations and transfer defendants to the ICTY and the ICTR.

The SCSL only has jurisdiction over natural persons who "bear the greatest responsibility" for committing crimes. Those that bear the greatest responsibility are generally those associated with the RUF (including Charles Taylor) or the CDF. However, there were also atrocities committed by ECOMOG troops sent to protect citizens. While peacekeepers are within the jurisdiction of the SCSL, the Court's statute assigns primary jurisdiction for these crimes to the sending state. Only if the sending state is unwilling or unable to prosecute and the Security Council gives consent can the SCSL prosecute peacekeepers (Cryer, 2001). This provision has been modeled on the language found in the ICC statute.

The Structure of the Extraordinary Chambers for Cambodia

The ECC has some unique features that have not been seen in the other tribunals. The Chambers will be composed of both international and Cambodian judges, but Cambodians will be in the majority. This places a larger burden on the domestic judicial system. The Secretary-General will nominate no less than seven international judges of which the Cambodian Supreme Council of the Magistracy will appoint five. It is ultimately the responsibility of the Cambodians to select the international judges from the list provided by the Secretary-General. The ECC will be composed of a trial chamber and a supreme court chamber. The trial chamber will be composed of three Cambodian judges and two international judges while the supreme court chamber will have four Cambodian judges and three international judges. Even though the composition of the Chambers gives a majority of the seats to Cambodian judges, decisions require a super-majority. In the case of the trial chamber, four judges must agree with the decision. In the case of the supreme court chamber, five judges have to issue an affirmative vote. This was an issue during the negotiations as the UN feared that the Cambodian judges might be unduly influenced by the government on issues of indictments, court proceedings and sentencing. All judges are expected to serve for the duration of the proceedings.

In addition to trial judges, the ECC will also have two investigating judges, one Cambodian and one international. The conduct of the prosecution will be the responsibility of co-prosecutors, one Cambodian and one international. The international investigating judge and the international prosecutor will be selected by the Cambodian Supreme Council of the Magistracy from a list of two candidates submitted by the Secretary-General. The investigating judges and co-prosecutors will have equal status in the ECC. This presents interesting challenges when a disagreement on investigations and prosecution of suspects occurs. However, as part of the negotiations between the UN and the Cambodian government, it was agreed that a pre-trial ruling by a chamber of five judges would determine how to proceed. In this case, a super-majority of four is also needed. However if there is not a super-majority decision, the investigation or prosecution must proceed.[23]

Article 1 of the agreement stipulates that the UN and the Cambodian government shall cooperate in "bringing to trial senior leaders of Democratic Kampuchea and those who were most responsible for the crimes and serious violations of Cambodian penal law, international humanitarian law and custom and international conventions recognized by Cambodia." In Cambodia, there is dissatisfaction with limiting trials to only senior officials of the Khmer Rouge, and there has been little clarification on how to determine those "most responsible." It is possible that between twenty to thirty senior Khmer Rouge leaders would be subject to prosecution, but this has not been finalized. In addition, it is important to remember that there are current members of the government who were part of the Khmer Rouge before they defected to Vietnam in 1977 and 1978.

According to Article 9 of the agreement, the subject matter jurisdiction of the Chambers will include both elements of international and domestic law. Among the types of crimes mentioned are the crime of genocide as defined by the 1948 Convention, crimes against humanity as defined by the ICC statute, grave breaches of the 1949 Geneva Conventions and other crimes defined in the Law on the Establishment of the Extraordinary Chambers passed by Cambodia in 2001. The procedures within the Chambers will be based on Cambodian law, but international standards will also be used where there are inconsistencies or no precedent in the Cambodian penal code (which dates back to 1956). In addition, the statute stipulates that the maximum penalty for a conviction, in accordance with Cambodian law, is life imprisonment.

Similar to the SCSL, the ECC does not have provisions regarding territorial jurisdiction. At present, most of the members of the Khmer Rouge leadership who could be indicted are within Cambodia or unknown locations. Extradition would become an issue if Khmer Rouge members fled to Thailand once indictments and orders of arrest are issued. This issue will be exacerbated if the ECC decides to revoke amnesties. At that point, individuals such as Nuon Chea, Khieu Samphan and Ieng Sary might flee to Thailand or other countries in the region, and it would be the responsibility of those governments to secure arrests and transfer suspects. As seen in the case of Sierra Leone, neighbors in the region might be reluctant to take these actions. Even if members of the Khmer Rouge do not flee and continue to reside in Cambodia, the government needs to have the political will to arrest these individuals.

The Current Status of the Special Court for Sierra Leone and Extraordinary Chambers for Cambodia

While there have been concerns over whether the SCSL would be a viable institution given financial, logistical and security concerns, the SCSL has moved very quickly to issue indictments and begin trials. The first seven indictments were handed down in March 2003, followed by four more issued from April through June as well as the unsealing of the indictment against Charles Taylor also in June 2003. There are currently eleven individuals indicted by the SCSL.[24] Ten of these individuals have been arrested and arraigned by the Court. Former coup leader Johnny Paul Koroma's whereabouts are unknown.

In October 2003, prosecutors filed a motion asking that all the accused persons in custody be tried in two groups. The prosecutors argued that joint trials would be more efficient and that they would reduce the burden on witnesses. The judges, led by President Justice Ayoola, agreed that joint trials would be in the interest of justice. They also stated that this would enable the accused to receive a fair and speedy trial. However, the judges ruled that the nine individuals detained at that point should be tried jointly in three groups, according to the faction to which they were alleged to have belonged. Indictees were placed in an RUF, CDF or AFRC group (three indictees in each group). While the indictees will be tried together, judges will render individual verdicts based on the evidence in the case. More than a year after the first indictment, the first trial of the CDF group began in June 2004 followed by the RUF group in July. The trial for the AFRC group began in March 2005 after the appointment of judges to a second chamber. Although this Court has acted very quickly to indict and begin the trial process, the key concern is whether the SCSL will be able to continue to secure financing to fulfill its mandate.

Legislation for the ECC was ratified by the Cambodian parliament in October 2004. The budget for the Chambers for three years was estimated at $56 million. Of this amount, the international community would provide $43 million while the Cambodian government would provide the remaining $13 million. By the middle of 2005, there had been enough contributions to cover the international commitment. However in August 2005, the Cambodian government stated that it could not fulfill its part of the financial commitment and has requested that the international community contribute another $11.5 million to the tribunal. Even with this setback, the process of nominating both international and Cambodian judges has begun.

One of the important issues that remains to be solved by the ECC in order to provide justice is what to do about the amnesties granted by the government. Iang Sery lives in Phnom Penh and Khieu Samphan and Nuon Chea continue to live close to the Thai border. Samphan has acknowledged that the regime committed genocide. Chea admits that "some mistakes" were made during Pol Pot's regime, but also contends that the killing field statistics are "exaggerated and require examination" (Pringle, 2004). Both deny that they were involved in the atrocities committed by the regime. No Khmer Rouge leader has ever been tried, though two of them, Ta Mok, known as the butcher of Cambodia and Kaing Khek Iev, are being held without charges.

While the SCSL in Sierra Leone has generally had wide support among the public and government leaders, the creation of the ECC has been stymied by the Sen government and is viewed with suspicion by all levels of Cambodian society. Not surprisingly given the level of support in the two countries, the SCSL has moved quickly in issuing indictments and arranging an effective trial process while the negotiations over the ECC have taken years just to establish the structure and the legal basis of the Chambers. Perhaps these difficulties reflect the fact that the ECC is the only tribunal which has jurisdiction over crimes committed during the Cold War. While the international system has fundamentally changed since 1991, Cambodian domestic politics reflect many of the same realities of the 1970s and 1980s. Indeed while judges began to be interviewed for ECC positions in December 2005, it is uncertain how many of the elderly Khmer Rouge indictees will actually be alive by the time the ECC becomes fully operational. While thwarting the establishment of the Chambers suits the political objectives of the Sen government, it undermines whatever reconciliation and justice that the process will eventually provide.

As with all institutions of justice, there is no one model which is preferable. These institutions must be crafted to exist within a political and a legal culture. That being said, these institutions are most desperately needed in states in which there is a lack of the rule of law as tribunals can provide judicial training and serve to assist in the reconstruction of the domestic legal system. The experience of the SCSL demonstrates that hybrid tribunals can be very effective institutions while the experience of Cambodia provides a counterexample. However, the concept of state sovereignty and the atrocities committed are different in Sierra Leone and Cambodia. Perhaps the weakness of the Sierra Leonean government was actually a benefit to the process of providing justice and ending the impunity of rebel and government leaders. As we discuss in Chapter 4, the even tougher stance that the Indonesian government has taken *vis-à-vis* crimes committed in East Timor is a reflection of the determination of the government to retain sovereignty even at the cost of justice.

Notes

1. While the official name of the territory of East Timor changed in November 2002 to Timor Leste, we use the name East Timor throughout the book for purposes of consistency.
2. There is no formally approved name for the tribunal in Cambodia. The authors use the title "Extraordinary Chambers for Cambodia" as this is the best description for the tribunal based on the statute.
3. The SCPET and Indonesian Human Rights Court will be dealt with in Chapter 4 as they provide a better comparison since they address the same conflict, namely the violence associated with the 1999 referendum for independence in East Timor.
4. The SCPET is different than the SCSL and the ECC in that the SCPET was created by UN Resolution 1272 which established the United Nations Transitional Administration of East Timor. This is why Linton argues that East Timor represents "the creation of an internationalised structure within the domestic criminal justice system" (2001, p. 232).
5. During our interviews and discussions in Cambodia, the role of Vietnam during the period of the Khmer Rouge was repeatedly addressed. Many Cambodians, even within the legal community, question why the ECC will not be able to try Vietnamese for crimes against humanity and genocide.
6. Before the May 1997 coup, there had been two other coup attempts against President Kabbah indicating the low level of support that he enjoyed among not only junior officers but senior military officials as well.
7. Financing the Court has been an ongoing problem. Initially, the estimates for the first three years of the Court were approximately $115 million with $30 million necessary for the first year. These estimates have been repeatedly scaled back. The SCSL currently has a short-fall of $85 million. Only thirty-three UN member-states have contributed to the Court. However, the UN has offered a subsidiary grant to compensate for the $85 million.

8. Under violations of international humanitarian law, the draft statute included the "abduction and forced recruitment of children under the age of 15 years into the armed forces or groups for the purpose of using them to participate actively in hostilities" (United Nations Doc., 2000).
9. The international recognition of the concept of amnesty is far from resolved. Gallagher (2000) argues that the amnesty provided in the Lomé Agreement should be distinguished from other more standard forms of amnesty. Most importantly, the amnesty granted in Sierra Leone was for non-state actors. Generally, amnesties are provided by the state for state actors or former governments.
10. In August 2001, the government of Sierra Leone sent a letter to the UN Legal Counsel requesting that the temporal jurisdiction be extended to March 1991. This request was denied.
11. The Khmer Rouge held Cambodia's seat in the UN until 1989.
12. The other groups represented the government, the royalists which supported Sinahouk and another group which opposed the Sen government.
13. Pol Pot ordered the assassination of Son Sen, a leading CPK official.
14. Following the 1993 elections, there was no super-majority in the parliament to form a government as required by the constitution. Therefore in order to obtain the required majority, the parties of Sen and Ranariddh agreed to a joint prime ministerial post.
15. The report also recommended the creation of a truth and reconciliation commission which so far has not been established.
16. Samphan was the public face of the Khmer Rouge for years as the movement's nominal leader. Chea was the Khmer Rouge's ideologue and also known as "Brother No. 2."
17. Interviews by the authors in Cambodia in May 2004 and March 2005.
18. In his report, the Secretary-General requested a second trial chamber. The Security Council rejected this request; however, a second chamber has now been added.
19. While the government is responsible for selecting the deputy prosecutor, there is no requirement that the individual be a Sierra Leonean. Deputy Prosecutor Desmond de Silva has British citizenship.
20. The International Crisis Group issued an excellent report that details the complicated relationship between the TRCSL and the SCSL, see ICG, 2002b.
21. Cryer (2001) notes that the definition of crimes against humanity while similar differ in every international and mixed tribunal.
22. At the time of this writing in May 2006, Charles Taylor had been apprehended attempting to flee Nigeria. The SCSL requested that he be tried at The Hague because of security concerns in Freetown. This request is being considered by the UN Security Council.
23. The Sen government, however, had proposed that the investigation or prosecution be stopped when a super-majority decision could not be achieved.
24. Two indictments have been withdrawn because the defendant died. Significantly, one of the most important indictees, Sankoh, died of natural causes while in prison in July 2003.

Chapter 4

Creating and Reasserting State Sovereignty: The Serious Crimes Panel for East Timor and the Indonesian Human Rights Court

As discussed in Chapter 3, the year 2000 brought about the creation of new tribunals for Sierra Leone, Cambodia, East Timor and Indonesia. While each of these tribunals has unique features regarding their jurisdiction, composition and financing, all of them constitute a movement away from the model established by the International Criminal Tribunal for the former Yugoslavia (ICTY) and the International Criminal Tribunal for Rwanda (ICTR)—a movement away from a purely international tribunal to a "hybrid" or "mixed" tribunal involving both international and domestic components, with the Indonesian Human Rights Court (IHRC) representing a purely domestic response to human rights violations.

While there may be compelling international and domestic political reasons for the creation of hybrid and domestic tribunals, the question remains whether these alternatives to international tribunals are as effective in providing justice and reconciliation. In all four cases, tribunals have been established in a conflict or a post-conflict environment in which the countries have undergone civil war.[1] The question that we will examine in this chapter is whether these forms of hybrid and domestic institutions as exemplified by the Serious Crimes Panel for East Timor (SCPET) and the IHRC are as, effective as international tribunals in providing reconciliation and in rendering justice defined in terms of indictments, prosecutions and sentences.

The SCPET and the IHRC are unique in that the same human rights violations have been tried by two countries, using different legal processes and arriving at different verdicts. While the cases presented to these tribunals are different, the violations stem from the same period and the same acts of violence. Therefore, these tribunals allow us to compare the verdicts and the sentencing to assess their ability to provide justice and accountability. Ultimately, hybrid and domestic human rights courts exist within a domestic environment in which political and financial concerns can often take priority over providing justice to victims.

This chapter is divided into four sections. First, we analyze the nature of the conflict in East Timor as well as the types of crimes which were committed. Second, we examine the debate over the creation of the tribunal in East Timor and Indonesia and some of the limitations brought about by the negotiations. Third, we discuss the structure of both tribunals and finally conclude by examining the ability of these tribunals to provide justice to victims, rights to the accused and ultimately a historical record of events. While it may not be surprising that the government in Jakarta has not supported a robust investigation and prosecution of crimes committed in East Timor, it is surprising that the government of East Timor has been much less enthusiastic about the process in Dili as well as the process in Jakarta than the international community.

The Nature of the Conflict in East Timor

For a number of centuries, East Timor was a colony of Portugal. Throughout this period, East Timor was exploited by the Portuguese first for sandalwood and later as an area for the cultivation of coffee and sugar cane (Pomeroy, 2001). While there were violent conflicts between the Portuguese and the native Timorese, particularly the 1912 Manufahi revolt, relations between the various ethnic groups, including ethnic Chinese traders, were largely peaceful. Typical of a colonial power, profits from agricultural products were exported back to Portugal so that by 1940, the capital of Dili had no running water or electricity.

In the 1960s, the Portuguese government attempted to develop the island through the introduction of three successive five-year plans. Also during this time, the United Nations (UN) recognized East Timor as a non self-governing territory under Portuguese administration; however, Portugal governed East Timor with a combination of direct and indirect rule, controlling the population through the traditional societal power structures. This situation continued until the April 1974 coup in Portugal in which the military withdrew its support of the Caetano regime (Opello, 1991). Within a short period of time, Portugal began to transition from authoritarianism to democracy which influenced not only the country's domestic politics but also its foreign policy.

The change in the Portuguese political system had a major impact on all of its colonies. For the first time, the Timorese were given the freedom to form their own political parties. After a series of alliances, the two main parties, the Timorese Democratic Union (UDT) and the *Frente Revolucionaria do Timor-Leste Independente* (Fretilin) formed a coalition. However in August 1975, the UDT, supported by the Indonesian government, launched a coup in an attempt to seize power from the Portuguese and halt the ascendancy of Fretilin.[2] In the power struggle, Fretilin was perceived to be the most popular Timorese party which was led by Xanana Gusmão. Ultimately, the coup failed, and the UDT forces fled to West Timor which was controlled by the Indonesians. Later as the Portuguese left East Timor, Fretilin gained *de facto* control of the island. In the power vacuum, Fretilin declared East Timor independent; however, the party had not yet developed a coherent set of economic policies or military resources, nor did it have the political experience to administer the island during a period of ever increasing encroachment by the Indonesian Military (TNI).

In December 1975, the TNI launched a full-scale invasion of East Timor under the pretext of President Suharto's "New Order" administration which was designed to prevent islands in the eastern archipelago from declaring independence. The UN did not recognize the annexation of East Timor by Indonesia; however due to Cold War politics, the Security Council failed to take any action (Jolliffe, 1978). At this time, the US was much more concerned with containing communism in Southeast Asia and assisting its key strategic ally, Indonesia, in combating communist insurgency. East Timor became the twenty-seventh province of Indonesia in July 1976.

Unlike the Portuguese, the Indonesians imposed direct and often brutal rule. During the early years of occupation, approximately 60,000 individuals were killed and many more were forced into resettlement villages. A small guerrilla army, the National Liberation Armed Forces of East Timor, was formed by Gusmão to fight for independence. Media coverage of events in East Timor, however, was extremely limited as the Indonesian government banned all media outlets. However, two events in the 1990s galvanized the demand for Timorese independence. In November 1991, thousands of individuals marched towards the Santa Cruz cemetery to mourn the death of Sebastião Gomes, a student protester who was killed by the military. As the Timorese entered the cemetery, the TNI opened fire and killed more than 200. The "Santa Cruz Massacre" marked a turning point in the occupation of East Timor. For the first time, the images of the killings were made public by the international media.[3] The public outcry over the treatment of the population and the bravery of the Timorese people and leadership led to Bishop Carlos Ximenes Belo, head of the Catholic Church, and José Ramos-Horta, an international spokesperson for the independence cause of East Timor being awarded the Nobel Peace Prize in 1996.

By 1998, there were increasing international calls for the withdrawal of the TNI from East Timor as well as the right of indigenous people to self-determination. The Suharto regime resisted any attempt to provide autonomy let along outright independence to East Timor. However, the Asian financial crisis quickly undermined the public's confidence in the Suharto regime and lead to widespread demands in Indonesia for a change in government. With the Cold War over, the US position on Suharto changed and without domestic or international support, he was forced to resign. He was replaced by B. J. Habibie who quickly offered a reform program which would allow the Timorese to decide between autonomy within Indonesia or outright independence.[4] Just as in 1974, the Timorese were quickly confronted with the prospect of self-government. While many Timorese welcomed this possibility, there was a vocal minority that sided with the Indonesian government and did not want independence (Jones, 2001). The TNI used this fact so that unlike the Portuguese, the Indonesians did not initially withdraw from East Timor.

Under the auspices of the UN, a referendum was scheduled for 30 August 1999 to decide whether East Timor would become autonomous or independent. During the pre-referendum period, armed groups representing both sides engaged in attacks.[5] The TNI was not a passive bystander but actively assisted the pro-Indonesian militia.[6] In fact, Smith argues that the agreement between the UN and Indonesia which established the referendum was flawed since "it gave in to Jakarta's refusal to allow UN 'blue beret' forces, and left security in Indonesian hands" (2004, p. 148). In the August referendum, turnout was just under 99 per cent, with 78.5 per cent voting against autonomy.

Shortly after the referendum, the violence in and around Dili increased dramatically. UN personnel withdrew and were eventually evacuated along with some Timorese civilians. During the ensuing violence, approximately 2,000 individuals were killed while 250,000 individuals fled to West Timor. Also during this period, approximately 70 per cent of East Timor's buildings and infrastructure were destroyed (Smith, 2004). The Security Council in September authorized the International Force for East Timor (INTERFET) to restore order (Linton, 2001). In October 1999, the Indonesian parliament recognized the result of the referendum, and the Security Council passed Resolution 1272 which established the United Nations Transitional Administration in East Timor (UNTAET) which took over from the INTERFET the responsibility of administering East Timor during its transition to independence. At that point, even though the East Timorese had voted for independence, the new state was not ready to assume total political control so the UNTAET assumed many government powers until 2002.[7] While the status of East Timor had been determined, it was unclear how individuals responsible for the human rights violations perpetrated during the referendum process would be brought to justice, including East Timorese and the TNI.

The culpability of TNI officers must be placed within the larger context of Indonesian civil-military relations. Suharto seized power in 1965 while a leading general in the TNI. Not surprisingly, Suharto's regime politicized the military. Several key cabinet posts (including historically the post of attorney general and minister of defense) as well as a number of legislative seats were allotted to the military and police forces. Suharto's party, Golkar, was composed of senior military officers, and therefore like any authoritarian regime, military support was paramount to maintaining political power. While Suharto's immediate successor, Habibie, instituted reforms designed to reduce the influence of the military, these reforms were piecemeal and did not change the fundamental power of the TNI.[8]

Negotiating the Special Crimes Panel for East Timor

After the violence in East Timor, there was an outcry by the international community to bring to justice those responsible for the human rights violations. The UN Commission on Human Rights (UNCHR) met at a special session in September 1999 and called upon the Secretary-General to establish an International Commission of Inquiry (ICI) and discuss the possibility of an international tribunal. The ICI compiled information on possible violations of human rights and acts that may have constituted breaches of international humanitarian law committed in East Timor after January 1999.[9] The ICI visited East Timor and Indonesia in November and December 1999 and delivered a report to the UN Secretary-General in January 2000. Even though the Indonesian government denied the Commission access to military files, the

ICI report concluded that the incidents of wide-spread and systematic attacks on the civilian population supported charges of crimes against humanity.[10] The three *rapporteurs* determined that there was enough evidence to assign responsibility to the Indonesian government and called for action by the government.[11] However based on the investigation, it was also recommended that an international tribunal be set up to try those involved in the 1999 violence (Rudolph, 2001).

For economic and political reasons, the Security Council did not respond to the report's call to create an international tribunal based on an ICTY and an ICTR model with Chapter VII authority. Instead, the UNTAET took the lead in designing the structure and the procedures that would guide the work of what would become a hybrid tribunal to prosecute those responsible for the violence (Cohen, 2002).[12] As part of the effort to begin the process of handing over power to the Timorese, the UNTAET established the National Consultative Council (NCC), a political body consisting of eleven Timorese and four UNTAET members, to oversee the decision-making process during the transition period. Decisions related to the creation of the hybrid tribunal involved the NCC (and therefore ostensibly Timorese). However, the UNTAET was criticized for not carrying out enough consultations related to the establishment of the tribunal which provoked the anger of judges, prosecutors and public defenders in the Dili District Court (Linton, 2002). In the end, there was very little consultation and negotiation between the Timorese and the UNTAET. Most of the negotiation concerning the establishment of the SCPET occurred either within the Security Council or within the UNTAET. While the Security Council refused to consider creating the SCPET under Chapter VII authority, the Council realized that the international community had to create a legal mechanism to address the human rights violations in East Timor. However while the SCPET appeared to be the appropriate mechanism to address the violence in East Timor, there was little discussion with the national leadership regarding the structure of the Tribunal.

Negotiating the Indonesian Human Rights Court

As previously mentioned in the wake of the post-referendum violence, a special session of the UNCHR was convened in Geneva to discuss the possibility of the creation of an international tribunal similar to the ICTY and the ICTR. The Indonesian government was reluctant to support the idea of the establishment of an international tribunal arguing that it would violate its sovereignty since the alleged crimes were committed on what was Indonesian soil. Moreover, the government maintained that the Indonesian legal system was capable of conducting trials and that national remedies had to be explored before an international process could even be considered (Rae, 2003). With the assistance of Asian bloc countries, Indonesia was able to convince the members of the UNHCR that the country was capable of prosecuting those accused of the pre and post-referendum violence (ICG, 2002a).

From the beginning, the creation of the IHRC was stymied by the government and especially the attorney general's office. In September 1999 as the UNCHR discussed the situation in East Timor, the National Human Rights Commission (KOMNAS HAM) appointed a Commission of Inquiry (KPP HAM) to investigate human rights violations in East Timor. The mandate of the KPP HAM was to gather evidence of human rights abuses since January 1999, investigate whether the state and national agencies were responsible for crimes and compile evidence to be used by a future human rights court (Cohen, 2003). In January 2000 as the ICI report was presented to the UN, the KPP HAM produced its own detailed report which recommended that more than 100 individuals be further investigated by the attorney general, including the four highest-ranking members of the TNI. The report also listed thirteen primary cases in which substantial evidence indicated that there had been a close relationship between Indonesian military leaders and Timorese militias.

Attorney General Marzuki Darusman argued that he could not proceed with prosecutions because existing Indonesian law contained no provisions for crimes against humanity, the main charge made in the KPP HAM report and by the ICI. Instead, he appointed an investigation team which took most of the year to examine the KPP HAM report. Rather than investigate all of the evidence cited by the report, Darusman announced that his office was giving priority to the investigation of only four of the primary cases listed in the report and significantly excluding from investigation the highest-ranking military officers. His decision had another important impact as the investigation into only four cases "immediately reduced the prospects for any systematic examination of the more general pattern of violence during 1999. In particular, it meant that there would be little investigation into the role of state policy that is critical to establishing a case for crimes against humanity, as opposed to an ordinary criminal case of murder" (ICG, 2002a, p. 4).

In November 2000, the Indonesian legislature passed Law 26 which incorporated the Rome Statute of the International Criminal Court (ICC) in order to provide a legal basis for trying human rights violations in a domestic process. The legislation also allowed the president to appoint by decree an *ad hoc* human rights court, based upon a request by the legislature with appointments made by the Supreme Court. In March 2001, President Abdurrahman Wahid issued a presidential decree (Decision 53) which authorized the creation of an *ad hoc* human rights court with jurisdiction over human rights violations committed only *after* the August referendum. In August 2001, President Megawati Sukarnoputri signed Decision 96 which extended the mandate of the *ad hoc* court to April 1999. However, it was left to new Attorney General M. A. Rahman to draft the indictments based upon the decree.[13]

The indictments were issued by the Ministry of Justice based on a narrow reading of Decision 96. Moreover, the presidential decree was considered by many human rights groups to be far too general and not incorporating specific elements of human rights violations. For example, the decree mandated an investigation of "gross human rights violations" without any specific mention of criminal elements including crimes against humanity, genocide or war crimes.[14] Much of the KPP HAM report never found its way into the decree, and as a consequence, several important issues and cases that the KPP HAM noted in its report were never investigated because of the restrictive and general nature of the decree and ultimately the law which established the IHRC's jurisdiction.

The Structure and Jurisdiction of the Serious Crimes Panel for East Timor

This hybrid tribunal was established through UNTAET Regulations 2000/11 (6 March 2000) and 2000/15 (6 June 2000) which contained the enabling legislation for investigation, prosecution and sentencing. The organization and the jurisdiction of the SCPET were outlined in Regulation 2000/15. The SCPET was given exclusive jurisdiction over genocide, war crimes and crimes against humanity (derived from the ICC's Statute) as well as murder, sexual offenses and torture (as defined by the Indonesian penal code). At this time, East Timor was using the inherited penal code from Indonesia.

As part of the structure of the legal process in East Timor, a Serious Crimes Unit (SCU) was established under regulation 2000/16 (6 June 2000). The SCU was responsible for conducting investigations and preparing indictments to bring to justice those responsible for crimes against humanity and other serious crimes. The SCU was divided into four regional teams comprised of UN prosecutors, legal officers, investigators and trainee staff with separate forensic investigation, evidence management and witness support teams. The regional investigation and prosecution teams covered all thirteen districts of East Timor. After the independence of East Timor in 2002, the SCU worked under the legal authority of the Timorese prosecutor-general.

Even though there had been numerous incidents of violence since Indonesia annexed East Timor in 1975, the SCPET and the SCU temporal authority was limited to the period of 1 January 1999 through 25 October 1999. This has brought about claims that "narrowing the time frame suppressed or ignored a broader truth" (Rae, 2003, p. 173). The UN's budget provided for two trial chambers, each composed of two international judges and one Timorese judge. They operated as part of the Dili court system. Therefore, the SCPET was established as part of the Timorese legal system. The appellate chamber was composed of two international judges and one Timorese. These judges were appointed by the Timorese Supreme Council of the Judiciary (de Bertodano, 2003).

Ten priority cases were identified as part of the work of the SCPET and the SCU. These included the Liquiça church attack, the Suai church massacre, the September attack on the compound of Bishop Belo, the Maliana police station attack and the TNI 745 Battalion killings. Within the ten priority cases, a total of 202 accused persons were charged with crimes against humanity (183 remain at-large in Indonesia). A national indictment issued on 24 February 2003 charged the former Indonesian minister of defense and commander of the armed forces, six high-ranking Indonesian military commanders and the former governor of East Timor with crimes against humanity for murder, deportation and persecution during 1999.

All investigations were completed on 30 November 2004, and the mandate of the SCU and the SCPET ended in May 2005.

The Structure and Jurisdiction of the Indonesian Human Rights Court

Under Law 26, the IHRC was created as a special chamber within the Indonesian domestic legal system. The Supreme Court established a special committee which was in charge of selecting candidates to be proposed to the legislature as judges for the IHRC. The candidates that were selected were a combination of career and non-career (*ad hoc*) judges. Some of the drafters of the law intended that non-career judges come from the ranks of human rights attorneys with experience in this area. This was seen as vital as no career judge had experience trying human rights cases. However, "instead, an obscure regulation was unearthed, requiring that any non-career judge serving in an Indonesian court be drawn from university law faculties" (ICG, 2002a, p. 4).

Some of these academics not only were often not versed in human rights law but had no training as a judge. Also, the academics had to be nominated by their respective universities and often the most qualified individual from a law faculty was not nominated by the university rector.[15] However, Cohen (2003) argues that some of these *ad hoc* judges did have training or experience in international human rights law and therefore played an important role in the most prominent convictions of the IHRC. On the other hand, others have argued that the lack of actual judicial administration and experience as a judge made the *ad hoc* judges "more afraid of the officers in the gallery."[16] Because many of the judges were inexperienced in the courtroom as well as inexperienced in international human rights law, the UN provided materials and training seminars, including a visit to the ICTY.[17]

Approximately thirty-two candidates were put forward to the legislature. In an open session, the legislature debated the list of proposed candidates. The chief judge of the IHRC was authorized to appoint a five-judge panel drawn from a combination of twelve career and thirteen non-career or *ad hoc* judges. Each trial panel consisted of three *ad hoc* and two career judges with a presiding career judge (Cohen, 2003). The Central Jakarta District Court served as the home of the IHRC within the Indonesian legal system. The appeals process included two panels of three judges, and cases could be appealed to the Supreme Court.[18]

The temporal jurisdiction allowed the prosecutor to bring indictments only in cases occurring between April and September 1999. Article 5 of Law 26 provides that the IHRC had the authority to hear and rule on cases of gross violations of human rights perpetrated by an Indonesian citizen outside the territorial boundaries of Indonesia. Article 7 of the law states that the definitions of the crime of genocide and crimes against humanity are in accordance with the ICC's Rome Statute. Law 26 lays out a very rigid and relatively quick process for disposing of cases. The law states that the investigator has thirty days to complete the preliminary inquiry and a total of 240 days for the investigation. The law also specified a time limit of 180 days for cases to be heard and ruled on by the IHRC and for appeals to both the appellate chamber and the Indonesian Supreme Court to be heard and ruled on within a period of ninety days. An Amnesty International report argued that "such time limits are useful as benchmarks, but they should not be mandatory" (Amnesty International, 2001, p. 6). The law also established sentencing guidelines in which the minimum sentence that could be imposed was ten years. This created a problem for some of the judges as they wanted sentencing discretion in order to impose terms of less than ten years.[19]

Issues of Concern and the Status of the Serious Crimes Panel for East Timor

From the beginning, observers identified several shortcomings with the Timorese tribunal. Before the end of its mandate, the SCU indicted a total of 391 individuals for crimes against humanity committed during and after the 1999 referendum; however, 290 of these individuals were in Indonesia with little chance of being transferred. The Indonesian government refused to act on several arrest warrants issued for Indonesian and Timorese citizens. These arrest warrants included thirty-seven Indonesian TNI military commanders and officers, four Indonesian chiefs of police, sixty Timorese TNI officers and soldiers, the former governor of East Timor and five former district administrators. Former Minister of Defense General Wiranto (a leading presidential candidate in 2004) was among the senior officers enjoying apparent immunity from prosecution. The Timorese government has been criticized for initially endorsing and then disavowing the indictment against General Wiranto.

By the end of its mandate in May 2005, the SCPET had handed down a total of eighty-four convictions and three acquittals. However, most of those who faced trials were lower-level Timorese militia members. The judiciary's shortage of personnel, as well as bureaucratic and managerial inefficiency, contributed to the inability to provide for prompt trials. From the beginning, UNTAET confronted a legal vacuum when it arrived in East Timor. Many of those with legal training working under the Indonesian government had fled after the referendum fearing retaliation (Katzenstein, 2003). None of the Timorese judges had any significant courtroom experience when they were appointed in 1999, and the fledgling judicial process was plagued by delays and claims by non-governmental organizations (NGOs) of poor decision-making. In addition, most trial judges and prosecutors were trained only in Indonesian law and received their legal education in the Indonesian language while most appellate judges and many senior government officials were trained elsewhere and spoke little or no Indonesian. These problems plagued the tribunal as all twenty-two Timorese judges, some of whom had been presiding over prosecutions for crimes against humanity in the SCPET, failed their probationary evaluation in February 2005 and were disqualified to hear cases. Until six judges were reappointed to finish their scheduled work on the SCPET and the appellate chamber, only four international judges had been able to hear cases in the two chambers throughout the court system.

Laws enacted by the Timorese parliament were intended to gradually replace the Indonesian penal code and UNTAET regulations. The problem is that the laws were published only in Portuguese, and many litigants, witnesses and criminal defendants were unable to read the laws. In addition as of 1 October 2004, a decision by the Superior Council of Magistrates required that trials be conducted solely in Portuguese and Tetum. The Judicial System Monitoring Program (a Timorese coordinated NGO) issued several reports regarding the functioning of the tribunal, questioning the impartiality of the SCPET, the competence of the defense counsel, the lack of transparency and information about the proceedings as well as the delays and interruptions in the trials. Various defense counsels were criticized on several fronts. For some, the high conviction rates indicated that the defense might not be zealously advocating for defendants. In addition while plea bargaining was used to expedite the legal process, there were indications that defendants did not understand that this entailed an admission of guilt. Public information about the trials and the process was lacking, and travel by the judges to the different locations of the court meant that cases were not heard in a timely manner, creating uncertainty and frustration for both defendants and witnesses.

Issues of Concern and the Status of the Indonesian Human Rights Court

Aside from the criticisms of the IHRC in terms of its temporal and criminal jurisdiction, the major criticisms of the IHRC process focused on the lack of convictions, unprofessional conduct of the judiciary and the prosecutorial teams and the flawed appeals process. Eighteen individuals were indicted with twelve eventually being acquitted. Of the six that were found guilty, the IHRC appellate chamber overturned the conviction of five high-ranking Indonesian security officials and cut in half the ten-year sentence of Eurico Guterres, Vice Commander of the *Pasukan Pejuang Integrasi* (Pro-Integration Troop) and former leader of the Aitarak militia in East Timor.[20] Thus only one of the eighteen who was originally tried by the IHRC is facing the possibility of being imprisoned.[21]

In our interviews with NGO leaders and members of the judiciary, they argued that the problems with the IHRC process were not specific to this institution or human rights issues in general but involved more systemic problems associated with the Indonesian judiciary and the need to reform civil-military relations. Because the attorney general had historically been a member of the military, it was difficult for the Ministry of Justice to conduct trials of military personnel. The NGOs hoped that the acquittals and reversals would lead to international involvement in future human rights trials. They felt that there needed to be established an international legal procedure and that an UN-appointed panel of experts would assist in creating a record of past abuses which could be the basis for further international action. The problem, however, is that Indonesian society is very much against an international process. Polling data indicate that 70 per cent of Indonesians are opposed to an international process to try the military.[22]

One of the criticisms that has been made of the process involves the lack of professionalism of the judges. The judges that we spoke to were very candid about their lack of expertise in international humanitarian law. The problem was that most of the career judges had no training in international law and that the *ad hoc* judges while sometimes academic experts in international law had never presided in a courtroom. The additional training received via the UN (including a visit to The Hague) was very important in their professionalization. The judges also explained that as a judge, they relied upon the prosecutors to provide sound indictments and indicated that because of political interference, prosecutors did not present strong cases. Under the constitution, the prosecutors are part of the executive branch, and for approximately thirty-two years, the attorney general was drawn from the military.[23] The judges indicated that while there was pressure from the TNI during the actual court proceedings, they did not encounter any political interference during their deliberations. When asked about the reversals, the judges indicated that they disagreed with many of the decisions but that it was ultimately up to the appeals judges to decide matters.

Additional criticisms of the process have been leveled at the incompetence of the prosecutors and their lack of concern in securing convictions. Several of the NGOs we spoke to made this criticism; however, they also pointed out that some of the prosecutors worked very hard under difficult circumstances. One of the concerns in establishing the IHRC was witness protection. Given that testimony was crucial to establishing a chain of events and that witnesses would be providing testimony against TNI officers as well as high-ranking civilians, there was a concern for witness safety. Law 26 was largely silent on the issue of witness protection and the use of testimony. The IHRC law relied on Indonesian domestic law to establish the code of conduct related to evidence.[24] Indonesian law does not allow video testimony, and thus there was the problem of bringing witnesses to Jakarta who were often scared and reluctant to leave East Timor. This was especially a concern given that 75 per cent of the court gallery consisted of TNI members who often brought guns and knives to the courtroom as part of their daily military attire.

Conclusions

The conflicts in 1999 and militia activity in 2000 and 2001 resulted in over 250,000 Timorese fleeing their homes. As a sign of the relative success of the new government by 2003, approximately 225,000 Timorese had returned. However, the end of the trials in East Timor means that the most high-profile person to be indicted, General Wiranto, will never be prosecuted in East Timor. If the IHRC process had led to prosecutions and sentences for those who were not transferred to Dili, then many might feel that justice had been rendered. Instead, the IHRC has been viewed by the Security Council, states and many Indonesian NGOs as a failure.

However, the IHRC must be placed within the broader political environment in Indonesia. The country is transitioning toward a stable democracy and rule of law after three decades of authoritarian rule. The problems of the IHRC are not unique but represent systemic problems of the Indonesian judiciary. As one individual from an Indonesian NGO argued "there can be no reconciliation without Indonesians going on trial."[25] The irony is that while the IHRC and the SCU were investigating the same crimes committed in East Timor, there was virtually no coordination between these bodies. In April 2000, a memorandum of understanding was signed between the Indonesian attorney general's office and the UNTAET to facilitate cooperation related to human rights matters. While the UNTAET assisted the Indonesian prosecution by providing witness testimony, the attorney general's office did not allow UNTAET to interview witnesses in Indonesia. Perhaps the lack of coordination is not surprising given the lack of political will not only in Jakarta but also Dili. This is a problem because many NGOs felt that the process in Dili needed to actually be strengthened in order to counteract the flawed process in Indonesia.[26]

The request that the SCU terminate its indictments in November 2004 led to increased Timorese public support for an international tribunal or some other mechanism to bring to justice those indictees who remained at large in Indonesia. At the same time, the government in Dili has indicated that it does not support an international process as it wants to further its relations with Indonesia. For its part, the international community is not convinced that the hybrid process in East Timor and especially the domestic process in Indonesia have resulted in justice for victims. The UN approved in February 2005 the creation of a Commission of Experts to evaluate the SCPET and the IHRC and to recommend further steps for achieving accountability. The report by the UN Commission described the SCPET and the IHRC efforts as inadequate and suggested that an international tribunal may be necessary to ensure justice is delivered. By whatever standard used to assess the Jakarta and the Dili trials, it is clear that they have failed to meet the demands made in Security Council Resolution 1272 that "all those responsible for such violence be brought to justice." However, Indonesia and East Timor have rejected the recommendation of the UN Commission, arguing that an international tribunal would undermine the improving relations between the two countries.

Would an international process have resulted in the prosecution of those most responsible for human rights violations in East Timor as well as ensured that the appeals process would not be subverted? Based on the history of the ICTY and the ICTR, the answer most likely would be yes. However, if an international tribunal had been established for East Timor, the situation would resemble the complexity and difficulties of the ICTY rather than the relatively easier situation of the ICTR. Ultimately, prosecuting high-level officials for human rights violations requires the cooperation of nation-states, and it is difficult to imagine a scenario in which the Indonesian government would have either transferred military officials or allowed an international process to occur within the country. So if one is to evaluate these tribunals based on the ability to deliver justice to victims, then the SCPET and the IHRC appear to be inferior options to international tribunals.

However in some important ways, both tribunals have served a broader purpose. The SCPET and the SCU have provided judicial training for a legal profession just emerging in East Timor while the IHRC has assisted in codifying into Indonesian law important human rights principles. Moreover the failures of both tribunals have focused important scrutiny on the legal processes in these countries as well as assisted NGOs in their calls for legal reforms. These tribunals and all legal processes are embedded within the larger society. The IHRC is a reflection of the limitations of justice in a post-authoritarian society while the problems of the SCPET reflect the pains of nation and state-building in East Timor.

On the broader issue of reconciliation and the establishment of a historical record of abuses, perhaps no tribunal model is totally effective. Clearly, the purely domestic IHRC has failed to provide a clear historical record of the abuses in East Timor. Perhaps this is why the call for a truth and reconciliation commission (TRC) is important. As demonstrated in TRCs ranging from South Africa to Sierra Leone, a TRC can provide a necessary forum for addressing human rights violations that in some cases may be superior to a legal process (we address this issue in greater detail in Chapter 7). While the governments of Indonesia and East Timor may want to put the past behind them and focus on economic cooperation, these states can only move forward when an account of the history of human rights violations in East Timor is established.

To that end, the leaders of Indonesia and East Timor, Susilo Bambang Yudhoyono and Gusmão, signed an agreement in March 2005 creating a bilateral Truth and Friendship Commission to provide justice without an accompanying legal mechanism. The head of Dili's Catholic Church, Bishop Alberto Ricardo da Silva, has stated his opposition to the Commission on the grounds that it leaves the quest for justice behind. However, East Timorese officials, such as Minister of Foreign Affairs José Ramos-Horta, have stated that independence itself was enough justice. Minister Ramos-Horta acknowledged that the government of East Timor is moving forward with the Commission even in the absence of a social consensus. The Commission, composed of five members from each country, started hearing witnesses and reviewing documentation in August 2005 without having the ability to refer individuals to a court of law to be tried for war crimes or crimes against humanity. While far from perfect, a TRC that promotes an account and examination of the events in 1999 is far preferable to the *status quo*.

Notes

1. In the case of Cambodia, the civil war had concluded decades before the creation of the Extraordinary Chambers for Cambodia while in the case of Indonesia and East Timor, tribunals have jurisdiction over crimes committed technically while East Timor was still a province of Indonesia, and thus the human rights violations can be characterized as intrastate and not interstate.
2. Fretilin and the UDT represented different social classes in Timor. Fretilin was a quasi-Marxist party inspired by independence movements in Africa while the UDT represented landowners.
3. A British television crew happened to be in East Timor when the massacre occurred.
4. Although many politicians were willing to let the Timorese decide their own fate, most senior military officials denounced the idea of independence and some even rejected the idea of autonomy (Huxley, 2002).

5. The violence occurred while the United Nations Assistance Mission for East Timor (UNAMET) organized the referendum.
6. The Indonesian army and the militia groups were assisted by West Timorese and Indonesian migrants.
7. East Timor became a fully independent nation-state in May 2002 following approximately two and a half years under the authority of UNTAET. While the UNTAET's mandate ended with independence, a successor organization, the UN Mission of Support in East Timor, was immediately established.
8. The reforms instituted by President Habibie included the reduction in legislative seats assigned to the military from seventy-five to thirty-eight, the distancing of Golkar from the military and the separation of the police force, Polri, from the military. Huxley (2002) argues that these reforms proved to be ineffective because of the all-pervasive structure of the armed forces, lack of political will to change civil-military relations and the fact that several cabinet ministers, even under President Megawati Sukarnoputri, were former generals.
9. The UNCHR also called for collaboration between the IHRC and the National Human Rights Commission (KOMNAS HAM) which conducted its own investigation through a Commission of Inquiry (KPP HAM).
10. KPP HAM in Indonesia came to a similar conclusion.
11. This provided the Indonesian government with the opportunity to initiate its own process.
12. UNTAET Resolution 2000/11 (6 March 2000) states that the creation of the SCPET does not preclude the establishment of an international tribunal.
13. Ifdhal Kasim, Executive Director of the Institute for Policy Research and Advocacy (ELSAM), interview with the authors, 23 November 2004.
14. Later, the crime of genocide and crimes against humanity were included in the subject matter jurisdiction. Significantly, war crimes were never included in the IHRC's jurisdiction.
15. Ifdhal Kasim, Executive Director of the Institute for Policy Research and Advocacy (ELSAM), interview with the authors, 23 November 2004.
16. Judge Roki Panjaitan, Former IHRC Judge, interview with the authors, Jakarta, 26 November 2004.
17. Ibid.
18. Ibid.
19. The issue of the minimum sentence became a basis for appeal. In one case, the five-judge panel sentenced a defendant to three years; however because of the minimum sentencing guidelines, the defendant appealed the conviction arguing that an illegal sentence had been imposed (ironically, a sentence far less than the minimum). At the time of this writing, the case was still on appeal.
20. The reduction in the minimum sentence of Guterres established his basis for appeal to the Supreme Court.
21. Those that have been found guilty at the trial-level have been almost exclusively ethnic Timorese not ethnic Indonesians.
22. Henry Simarmata, Indonesian Legal Aid and Human Rights Association, interview with the authors, Jakarta, 17 November 2004.
23. Ifdhal Kasim, Executive Director of the Institute for Policy Research and Advocacy (ELSAM), interview with the authors, 23 November 2004.
24. Ibid.
25. Henry Simarmata, Indonesian Legal Aid and Human Rights Association, interview with the authors, Jakarta, 17 November 2004.
26. Ibid.

Chapter 5

Financial Considerations in the Maintenance of International Tribunals

In the preceding chapters, we examined the political environment in which international tribunals have been established and have argued that these *judicial* institutions represent a *political* compromise among the international community and increasingly the host government in which issues of justice have sometimes become superseded by other concerns. As indicated throughout this book, the funding of tribunals has become a major focus of concern of United Nations (UN) member-states. The International Criminal Tribunal for the former Yugoslavia (ICTY) and the International Criminal Tribunal for Rwanda (ICTR) were authorized under UN Chapter VII authority which guarantees funding as an assessed share of the UN budget. Over the last decade, the two tribunals received over $4.5 billion through Chapter VII financing (see Table 5.1). As discussed in the next chapter, the Completion Strategy for the ICTY and the ICTR and the termination of these tribunals by 2010 has been largely motivated by a concern of the considerable sums of money that the tribunals have spent over the last decade.

Moreover as discussed in Chapter 3 because of the costs associated with Chapter VII funded tribunals, some Security Council members were unwilling to establish later tribunals as auxiliary organs of the UN with guaranteed funding, including the Special Court for Sierra Leone (SCSL) and the Extraordinary Chambers for Cambodia (ECC). Instead, member-states called for voluntary contributions from the international community to finance these tribunals. As a consequence, much of the discussion on the funding of tribunals has focused on so-called "donor fatigue" in which some states have become overwhelmed by tribunal financing. It is this fatigue which has caused states to withdraw support for Chapter VII tribunals and turn to voluntarily funded tribunals such as the SCSL and the ECC.[1]

However recently, the Cambodian government has indicated that it is experiencing its own form of fatigue and is unsure whether it will fulfill its prior financial commitment to the ECC. In August 2005, Prime Minister Hun Sen demanded that the international community increase its contribution above the agreed $43 million. Moreover, the Cambodian government has announced that it will only contribute $1.5 million to the tribunal which is well short of the $13 million it had earlier pledged. Sen went so far as to state that "if they don't give money, no trial will be convened" (BBC News, 2005).

Irrespective of the situation in Cambodia, the evidence is clear that for some states, the creation of hybrid tribunals and the termination of Chapter VII tribunals is a cost saving measure. What is less clear is why states on a bilateral basis provide contributions to these tribunals.[2] This chapter examines the financing of tribunals and focuses on those factors which are associated with tribunal funding. Specifically, we examine why countries voluntarily contribute to tribunals, especially in the case of those tribunals which have guaranteed funding through Chapter VII financing. We seek to place tribunal funding within the broader foreign assistance literature in order to explain the motivations of donor countries in providing voluntary contributions.

We believe that the funding of tribunals, as an example of foreign assistance, is particularly interesting as it involves the interaction of bilateral and multilateral assistance. Especially in the case of those tribunals which are funded through Chapter VII appropriations such as the ICTY and the ICTR, states have a powerful incentive to free ride and provide no voluntary contribution. In these two cases, the state is already providing funding to the tribunal through Chapter VII budgetary requirements. Why then would states contribute additional funding to tribunals which they have in essence already funded? This is a particularly relevant question as the same member-states have also been asked to make a contribution to national courts. The inauguration of the War Crimes Chamber (WCC) in the Court of Bosnia and Herzegovina (BiH) in March 2005 is the most publicized example of national court development through state contributions (an issue that we address as part of the ICTY's Completion Strategy in Chapter 6).

Table 5.1 Chapter VII and Voluntary Contribution Amounts for Tribunals[1]

Year	ICTY (1993-2005)		ICTR (1994-2005)		SCSL (2002-2005)	ECC (2005)
	Chapter VII	Voluntary	Chapter VII	Voluntary	Voluntary	Voluntary
1993	276,000	NA				
1994-1995	36,100,000	6,449,794	NA	5,177,418		
1996-1997	84,017,622	2,487,259[2]	72,444,500	2,214,168		
1998-1999	158,879,100	8,181,173	119,411,000	459,983		
2000-2001	192,386,500	14,150,730	166,526,300	200,000		
2002-2003	223,169,800	6,192,000	177,739,400	50,000	16,278,502[3]	
2004-2005	271,854,600	NA	NA	943,577	NA	43,000,000[4]

Note: Data compiled by authors.
[1]Amounts shown are in USD.
[2]1996 data not available.
[3]Funding only for 2003.
[4]Funding only for 2005.

In this chapter, we also examine the case of those tribunals which rely exclusively on voluntary funding, such as the SCSL and the ECC, and ask why donors contribute to tribunals which are located in states which offer few economic and strategic advantages. Indeed an examination of those countries which provided voluntary contributions shows a diverse cross section of countries that might not have

Table 5.2 Number of Tribunals and Amount Voluntarily Funded by Donor Country

Country	Number of Tribunals	Total Voluntary Amount (USD)
Australia	2	2,403,887
Austria	2	468,547
Belgium	4	3,092,280
Cambodia	1	5,000
Canada	4	5,139,643
Chile	3	11,000
Cyprus	2	24,000
Czech Republic	2	110,000
Denmark	4	1,076,873
Egypt	1	11,000
Finland	3	1,181,262
France	1	4,800,000
Germany	3	4,151,198
Greece	2	30,000
Hungary	1	12,000
Ireland	3	474,054
Israel	2	15,000
Italy	2	2,193,709
Japan	2	21,500,000
Lebanon	1	3,000
Lesotho	1	40,549
Liechtenstein	2	9,985
Luxembourg	3	351,775
Malaysia	2	2,550,000
Malta	1	1,500
Mauritius	1	1,500
Mexico	1	6,000
Namibia	1	500
Netherlands	4	11,477,831
New Zealand	3	549,452
Nigeria	1	10,000
Norway	4	3,189,241
Pakistan	1	1,000,000
Philippines	1	961
Poland	1	12,000
Portugal	1	20,000
Saudi Arabia	1	300,000
Singapore	1	15,000
Slovenia	1	10,000
South Africa	1	10,000
South Korea	1	150,000
Spain	2	163,725
Sweden	4	1,479,429
UK	4	11,668,104
USA	3	22,266,298
AVERAGE	2.02	2,212,942

Note: Data compiled by authors.

been anticipated (see Table 5.2). Interestingly in the case of Cambodia (a country which will be a recipient of voluntary contributions), it was one of the first countries to provide a voluntary contribution to the ICTY. As Table 5.2 shows while many states have provided a contribution, most of the contributions have been rather modest. In addition, many states have contributed to only one of the tribunals.

The Motivations for Foreign Assistance

While we view the funding of tribunals as a form of foreign assistance, we recognize that this form of assistance would generally not be included in the definition provided by the Development Assistance Committee (DAC) of the Organization for Economic Cooperation and Development. For the DAC, foreign assistance qualifies as official development assistance based on the following criteria: The assistance is undertaken by official agencies, promotes economic development and welfare as its main objectives and has a grant element of 25 per cent or more.[3] Tribunal financing is not targeted at poverty reduction, macroeconomic policy and is only tangentially related to state and democracy-building. However, Duffield (2001) suggests that a new development-security environment emerged in the 1990s and that foreign assistance plays a key role in global governance. Duffield and others argue that the definition of foreign assistance is now much broader than purely economic development. Assistance targets conflict prevention and resolution, strengthening civil and representative institutions, promoting the rule of law and security sector reform. Donors have given a high priority to strengthening and developing political and administrative institutions in recipient countries, including reform of the judicial system (an issued addressed in Chapter 6). We believe that tribunal funding fits within this broader notion of foreign assistance, and therefore we seek to determine if tribunal financing is motivated by considerations generally found in the foreign assistance literature.

Foreign assistance has often been referred to in the literature as a puzzle because of the various forms it can take, the different motivations for donors and the diverse characteristics of recipients (Schraeder, Hook and Taylor, 1998; Boulding, 2004). Donor motivations vary by country. One of the most obvious motivations for providing foreign assistance is to promote the so-called "national interest." Donors provide greater support to states which enhance their political, economic, military or cultural interests (Tisch and Wallace, 1994). For example, Japan concentrates its aid in the Asian region in order to promote economic and cultural benefits (Schraeder, Hook and Taylor, 1998). Former colonial powers such as Britain and France have not only concentrated their foreign assistance in their former colonies because of cultural ties but also to maintain privileged access to resources and markets in the decolonized areas (Degnbol-Martinussen and Engberg-Pedersen, 2003). For the US, strategic benefits have historically been important, especially during the Cold War (Grant and Nijman, 1997). Therefore, examining the motivations for financing is part of the so-called pragmatist approach to transitional justice and tribunals which examines the self-interest considerations of political actors (Vinjamuri and Synder, 2004).

The foreign assistance literature tends to focus either on the effect of the assistance on the recipient country or the determinants of foreign assistance by examining donor motivations. We are interested in which factors account for the voluntary contributions made by donor countries, and therefore examine characteristics of the donor rather than the recipient country. We felt that this was appropriate given that on many measures, our recipient countries (*e.g.*, Rwanda, Sierra Leone and Cambodia) were similar in their level of economic and political development and did not vary on key recipient characteristics. We are interested in explaining those factors associated with contribution levels among states which contribute to tribunals. Our discussion does not address why a state contributes (as most states do not contribute). Instead, we endeavor to establish whether there is a pattern of contributions among donors.

The funding of tribunals can take three different forms. As indicated in previous chapters, those tribunals which are authorized by the Security Council under Chapter VII authority are funded as an organ of the UN through the general budget. The ICTY and the ICTR fall within this category. A second form of funding involves voluntary monetary contributions. This form of contribution can be provided to any tribunal, but in the case of the SCSL and the ECC, this is the main form of funding. Finally, states have been encouraged to provide in-kind contributions to tribunals which can take the form of personnel and equipment. These in-kind contributions have been extremely important in the maintenance of facilities for the ICTY trial chambers and the ICTY and the ICTR appellate chambers.[4] In order to determine whether voluntary contributions fit within a general pattern of foreign assistance, we examine the relationship between factors associated with foreign assistance and the level of state monetary contribution to international tribunals. Most studies of foreign assistance have conceptualized assistance as a decision-making process (Cingranelli and Pasquarello, 1985). Thus, we do not include in the discussion Chapter VII funding as it is non-discretionary and therefore requires no decision-making on the part of the donor country. We also exclude in-kind contributions because often the information about these contributions is under-reported. While these in-kind contributions can be very important, information on this kind of contribution is much less precise and seldom available.

Therefore, we examine the voluntary contributions provided by donor states for the ICTY, the ICTR, the SCSL and the ECC[5] tribunals. We do not discuss the funding of the SCPET as information on this tribunal was unavailable. Moreover, the SCPET is an unusual case in that it was indirectly funded under Chapter VII authority and does not clearly fit any category.[6] Based on annual reports filed by the various tribunals, we have been able to determine the voluntary contributions covering the period of 1994 through 2005. We have data for the ICTY from 1994[7] through 2003, the ICTR from 1994 through 2005, the SCSL for 2003 and the ECC for 2005.

In order to examine whether tribunal contributions fit within a general pattern of foreign assistance, we analyze several factors associated with foreign assistance. In order to assess whether funding was a form of state prestige, we analyze Security

Council membership (Wang, 1999). We are interested in determining whether those countries which provided a contribution were more likely to provide a larger contribution when members of the Security Council. As Security Council members, donors would be involved in debating tribunal resolutions and reports which would enhance their prestige within the international community. Several studies going back to the early work of Morgenthau (1962) find that "prestige aid" is an important motivator for donor countries. Orr (1988, p. 34) argues that foreign assistance not only cultivates prestige but can even be used to create a "great power status."

The second factor that we examine is regional affiliation. Schraeder, Hook and Taylor (1998) note that foreign assistance can be provided to states due to regional identification. States that share a "natural collective" may be more likely to provide assistance to countries in their region than countries outside their region. In addition, foreign assistance may be given by regional powers in order to affect a change in policy or to exert further control within the region. We examine whether those countries that provided a contribution are more likely to be from the same region as the tribunal.

Another factor that we also consider is the colonial past. We want to assess whether the influence of cultural similarity, specifically defined as the colonial past, influenced the amount that donor countries provided.[8] Alesina and Dollar (2000) find that the colonial past as a motivation for foreign assistance varies widely among states.[9] Given that two of the tribunals were established in Africa, we want to examine whether the status as the former colonial power provided a motivation for tribunal funding.[10] Finally, we explore if financing tribunals is a function of the size of the donor's economy. We view this factor as a possible means to measure the general foreign assistance provided by countries. We feel that countries which provide financing to tribunals do so as part of their normal practice of foreign assistance. While most studies of foreign assistance analyze the economic motivation of donor countries, we consider the possibility that tribunal contributions are based on the economic self-interest of the donor country to be negligible. Given the relatively insignificant import and export market of Rwanda, Sierra Leone and Cambodia, it is doubtful that countries such as the US would be inclined to provide a contribution to a tribunal based on economic interests.

Motivations for Voluntary Tribunal Contributions

Based on our analysis of the information found in the annual tribunal reports as well as the factors previously identified as associated with foreign assistance, we find that there is very little relationship between the factors commonly found in the foreign assistance literature and motivation for contributions to tribunals. That being said, there are some interesting patterns which emerge. In our analysis of all the tribunals, Security Council membership and size of the economy were important in the case of the ICTY and the SCSL.[11] Countries which gave a contribution to these tribunals were likely to give more while occupying a Security Council seat. We believe that this indicates that tribunal contributions served as a prestige factor for countries that were on the Security Council. Conversely, one might argue that Council membership itself was the "prestige" and provided a norm of behavior which compelled countries to provide even larger contributions during their membership.

In addition, the size of the economy was important for most tribunal contributions—countries with a larger economy were more likely to provide a larger contribution to tribunals. We believe that this means that countries which normally gave large amounts of foreign assistance are more likely to give a larger amount of assistance for tribunals. As indicated previously, while the list of countries which provided a tribunal contribution is somewhat surprising, this finding is not surprising. As shown in Table 5.2 while countries such as Egypt, Lesotho and Namibia provided a tribunal contribution, the amounts that they provided were rather small (for example, Namibia's total contribution to all tribunals was $500).

Not surprisingly, the factors most associated with contributions to the ICTR and the SCSL were largely similar and showed a relationship between the former colonial power and the amount of the contribution which was provided. A cursory examination of the amounts provided by the Belgian government for the ICTR and the British government for the SCSL confirms that as former colonial powers, they provided large contributions. Belgium provided over 30 per cent of the total contribution for the ICTR, and the UK provided almost 23 per cent of the total for the SCSL.

Conclusions

Those factors which are most often cited in the foreign assistance literature as significant motivations for donor countries proved to be only marginally important in the case of overall tribunal funding. The factor that appears to be most important in accounting for tribunal contributions is GDP. Those countries that have the largest economies make the largest contribution to tribunals. We believe that this indicates that tribunal financing fits within a general pattern of foreign assistance. However, this conclusion tells us very little about why countries provide additional financing to Chapter VII tribunals or contribute to voluntarily funded tribunals. We can rule out membership in the Security Council, regionalism and colonialism as having an appreciable effect among *all* tribunals.

One might argue that our results indicate that tribunal financing is not a case of foreign assistance. While a possibility, our view is that tribunal financing is a form of bilateral foreign assistance within a multilateral framework. It is difficult to argue that a tribunal contribution is not a form of foreign assistance. Moreover even if tribunal financing is not foreign assistance, we contend that it would be logical to investigate whether tribunal contributions were provided because of prestige, regional and colonial concerns. Therefore, we believe that we have identified those factors that one would have *a priori* associated with contribution amounts.

That being said, we are surprised at the lack of relationship between funding and these key factors and wonder what additional factors might account for the variation in contribution amounts. One possibility worth exploring in the future is the role of domestic politics, elections and interest groups in tribunal contribution amounts (Cassen, 1994). Because the tribunals involved cases of gross human rights abuses, domestic constituencies in donor countries were often mobilized in support of a mechanism to bring perpetrators to justice. Perhaps the mode of contribution and amount reflects the pressure that groups placed on politicians before and during an election cycle. Certainly there are cases in which countries were consistent over time in their support of tribunals. However in the case of the ICTY and the ICTR, there are many examples in which countries gave one year, and then might go two or three years before providing another contribution. This seemingly random behavior might be explained by the election cycle in the country or domestic politics more generally. Unfortunately at this point, the foreign assistance puzzle for international tribunals remains a mystery. However, this chapter has ruled out several logical explanations behind state behavior in providing bilateral foreign assistance in a multilateral setting.

Notes

1. For example, the Cambodian government has agreed to cover the costs of the location for the ECC as well as those associated with Cambodian personnel while the UN will finance the international personnel, witness and defense expenses and safety and security equipment through voluntary contributions.
2. While voluntary financing is bilateral, it is also channeled through multilateral organizations such as the UN.
3. While the DAC definition of assistance emphasizes economic development, the DAC recognizes that assistance includes several facets such as emergency relief, humanitarian and environmental assistance and gender equality. Therefore, economic development is only one aspect of foreign assistance.
4. The Netherlands is one of the primary in-kind contributors. It is also a major cash contributor which shows that the two forms of contribution are not mutually exclusive.
5. In the case of the ECC, the contribution amount is actually a pledge as the tribunal has not officially begun.
6. As indicated in Chapter 4, in 1999 the Security Council passed Resolution 1272 which established the United Nations Transitional Administration in East Timor (UNTAET) which was authorized to administer East Timor during its transition to independence. At that point, even though the East Timorese had voted for independence, the new state was not ready to assume total political control so the UNTAET assumed many government powers until 2002. The SCPET was administered and funded by UNTAET, and therefore even though the SCPET was not considered an auxiliary organ of the UN in the same manner at the ICTY and the ICTR, in reality the SCPET's primary mode of financing was through Chapter VII funding.
7. The ICTY's annual report for 1996 neglected to include a list of voluntary contributions, and therefore, this year has been omitted from our data set.

8. Cultural similarity is a much broader concept than colonial past. In the case of the colonial past, there is usually a generally recognized former colonial power. Cultural similarity, however, can be group, tribe or clan-based and more difficult to establish. We decided to examine the more restrictive concept of colonial past. We recognize that this concept excludes several interesting cases such as the fact that several Islamic countries provided contributions to the ICTY in all likelihood because of the atrocities committed against Bosnian Muslims.
9. Of course in some cases such as Canada and Sweden, the donor country had no colonies and colonial past.
10. For Sierra Leone, Cambodia and Rwanda, there was an obvious former colonial power; in the case of the former Yugoslavia, the situation is more complex.
11. The data set that we have compiled is available at: www.ux1.eiu.edu/~sdroper/justice.htm. We are conducting a more thorough statistical analysis of the data.

Chapter 6

The Completion Strategy for the International Criminal Tribunal for the former Yugoslavia and the International Criminal Tribunal for Rwanda

This chapter examines the issues related to the Completion Strategy of the International Criminal Tribunal for the former Yugoslavia (ICTY) and the International Criminal Tribunal for Rwanda (ICTR). Passed in 2003, United Nations (UN) Security Council Resolution 1503 affirmed the ICTY's Completion Strategy and requested the ICTR to formalize a strategy based on the ICTY model. The Completion Strategy of the ICTY and the ICTR calls for a completion of all investigations by 2004, trials by 2008 and appeals by 2010.[1] The Completion Strategies involve several inter-related issues including the financing of the tribunals, the further development of national courts as venues for transferred cases and the use of plea bargaining as a tool to reduce the backlog of tribunal cases. Some have argued that these "practical considerations" have impinged on the ability of the tribunals to provide justice to victims as well as to develop a historical record of the atrocities which were committed. While the motivation for the Completion Strategies varies, many have argued that the deadlines that have been established fail to appreciate the difficulty of terminating the process by 2010. Some have gone so far as to call the strategies "junk justice" which place financial considerations above the goals of justice and reconciliation.[2]

As part of the Completion Strategy of the ICTY and the ICTR, national courts are encouraged to accept transferred cases from the tribunals in order to ease the backlog. To that end, the tribunals have been working with national courts to implement reforms of the penal code, training judges and attorneys as well as strengthening witness protection laws. The development of capacity-building in the national courts in the former Yugoslavia[3] and in Rwanda is a necessary component of reconciliation among divided communities; however, the question remains whether the current national courts have sufficient resources and personnel to prosecute the large number of indictees still awaiting trial. Moreover, there is also the question of whether the political will exists in the various governments, particularly in the *Republika Srpska* (RS)[4], to work with other political entities and ensure that trials meet international standards.

As discussed in Chapter 5, the termination of the tribunals by 2010 is part of the larger issue of financing tribunals and donor fatigue, particularly of the US.

Transferring cases to national courts is viewed as a more cost effective means for dealing with cases. Indeed, since the creation of the ICTY and the ICTR, we have seen a gradual shift of financing and court administration to states. The Special Court for Sierra Leone (SCSL), the Serious Crimes Panel for East Timor (SCPET) and the Extraordinary Chambers for Cambodia (ECC) are examples of hybrid tribunals in which the use of state resources reduces the overall financial burden of the international community. The movement towards a purely national process is seen as a logical next step in reducing the international financial burden. The question remains whether the goals of the ICTY and ICTR as set forth in authorizing Resolution 827 and 955 can be fulfilled with a reduction in financing and a movement of trials to national courts. In this chapter, we examine the Completion Strategy of these two tribunals and specifically address the capacity of the national courts in the former Yugoslavia and Rwanda to administer justice not only in the cases which are transferred but more generally in cases which involve war crimes indictments.

The "Rules of the Road" Process for Reviewing Cases in National Courts

In order to be able to appreciate the components of the ICTY Completion Strategy, it is necessary to review the relationship between the ICTY and the national courts of Bosnia and Herzegovina (BiH). The discussion concerning the relationship between the ICTY and new national courts such as the War Crimes Chamber (WCC) might leave the impression that only recently has the ICTY developed links with national courts. In reality, the relationship between the Tribunal and national courts in the former Yugoslavia goes back to the creation of the ICTY in 1993. Even as the war was raging in 1993 and 1994, national courts were busy issuing indictments and conducting trials (largely *in absentia*). As these trials were conducted in a war-time environment, it is not surprising that standards of justice and fairness were compromised. For example, the Organization for Security and Co-operation in Europe (OSCE) reports that between 1993 and 1995 in the military court in the Municipality of Orašje, forty-seven suspects were convicted *in absentia* with several receiving the death sentence.[5]

The arbitrary arrests and unfair trials had a chilling effect on the return of civilians to their homes as well as travel throughout BiH. As the Dayton Peace Agreement of 1995 envisioned the free movement of refugees and displayed persons, it was critical that a process be established to assist the national courts in meeting international standards of justice. As part of the Rome Agreement signed in February 1996 by the presidents of BiH, Croatia and the Federal Republic of Yugoslavia, the so-called "rules of the road" (RoR) procedure was introduced to ensure that national courts met international legal standards. The RoR procedure required that national authorities submit their case to the ICTY's Office of the Prosecutor (OTP) for approval before the indictment and arrest of suspects (or continuing detention of suspects). Between 1996 and 2004, the OTP's special RoR unit reviewed files for 5,789 suspects with 3,489 cases referred back to the national authorities (OSCE, 2005a, p. 6).

Cases referred back to the national authorities for review were categorized either "A," "B" or "C." Category A referrals indicated that the evidence against the suspect was sufficient to justify an indictment. Category B referrals indicated that the evidence was insufficient to meet international standards while Category C cases indicated that the RoR unit was unable to determine whether there was sufficient evidence in which case authorities could gather additional evidence and re-submit the case to the ICTY for re-categorization. The vast majority of cases that were sent back to national authorities were categorized as "B." Of the 3,489 cases that were referred back to national authorities, 846 cases were categorized as "A" while 2,346 were categorized as "B" and 675 as "C." One of the problems with the RoR process has been that when cases are referred back to BiH, the ICTY never stipulated the territorial jurisdiction of a case (*i.e.*, where the case had to be tried). Rather, the case was referred back to the court which submitted the application, and as the OSCE (2005b, p. 15) notes, "[b]ecause BiH was so ethnically divided in the aftermath of the conflict, the respective authorities had little faith that cases returned to the courts with appropriate jurisdiction would proceed to trial effectively or at all." Generally, those trials which have occurred via the RoR process try the ethnic minority in the region in which the case was initiated.

As part of the Completion Strategy, the ICTY in 2004 transferred the RoR review process to state authorities in the former Yugoslavia. For example in BiH, prosecutors at lower levels including cantons and districts now submit the application for review to the prosecutor's office in BiH. While thousands of cases will eventually be tried in BiH, only select cases will be tried at the state level with most cases tried in local courts. In order to meet the demands that these cases will place upon the judiciary, the ICTY and the OSCE have offered a number of training programs designed to assist the courts in meeting international standards of fairness. However even with these training and monitoring programs, Judge Theodor Meron, President of the ICTY, admitted that at "the moment, there are still doubts that credible war crimes trials can take place in the national jurisdictions of Croatia and Serbia and Montenegro" (2005). While the situation in the Federation of Bosnia and Herzegovina (a constituent part of BiH) is considered to be much better, by "contrast to the Federation, the RS has made little progress on war crimes prosecutions and has conveyed its lack of interest in, if not hostility towards them" (Zoglin, 2005, p. 49).

The Impact of the International Criminal Tribunal for the former Yugoslavia's Completion Strategy on Delivering Justice

Transferring the RoR procedure to the state judicial systems in the former Yugoslavia was an important component of the ICTY's Completion Strategy as it relieved the responsibility of reviewing hundreds if not potentially thousands of cases brought by national prosecutors. The transfer of the RoR procedure to the national judiciaries is part of a larger effort by the ICTY to reduce the backlog of cases which has created logistical, tactical and financial problems. The first few years of the Tribunal marked a process of institution-building in which few indictees were apprehended and most cases involved lower-ranking persons. However over the last few years, the Tribunal has been much more effective in securing the arrest of high-ranking indictees which has created the problem of increasing the length of the pre-trial and trial processes. In general, these trials are time-consuming because of the complexity of the crimes, problems associated with the use of witness testimony as well as the length of time between the perpetration of the crime and trial.

The development of the Completion Strategy began as early as 1999 when an Expert Group was commissioned by the UN Security Council to report on the functioning of the ICTY and the ICTR. In the November 1999 Expert Group report, forty-six recommendations identified institutional and procedural issues which needed to be reformed in order to expedite the pre-trial and eventually the trial process. While the Expert Group did not propose a specific completion date, the Group urged the tribunals to implement the changes to stream-line the process with a goal of disposing of cases quicker. Commenting on the report, Judge Claude Jorda, then President of the ICTY, stated that given the reforms discussed in the report, the mandate of the Tribunal could be shortened to 2007. In his address to the Security Council on 27 November 2001, Jorda indicated that the ICTY was considering "relocating" lower-level cases to the national courts of the former Yugoslavia only with assurances that the trials would meet international standards. Chief Prosecutor Carla Del Ponte had already indicated that she would consider transferring lower-level cases back to the former Yugoslavia.

Transferring cases to national courts had several advantages. First, transferring lower-level cases would reduce the backlog of ICTY cases and allow the Tribunal to complete its mandate sooner. Second, UN member-states believed that this process would reduce their overall financial burden as the mandate the ICTY would end quicker. Third, Jorda and others argued that trials in the former Yugoslavia would increase the transparency of the process, dispel notions of bias in the prosecution of ethnic Serbs and enhance the overall level of public confidence in the process. While there were several advantages in transferring cases to national courts, there was scepticism that the courts in the former Yugoslavia would be able to render verdicts that complied with international standards. The experience with the RoR procedure had demonstrated that there were still significant problems in relying on national courts to try war crimes.

In May 2002, a report commissioned by the Office of the High Representative (OHR), the chief civilian peace implementation agency in BiH, examined the feasibility of transferring lower-levels cases from the ICTY to national courts. One of the tasks of the experts commissioned by the OHR was to address the forum in which the trials should occur. The concern was that previous trials at the canton or district-level "had, however, proved inadequate and was often regarded as an occasion for dispensing 'ethnic' justice or exacting revenge. The trials were politically explosive, especially as various past and present national leaders were among those indicted or likely to be indicted" (Bohlander, 2004, p. 4). Because of these concerns, the report proposed the creation of an international humanitarian law (IHL) division within the

State Court of BiH. Furthermore, the report recommended that the IHL division be staffed by national and international judges and prosecutors, applying newly adopted criminal codes as well as certain aspects of case law developed at the ICTY. The IHL prosecutor has discretion involving lower-level cases to either try the cases within the IHL division or lower-level courts.

The report contained a number of recommendations involving strengthening judicial institutions as well as noting areas of concern regarding witness protection and the legal procedures and codes. In order to be able to meet the challenges of prosecuting both transferred ICTY cases as well as RoR cases, the OHR in 2003 proposed several amendments to the BiH legal system.[6] The courts and prosecutors' offices were restructured, and all judges and prosecutors went through a re-appointment process. The changes in the legal structure in BiH were an important component in the ability of the ICTY to transfer cases. Security Council Resolution 1503 noted that:

> the strengthening of national judicial systems is crucially important to the rule of law in general and to the implementation of the ICTY and ICTR Completion Strategies in particular . . . an essential prerequisite to achieving the objectives of the ICTY Completion Strategy is the expeditious establishment . . . and early functioning of a special chamber within the State Court of Bosnia and Herzegovina (the "War Crimes Chamber") and the subsequent referral by the ICTY of cases of lower- or intermediate-rank accused to the Chamber.

The statute of the ICTY also had to be changed to allow for the transferring of cases to national courts. Specifically, Rule 11*bis* had to be broadened to allow for referral of current pre-trial cases to a national court as well as accused not in the custody of the ICTY. The 30 September 2002 revision to the Rule included the creation of a special trial chamber known as a "Referral Bench" to consider all requests from the OTP to transfer a case to a national court. The Referral Bench is guided in its decision based on whether the accused will receive a fair trial without the imposition of the death penalty as well as the gravity of the crime. The cases referred from the ICTY are then transferred to the WCC for final disposition. While war crimes cases can generally be heard in canton and district courts throughout BiH, the WCC is the only court that can hear cases transferred from the ICTY (as well as those cases in which the ICTY's OTP has not issued an indictment and defers to the WCC).[7]

In February 2003, the OHR and the ICTY issued a joint decision regarding the necessity for the creation of the WCC. At a donors conference in October that year, €16.1 million were pledged for the construction and staffing of the WCC. The WCC's jurisdiction includes not only ICTY transferred cases but also the most sensitive cases in BiH. The creation of the WCC is part of a broader process of strengthening judicial institutions in BiH, and therefore the WCC will evolve as the legal capacity within BiH continues to develop. During the first phase which is scheduled until 2007, the trial and appeals panel consists of two international judges and one national judge. A majority of seven international prosecutors will initially form the Chamber's OTP. The panels and the OTP will later evolve into a majority of national judges and prosecutors with the final phase to be completed within five years of exclusively national judges and prosecutors.[8]

In March 2005, the WCC offices were inaugurated and in September 2005, the first case was transferred from the ICTY to the WCC. The transfer of Radovan Stankovic to the WCC was the first of fourteen cases scheduled to be transferred to the WCC. While the Referral Bench has generally agreed with requests from the ICTY's OTP to transfer cases, it would be incorrect to view the decision to transfer a case as automatic. In June 2005, the Referral Bench allowed Del Ponte to withdraw her request for a proposed transfer of the case involving the so-called "Vukovar Three" to either Croatia or Serbia and Montenegro concluding that the intensity of the feelings of the public concerning this case "brings into sharp focus the question of whether, even today, a trial held in either country would be generally acceptable as reflecting the fair administration of justice" (OSCE, 2005a).

The ICTY's Completion Strategy and the transferring of cases to national courts have come under criticism from various quarters. The US has been one of the strongest supporters of the Completion Strategy as a means for strengthening judicial capacity in the former Yugoslavia as well as a means by which to reduce the international community's tribunal financial burden.[9] Therefore, it is not surprising that the US has been a vocal critic of any new indictments which might interfere with the Completion Strategy timetable. For example in response to Prosecutor Del Ponte's report to the Security Council in 2003 in which she outlined fourteen new and additional indictments, US OSCE Ambassador Stephan Minikes (2003, p. 1) argued that "it appears the Prosecutor has indicated an approach that complicates and puts at risk the timeline set out in the Completion Strategy."[10]

Indeed in his semi-annual report to the Security Council, ICTY President Meron indicated that the arrival of twenty-two accused since November 2004 placed significant burdens on the ICTY and required that the trial period be extended from 2008 to at least the end of 2009. Moreover, the Completion Strategy's end date of 2010 can only be fulfilled with the timely arrest of the two remaining most sought after fugitives (Radovan Karadzic and Ratko Mladic). Meron (2005) was unequivocal when he stated that "the Tribunal will not have fulfilled its historic mission, and it will not close its doors, until Karadzic [and] Mladic . . . have been arrested, brought to The Hague and tried before the Tribunal in accordance with the full procedural protections recognized by our jurisprudence."

While some such as the US have been critical of the ICTY for not fulfilling the timeline established by the Completion Strategy, others have been critical of the very concept of the Completion Strategy. Given the atrocities which were committed, the complexity of the cases and the lack of reconciliation among the ethnic groups, it is questionable whether transferring ICTY cases as well as the RoR procedure to the states of the former Yugoslavia is desirable. For example, the OSCE Mission to Croatia reports that in its monitored proceedings in 2004, 75 per cent of the accused were Serbs and that there was a noticeable difference in the type of behavior for which Serbs and Croats are charged, with Serbs being accused of a wider range of criminal acts.

For many, the transfer of cases to the national courts is "penny wise but pound foolish." Zoglin (2005, p. 75) argues that the "determination to return . . . cases to national courts merely was a way for the international community to wash its hands of an expensive problem." While building the judiciary in the former Yugoslavia is an important goal, it is questionable whether the judiciaries in BiH, Croatia and Serbia and Montenegro have the capacity and political will at this point to fully engage in fair trials. Moreover for judiciaries that are in a process of re-building, it is hard to imagine how they will be able to cope with the remaining thousands of pending cases involving complex legal and forensic issues. While the ICTY was first to submit a Completion Strategy, it is surprising that more attention has not been paid to the ICTR because it has been functioning alongside a national process since its inception. Instead, most of the media's attention has been focused on the Completion Strategy of the ICTY. What lessons from the experience of the ICTR might help us to understand the future direction of the ICTY's national judiciary strategy?

National and *Gacaca* Courts in Rwanda

While the atrocities of genocide and war crimes are similar in the former Yugoslavia and Rwanda, the scale of events in Rwanda and its rapidity placed additional burdens on the development of national courts as a forum for the prosecution of cases. Approximately 80,000 prisoners await trial in Rwanda, some having been in jail since 1994. This figure includes the release of approximately 25,000 prisoners in early 2003.[11] By 2004, only 9,000 individuals had been tried in the national court system, and approximately 10 per cent had received the death sentence (Amnesty International, 2002). This low number of trials is not surprising given the destruction of the Rwandan legal system during the genocide. Corey and Joireman (2004) quote an Amnesty International report which indicates that only ten attorneys were left in the country following the 1994 genocide. By mid-1997, the Rwandan Bar Association had only forty-four members, and almost none of them would defend those accused of genocide either because they felt that the suspects were guilty or because of the personal danger involved (Amnesty International, 2002).

As noted in Chapter 2, Rwandan national courts can impose the death penalty in cases in which individuals are convicted for participating in the genocide. In 1998, the first executions of some twenty-two prisoners occurred, and since then, hundreds more have been sentenced to death. Because these national courts can impose the death penalty, it is imperative that the trials be conducted according to international standards with competent legal counsel provided. However, human rights organizations which monitored these trials report that the proceedings were grossly unfair (Amnesty International, 1998). While the charges of ethnically-based trials exists in both the former Yugoslavia and Rwanda, the lack of a death penalty as well as the international institutions of the OHR and the OSCE provide a greater level of protection in the former Yugoslavia than in Rwanda. However in both of these countries, it is difficult to imagine national courts being able to process the thousands, and in the case of Rwanda tens of thousands, of cases pending. Moreover without donor funding, it is doubtful that the Rwandan judiciary would have been able to process the number of cases it has to this point.

In order to cope with the tremendous backlog of cases, the Rwandan government passed an organic law in 2000 which established village courts known as *gacaca* courts. These "courts" were used during the pre-colonial period to resolve local disputes between and within families dealing with a variety of issues including property rights and farming. As Corey and Joireman (2004) note, the current process in Rwanda differs from the traditional *gacaca* courts. The current version is much more institutionalized and involves involuntary participation. Most cases currently at the formal national courts will be transferred to the *gacaca* courts which will hear cases involving individuals accused of crimes under the new legal code (categories two through four which include murder, assault and theft). Those accused of category one offenses (*e.g.*, planning or instigating the genocide as well as sexual torture and violence) will be tried within the formal national courts.

In order to facilitate such a large patchwork of more informal courts, the government held elections for *gacaca* judges in 2001 in which thousands of individuals were selected (Daly, 2002). These judges have only very limited informal training provided by the government and many, if not all, were directly affected by the genocide which calls into question their ability to be impartial. During the trials, the local community serves as witnesses and is allowed to openly confront the accused. The argument is that "their active participation contributes to political and personal reconciliation within the Rwandan population, since people are given the opportunity to confront their attacker" (Corey and Joireman, 2004, p. 82). However, the new *gacaca* courts are national not local community creations with an amalgamation of traditional *gacaca* justice combined with norms of international humanitarian and human rights legal codes. Many question if this hybrid *gacaca* court can serve the function of reconciliation as well as meet international standards of justice. Amnesty International notes that the:

> significant differences existing between customary and contemporary forms of *gacaca* force the question of whether these differences negate the anticipated results: justice, the uncovering of truth and national reconciliation. If reconciliation is an essentially personal interaction between victim and perpetrator, one can see how *gacaca*, as previously practiced, would promote it. It is less clear that the state-mandated *Gacaca* Jurisdictions whose focus remains on retributive justice will achieve the same end (2002, p. 6).

Although a *gacaca* court pilot project was completed in 2002, there have been continual delays with trials only slated to begin in 2006. Even with the limitations discussed above, Rwandan authorities believe that one million suspects will go through the *gacaca* process (Schabas, 2005). However Fierens (2005) argues that by combining judicial, social and traditional concerns, the *gacaca* courts fail to meet the needs of the community as well as broader judicial principles. Corey and Joireman are more sanguine in their assessment of the courts. They argue that *gacaca* courts "may undermine the security of all Rwandans because it will aggravate ethnic fault lines in society. It will serve a retributive function for Tutsis" (2004, p. 89).

The Impact of the International Criminal Tribunal for Rwanda's Completion Strategy on Delivering Justice

Given the significant backlog in the Rwandan court system, the ICTR's Completion Strategy which envisions transferring approximately twenty cases to the national courts does not represent an undue burden on the judiciary. Rather, the ICTR's Completion Strategy calls into question whether cases should be transferred from an UN organ to a nation-state which imposes the death penalty. Also because the ICTR and the ICTY share the same appeals process, there is the concern of whether the appeals chambers can complete their hearings by 2010. Finally because some trials of at-large suspects may occur in third-party states, there is the question of whether judicial systems in these countries have sufficient capacity to hear such complex cases.

Security Council Resolution 1503 called upon the ICTR to formalize a Completion Strategy based on an ICTY model in which lower-ranked cases would be transferred to national courts. However as noted in Chapter 2, the ICTR was charged with the task of prosecuting only those deemed most responsible for the 1994 genocide which makes the Completion Strategy methodology for determining the importance of cases problematic. As part of the Resolution, the UN authorized the creation of a separate chief prosecutor for the ICTR to expedite the handling of cases; however, the UN did not provide for additional trial and appeals chambers. Security Council Resolution 1534 passed in March 2004 required that each Tribunal make a report to the Council on the progress of fulfilling the timeline as established in Resolution 1503.

The report submitted by Erik Møse, President of the ICTR, in May 2005 outlined the status of transferring cases to the national courts as well as the status of current and future ICTR trials. Unlike the report issued by President Meron of the ICTY, the ICTR report is more optimistic about the ability to complete all trials by 2008. The ICTR OTP intends to transfer forty-one cases to various national judiciaries (including Rwanda). While the report indicates that five of the current detainees will be transferred to national judiciaries (fifteen cases have already been transferred to Rwanda), the report never specifies how many cases will be transferred to Rwanda or which states aside from Rwanda might receive the transferred cases.

As an organ of the UN, the ICTR is prohibited from imposing a death sentence. As indicated in Chapter 2, initially the Rwandan government was reluctant to endorse the creation of the ICTR because the death penalty was prohibited. While relatively few death penalty sentences have been handed down by the national courts and even fewer individuals have been actually executed when compared to those arrested, the Rwandan government has maintained that the availability of the death penalty is an important component of post-genocide justice. Therefore, it is questionable whether defendants should be transferred from a forum in which the death penalty is not a possibility to one in which the death penalty can be imposed. Especially in light of the nature of the defendants before the ICTR, one would imagine that these individuals would have a higher probability of receiving the death penalty compared to others. Therefore, it is somewhat surprising that in his report, President Møse (2005, p. 4) makes only a passing comment on this issue: "Transfer of cases to Rwanda raises several issues. One involves the death penalty which has been imposed in genocide cases, though only rarely implemented." This is the only discussion in the report on this sensitive issue.

While the ICTR trials should be able to be completed by the 2008 deadline, it is questionable whether appeals will be completed by 2010 because of the shared appellate process with the ICTY. The majority of convictions have been appealed, and appeals can be lodged by multiple parties in a multi-accused case. Møse's report indicates that it is "difficult at this stage to indicate a completion strategy for the ICTR Appeals Chamber, as it is linked to the ICTY completion strategy ... the focus will shift to the Appeals Chamber where a drastic increase in work is anticipated" (2005, p. 9). Clearly as the ICTR and the ICTY attempt to complete all trials and appeals by 2010, the creation of additional trial and appellate chambers will become necessary. Unfortunately, these financial needs come at a time in which the international community is attempting to distance itself from the financial obligations of the tribunals as part of the UN system.

Conclusions

The Completion Strategy of the ICTY and the ICTR envision the completion of the work of the tribunals by 2010. Given the reports of both presidents in mid-2005, it is doubtful whether this target date will be fulfilled. Some question whether it is even advisable that the tribunals should attempt to complete their work under such a prescribed timetable. While the creation of the timetables was motivated by a concern of the international community regarding the substantial costs associated with Chapter VII funded tribunals, the Completion Strategy involves more basic questions of whether justice can be rendered by fragile national judiciaries in countries in which ethnic rivalry is still so intense. While assisting the national judiciaries in further developing capacity is a laudable and a necessary goal of the international community, it is questionable whether this goal should be linked to transferring some of the most complex and sensitive types of cases involving war crimes, crimes against humanity and genocide to judiciaries that are in the process of re-building.

Notes

1. The Completion Strategy of the Special Court for Sierra Leone (SCSL) was contemplated even during its creation and approved less than two years after the Court

had been established. The SCSL Completion Strategy does not outline specific target dates; however, the SCSL trials are due to be completed by the end of 2006.

2. For a critical assessment of the ICTY's Completion Strategy see, Zoglin (2005).
3. The former Yugoslavia includes Bosnia and Herzegovina (BiH), Croatia, Kosovo and Serbia and Montenegro.
4. The state of BiH consists of the Federation of the Bosnia and Herzegovina, the *Republika Srpska* and the autonomous district of Brčko.
5. The OSCE has been monitoring these trials for a number of years. For more information see, OSCE (2005a) and OSCE (2005b).
6. One of the changes to the legal code included a provision regarding plea bargaining which was viewed as a necessary device in order to process thousands of national cases in BiH. While plea bargains involving sentences as well as charges have been used at the ICTY, many question whether plea bargains are appropriate for war crimes. For a criticism regarding the use of plea bargaining at the ICTY see, Scarf (2004).
7. While the WCC is responsible for hearing ICTY transferred cases within BiH, changes in Rule 11*bis* allow for cases to also be transferred elsewhere within the former Yugoslavia. In September 2005, the ICTY's OTP announced the first transfer of a war crimes case to Croatia involving General Rahim Ademi and General Mirko Norac. While cases can be transferred to Croatia and Serbia and Montenegro, the vast majority of cases will be transferred to the BiH WCC.
8. For a complete discussion of the creation of the WCC, including administrative and financial issues see, Office of High Representative (2004).
9. Ambassador Pierre-Richard Prosper, Ambassador-at-Large for War Crimes Issues, interview with the authors, 31 August 2005.
10. Since this speech in 2003, Prosecutor Del Ponte continued to issue new indictments through early 2005. In March 2005, the OTP confirmed that no new indictments would be issued.
11. Reports indicate that nearly 5,000 individuals were re-imprisoned on other charges shortly after having been released.

Chapter 7

Understanding the Effectiveness of International, Hybrid and Domestic Tribunals

While the international community over the past decade has determined that tribunals are an appropriate mechanism for dealing with violations of human rights, there has been far less agreement among legal scholars and the human rights community on how to evaluate the role and the effectiveness of these tribunals. Some of the literature has regarded international and hybrid tribunals as ineffective institutions for the promotion of international justice; however, one of the major problems with this literature is that there is no accepted standard for measuring effectiveness or success. Another difficulty in judging the success of these tribunals involves the counterfactual example of what would be the current peace-building and justice efforts in the former Yugoslavia, Rwanda, Sierra Leone and East Timor without the creation of the tribunals. In other words while the tribunals may not have completely fulfilled their mandates, the International Criminal Tribunal for the former Yugoslavia (ICTY), the International Criminal Tribunal for Rwanda (ICTR), the Special Court for Sierra Leone (SCSL) and the Serious Crimes Panel for East Timor (SCPET) have provided more security and justice than the national courts would have been able to provide.[1] What should be the basis for measuring and defining the effectiveness or success of these or any international tribunals?

This question is difficult to answer because of the different interpretations of the rationale for establishing these tribunals. Some argue that these tribunals should be judged by their ability to provide for international peace and security (Shinoda, 2002) or to deter future atrocities (Morris, 1997) or even to reintegrate societies (Drumbl, 2000). Yacoubian (1998), for example, argues that deterrence is one of the three possible justifications given for the creation of the tribunals under international penal theory.[2] Although court decisions of the ICTY and the ICTR have referred to the deterrent effect of the tribunals, they are not a forum that can provide general deterrence.[3] Certainly one may infer that the creation of a tribunal expresses international condemnation of acts such as genocide which would hopefully have a deterrent effect on future crimes.

It is understandable that there are vastly different standards used to judge the relative success of these tribunals. The SCSL and the SCPET were established at the time of post-conflict state-building, and in the case of East Timor, the Tribunal was established even before statehood. In addition, the ICTY and the ICTR were established to deal with some of the worse atrocities seen since World War II. The government-sponsored ethnic cleansing policies in the former Yugoslavia lasted for several years while the number that died in the Rwandan genocide is almost unimaginable. Given the complexity of the crimes, the magnitude of the human rights violations and the nature of the conflicts it is not surprising that varying standards are used to judge these tribunals, nor is it surprising that many authors are critical of the tribunals.

Rather than relying on a subjective standard, this concluding chapter takes a different approach to examining the success of these tribunals. We begin this chapter examining the ICTY and the ICTR authorizing resolutions in order to understand the goals of the international community in establishing these two tribunals. By examining the "black letter" of the law, we are able to be more specific in our judgment of the success of these tribunals. The United Nations (UN) resolutions contain specific language which describes the international community's rationale for establishing these tribunals. Even though our approach is different than other authors, we also find that the ICTY and the ICTR have a mixed record of fulfilling their mandates. This has less to do with the institutions and more to do with the broad nature of their mandates. The UN Security Council saw these tribunals as having a multi-faceted mandate. For example, Resolution 955 establishes three reasons for the creation of the ICTR including (1) the "maintenance of peace," (2) ensuring "that such violations are halted and effectively redressed" and (3) leading to a "process of national reconciliation."

While the first two mandates are similar for the ICTY, Shinoda (2002) notes that the ICTR was the first international Tribunal established for the purpose of national reconciliation. However, if these are the goals of international tribunals, then they should be the basis upon which we judge their relative success and failure. It is with these goals in mind that we analyze the effectiveness of the ICTY and the ICTR. We examine the record of arrests and the length of trials in order to understand the effectiveness of the tribunals as judicial institutions. Later in the chapter, we discuss the effectiveness of hybrid tribunals such as the SCSL, the SCPET and the Extraordinary Chambers for Cambodia (ECC) and examine how the international and national component of these tribunals influences their effectiveness. Finally, we examine the Indonesian Human Rights Court (IHRC) as an example of a purely domestic process and note both its limitations and potential ability to contribute to judicial reform and human rights development. We conclude the chapter by noting that there is no institutional template that works in all situations. These institutions of justice must be crafted to reflect the post-conflict environment and the sincerity of the host state and the international community in establishing effective institutions to address violations of international law.

Measuring the Effectiveness of International Tribunals: The Maintenance of Peace

In society, judicial institutions are not viewed as organs of peace and security; instead, law enforcement agencies are responsible for providing law and order and maintaining the peace. However in an international context, judicial institutions, such as international tribunals, have been viewed as an essential component to promoting peace and security. The question remains whether these legal bodies can actually provide peace and security. For example Roberts (1998a) argues that neither tribunal (*i.e.*, the ICTY and the ICTR) has been successful at maintaining peace. He notes that the ICTY did not contribute to peace-building efforts and in the case of the ICTR, he argues that the "continuing bitter conflicts in the African Great Lakes region, including Hutu-Tutsi killings within Rwanda, do not suggest that the Tribunal has yet had a significant effect" (1998a, p. 274). Shinoda also questions whether peace-building "might collide with purely judicial needs . . . Does justice really contribute to peace? Should we reject unjust peace even in post-conflict regions?" (2002, p. 45).

The goal of peace is an understandable mandate of the ICTY since this Tribunal was created during the conflict as an element of the international community's peace-building initiatives. In 1993, when the Security Council approved the creation of the Tribunal, the conflict within Bosnia and Herzegovina (BiH) was still raging. If we are to define peace as the absence of war, we can initially conclude that the ICTY's goal to maintain peace was not achieved. Even though the Tribunal began operations in mid-November 1993, the conflict within BiH continued until the end of 1995, when the Dayton Peace Accord was signed by the conflicting parties—the existence of the Tribunal and the possibility of being indicted did not lead to the ending of hostilities.[4] As discussed in Chapter 2, the mandate of the ICTY was expanded in 1999 to include the Kosovo conflict and it appears that the Serbs were not concerned about the possibility of a change in the mandate of the ICTY to include this conflict.

Although the ICTR was established in a "post-conflict" environment, the international community was concerned that revenge killings on the part of the Tutsis would undermine peace in the region. Since the establishment of the ICTR, estimates are that tens of thousands have perished in clashes between Hutus and Tutsis. While BiH and Kosovo have received international peacekeepers,[5] there has not been a peacekeeping presence in Rwanda. Even with peacekeepers, judicial institutions will only be effective at promoting peace and security with the cooperation of law enforcement agencies. Indeed, the efforts of the tribunals have been stymied by not having their own law enforcement personnel. It would appear that the ability of either tribunal to maintain and promote peace-building measures is limited by the level of assistance provided by the international community and the host state.

However what would be the peace-building and security level without the tribunals? Akhavan (2001) argues that while conflict continued in Rwanda, the extent of revenge killings would be far greater in the absence of the ICTR. "Notwithstanding the various conflicts between the ICTR and the Rwandese government . . . this policy of accountability, aimed at discrediting the Hutu extremists, has also restrained the extent of anti-Hutu vengeance killings . . . the shadow of the ICTR proceedings . . . have exercised a moderating influence in the post-conflict peace-building process" (p. 23).

Measuring the Effectiveness of International Tribunals: The First Period of Apprehension and Transfer to the International Tribunals

In the following sections, we briefly outline some of the issues involved in tribunal justice. Perhaps no other aspect of the tribunals has received so much criticism as their ability to provide justice to victims as well as to ensure the rights of defendants. While the initial use of national courts in Rwanda made the achievement of justice different than the former Yugoslavia, the rules of evidence, due process and appellate jurisdiction of the tribunals is almost identical. One of the major issues for both tribunals has been the apprehension of defendants in order to ensure that human rights violations are redressed. There have been two distinct periods involving the ability of the tribunals to apprehend suspects. From the mid to late 1990s, both tribunals, especially the ICTY, were ineffective in apprehending suspects. Most of those who were tried at the ICTY prior to 2000 were lower-rank indictees. However in the second period since the early 2000s, the tribunals have been very successful in apprehending suspects (many of whom have voluntarily surrendered). As discussed in the previous chapter, the large number of apprehensions has created the unintended negative consequence of greatly increasing the backlog of tribunal cases.

ICTY Security Council Resolution 827 clearly states that " all states shall cooperate fully with the International Tribunal ... including the obligation of states to comply with the requests for assistance or orders issued by a Trial Chamber under Article 29 of the Statute."[6] However, the ICTY encountered continuous resistance in the apprehension and transferring of indictees, both from the parties to the conflict and by other states (Meron, 1997). In the Dayton Accords of 1995, BiH, Croatia and the Federal Republic of Yugoslavia (FRY) specifically agreed to assist the Tribunal in accomplishing its mandate. Afterwards, BiH and the FRY each transferred an indictee captured by the national police force in 1996. Croatia transferred an indictee for the first time only in August 1997. In each case, domestic efforts between 1993 and 2002 resulted in only six individuals transferred to the Tribunal from the FRY, two from BiH and three from Croatia.

While the number of apprehensions was few, the ICTY was prolific in issuing indictments in its first few years. Between 1994 and 1996, it issued forty-four public indictments. Between 1997 and 1999, the number decreased to seventeen, with a similar number between 2000 and 2002. However, there were only eight arrests by the end of 1996. The numbers began to increase, with thirty-one arrests between 1997 and 1999 and thirty-four between 1999 and 2002. About 44 per cent of those in custody at the Tribunal had voluntarily surrendered while approximately 34 per cent had been captured by the Stabilization Force or SFOR (Akhavan, 1998). ICTY indictees have been arrested in Austria, BiH, Croatia, Serbia and Germany.

One problem in gauging the early success of the ICTY in apprehending indicted individuals was the practice by the prosecution to request sealed indictments (Murphy, 1999). When submitting an indictment to a judge for confirmation, the prosecutor could request under ICTY Rule 53 that the indictment not be publicly disclosed on the grounds that doing so would make it more likely that the accused would evade apprehension. Therefore, sealed indictments were used as a tool of the prosecution to increase the speed by which defendants were apprehended. While the number of persons publicly indicted was known, the number of persons indicted under seal was not. However, Akhavan (1996) argues that the difficulty in capturing indicted individuals should not be considered a failure, since "interim justice" can take place through the restriction of travel and depravation of freedom of movement, as well as removal of suspects from public office.

As discussed in Chapter 6, the difficulty of the ICTY to apprehend high-ranking officials meant that during the first years of the Tribunal, resources were disproportionately allocated to investigating low-ranking perpetrators involved in the direct commission of crimes such as murder which were familiar to prosecutors and investigators in the context of domestic law enforcement. While there are benefits to prosecuting low-level perpetrators that have a direct link with victims, most analysts have stressed that the ICTY's value is ultimately based on its ability to successfully prosecute those at the highest level. Given the difficulty involved in arresting indicted war criminals, the ICTY established Rule 61 (under Article 15 of Resolution 827) which provided for a "super-indictment' in certain circumstances. The purpose of this Rule was to broaden awareness of the perpetrators' actions. It allowed the prosecutor to present the indictment and all supporting evidence to the Tribunal in an open court session. This could include examination of witnesses whose testimony would become part of the record. Under the provisions of Rule 61, the prosecution could present highlights of the case in the absence of the accused, essentially for the media.[7]

In the case of Rwanda, the initial effectiveness of the Tribunal was also greatly undermined by the lack of cooperation from other countries. Article 28 of Resolution 955 specifically requires all UN member-states to provide full cooperation including the surrender of individuals to the ICTR. Several African countries, mostly notably Kenya and the former Zaire (now the Democratic Republic of Congo), refused requests to transfer suspects.[8] Both countries accepted a large number of Hutu refugees, including several of the leading planners of the genocide. Part of this reluctance to transfer suspects was due to the balance of power struggle that had engulfed Central Africa since the mid-1990s. As Magnarella notes "they [Kenya and Zaire] supported Rwanda's former rulers because they regarded the successor RPF-led government as a client of Uganda's President Yoweri Museveni, their rival for leadership in East and Central Africa" (2000, p. 51).

Measuring the Effectiveness of International Tribunals: The Second Period of Apprehension and Transfer to the International Tribunals

While the ICTY failed to indict Croatian President Franjo Tudman, his Defense Minister Gojko Susak and former Bosnian Croat leader Mate Boban prior to their respective deaths, apprehensions of high-ranking officials gathered momentum after 2000. In April 2000, French commandos belonging to the SFOR in BiH arrested Momcilo Krajisnik, President of the Bosnian Serb Assembly from 1990 to 1995. After Bosnian Serb President Radovan Karadzic, Krajisnik was the most influential wartime ultranationalist still active. In January 2001, Biljana Plavšić, former deputy to Karadzic and former Bosnian Serb President was arrested.[9] The arrest of Slobodan Milošević by Yugoslav police on 1 April 2001 and his subsequent transfer to The Hague on 28 June 2001 represented a landmark for the Tribunal (Rudolph, 2001). Milošević was the first head of state to face trial in an international court (his death in March 2006 deprived thousands of victims' closure and justice). By 2006, the Tribunal's rate of apprehension of indicted individuals was over 94 per cent, with seventy-five trials either taking place or completed. The capture of former Croatian General Ante Gotovina in December 2005 means that only nine indictees remain at-large.

In terms of the ICTR, some of these early problems with the Tribunal have been worked-out, and it has been much more successful at apprehending defendants. So far, twenty-one countries have transferred indictees to the ICTR. Significantly in 2002, the Democratic Republic of Congo, a haven for Hutu refugees, surrendered its first two defendants. Approximately 89 per cent of those indicted by the Tribunal have been arrested, and approximately half of those arrested have either been tried or are currently in the trial process (see Table 7.1 and 7.2). The ICTR's defendants include eleven ministers of the 1994 interim government as well as the former president of the National Assembly, thirteen military leaders and fourteen senior government administrators. Significantly, the former Prime Minister Jean Kambanda has been convicted for genocide. This verdict, along with the conviction of former Bosnian Serb President Plavšić for crimes against humanity, are so far two of the most important convictions in the history of international humanitarian law.

Measuring the Effectiveness of International Tribunals: Providing Justice through a Speedy Trial

Resolution 827 guarantees the accused the right to a trial without delay. A speedy trial is a prerequisite for justice for the accused (Mundis, 2000). Unlike the tribunals established to deal with Germany and Japan after World War II, where activities by the accused were carefully documented, in the case of the former Yugoslavia the prosecutor has had to rely on eyewitness accounts which is time consuming and expensive. The collection of evidence becomes more difficult with the passage of time, as the recollections of the victims become more unclear. In addition, there has been concern expressed by witnesses for their protection after testifying, particularly since the focus of the tribunals is now the prosecution of high-ranking political and military leaders. One of the practices of the ICTY that has also been criticized is the use of unnamed witnesses (Leigh, 1996). During the discussion of the creation of the Tribunal, trials *in absentia* were debated, with France favoring them in some circumstances. The Italian government voiced concern over this procedure, and its position ultimately prevailed (Burns, 1996).

Table 7.1 International Tribunal Indictments and Arrests

	Yugoslavia	Rwanda
Individuals indicted	162	80
Individuals arrested	153	71
Individuals at large	9	9
Per cent arrested	94	89

Note: Data compiled by authors in January 2006.

Table 7.2 Status of International Tribunal Trials[1]

In Trial Chambers		
	Yugoslavia	Rwanda
Trials in progress	19	26
Number of trials completed	51	15
Convictions	39	12
Acquitals	12	3

Note: Data compiled by authors in April 2006.
[1]These numbers exclude the appeals process and only reflect trial deliberations.

The ICTY trials have taken on average three and half years from arrest through appeal to complete. In an effort to provide a speedier trial, the Tribunal began in 2002 to conduct six simultaneous trials instead of four which had been the previous practice (United Nations Doc., 2002b). Even with the increase in the number of judges in 2000 and the use of multiple trials, there is concern over whether trials can be completed by 2008 with appeals complete by 2010. Of those indicted, nine still remain at large (most notably Radovan Karadzic and Ratko Mladic, the political and military leaders of the Bosnian Serbs), forty-eight are currently at the pre-trial stage and nineteen trials are still being conducted as of April 2006.

The ICTR's Resolution 955 also includes language that requires that an individual be tried without delay. So far of those trials that have been completed, it has taken an average of four and a half years from arrest through appeal. One of the concerns of the ICTR is that as more individuals have been apprehended, the waiting time for detainees has increased. Current detainees could be scheduled for trial, but there is a lack of space on the trial docket. A report by former ICTR President Navanethem Pillay acknowledged that the process was unduly long. "Despite efforts of the judges and of all support sections, trials continue to be long drawn out and often defy the best-laid plans" (United Nations Doc., 2002a, p. 4). However, the report noted that the trial and appellate proceedings are lengthy because "judicial proceedings at the international level are far more complicated than proceedings at the national level" (United Nations Doc., 2002a, p. 4). The report goes on to cite the problem of translating documents, interpretation of the trial proceedings into three languages as well as the non-appearance of witnesses from Rwanda as the principal reasons why the process has been so slow. The lack of a speedy trial is not only problematic for the defendant but also the victim as it compounds the problem of national reconciliation. This is why the Completion Strategy has become an important mechanism for alleviating the backlog of cases and providing a speedier trial at the international level.

Measuring the Effectiveness of International Tribunals: The Process of National Reconciliation

The goal of national reconciliation was not expressly mentioned in the mandate of the ICTY. However, national reconciliation is a precondition for a permanent peace (Shinoda, 2002). The ability of individuals involved in the conflict to return to a normal life, living side by side with those they once fought is important to maintaining peace. After the conflict in the former Yugoslavia, nearly two million people returned to their countries and homes. However, approximately one and a half million people are still displaced, including 230,000 ethnic Serbs, Roma and other minorities who fled Kosovo. The FRY continues to host 390,000 refugees, the largest single refugee community in Europe. Refugees are concerned about returning to their homes in Croatia, BiH and Kosovo because of fear of retaliation from other ethnic and religious groups. Since BiH is divided into a Muslim-Croatian Federation and the *Republika Srpska* under the Dayton Accords, a large number of people fear going back to areas now controlled by opposing ethnic factions. About 250,000 Croatian Serbs remain in exile mostly in the FRY (United Nations High Commission for Refugees, 2003).

The goal of national reconciliation is specifically mentioned in Resolution 955 and is a unique feature of the mandate of the ICTR. It is a broad goal and Shinoda argues that the Security Council "did not unequivocally address a logical link between international peace and national reconciliation through such a compulsory tribunal" (2002, p. 49). In the Security Council debate over Resolution 955, Howland and Calathes quote the Czech Republic representative who argued that the ICTR "is hardly designed as a vehicle for reconciliation . . . Reconciliation is a much more complicated process" (1998, p. 144). Fundamentally, *national* reconciliation is an internal, domestic process. The ICTR represents an *international* attempt to forge national reconciliation because the national courts and government are either institutionally weak or not disposed to healing the society.[10]

In Rwanda, there have been well-publicized conflicts between the national courts and the ICTR. These conflicts have undermined the credibility of the ICTR within Rwanda. Because of its location in Arusha, the ICTR has been accused of being too remote from the people (both Tutsis and Hutus) to facilitate national reconciliation. Moreover, some have criticized the Tribunal because the majority of those who are convicted have not served sentences in Rwanda. At this point, a majority of those convicted are serving their sentences in Mali. Three other countries including Benin, Swaziland and most recently France have also agreed to accept ICTR convicts.

Fundamentally, national reconciliation can only occur in an environment in which both sides feel that justice is being fulfilled. In order to promote national reconciliation, there cannot be "victor's justice," and this is part of the problem with the stratified concurrent jurisdiction of the ICTR and the national courts. Morris (1997) argues that as long as individuals perceive that international as well as domestic judicial institutions are systematically biased towards one group, reconciliation will never occur. "If the leaders are away receiving 'international justice' which is perceived as lenient, and the followers are at home getting 'bargains' in the national justice system, then no one is punished fully and severely, relative to national standards, for the horrors that were committed" (p. 365).

As in the case of the former Yugoslavia, one important aspect of national reconciliation involves the return of Hutu and Tutsi refugees. Hundreds of thousands of Tutsis fled the country in the 1960s and remained refugees until after 1994. Following the Rwandan Patriotic Front's (RPF) capture of Kigali in July 1994, more than two million Hutus fled the country. Immediately after the RPF's return, Tutsi refugees began to return to Rwanda followed later in 1995 and 1996 by a large number of Hutus. Estimates are that at least two and half million Hutu and Tutsi refugees have re-entered the country since 1994. On this basis, national reconciliation has been occurring and has been much more successful than in the former Yugoslavia where refugees have been much slower to return.

However, it is doubtful that the Tribunal can be credited for the return of refugees. The return of refugees has been based on policies by the post-genocide governments as well as support from the international community. Once it became clear that there was going to be a significant return of refugees, the Rwandan government began a program called "villagization" in order to re-organize the system of villages to cope with the returning refugees. The program has been criticized by many human rights organizations and aid agencies as creating new "internally displaced former refugees." However, the program has not based re-location on tribal distinction which at least has fostered greater goodwill among all Rwandans. While the Tribunal establishes the international community's interest in conflict resolution, the Tribunal is too far removed to be an effective agent of reconciliation.

Re-Conceptualizing International Tribunals

Up to this point we have explored the rationale and mandates of the ICTY and the ICTR and analyzed how effective these tribunals have been in fulfilling their mandates. Early in their development, both tribunals were criticized for the failure to apprehend indictees—today, few individuals remain at large. Ironically, the tribunals are a victim of their own success as the backlog of cases increases the pre-trial wait period and the duration of trials (problems that the Complete Strategies are designed to alleviate). While the establishment of a tribunal is a better option than no action on the part of the international community, systems of justice can only be effective when all parties recognize the legitimacy of the judicial process (something that has been especially lacking in the case of the ICTY). Moreover any system of justice, whether international or national in scope, cannot fulfill its mandate with administrative problems brought about either because of limited trial chambers or the inability to work with law enforcement personnel.

Some of the problems of the tribunals can be attributed to the nature of international humanitarian law and their broad mandates. Whether these tribunals could ever become instruments of peace and security is highly debatable. Moreover, it is difficult to imagine circumstances in which *national* reconciliation can be created by an *international* institution. This is not to say that organizations like the Council of Europe or the Organization for Security and Co-operation in Europe (OSCE) have not been instrumental in resolving national disputes and fostering post conflict peace-building measures. However, the ICTY and the ICTR had very broad mandates following some of the worse atrocities seen since World War II. Any institution, no matter how well designed, would have difficulty in providing peace and security as well as reconciliation.

We also believe that the problems with these tribunals have as much to do with design as purpose. Given the nature of the crimes and the number of possible indictees, the international community was extremely short-sighted in creating tribunals with such a small number of judges and chambers. We see just how limited the resources of the tribunals are now that they are more effective in apprehending and trying defendants. Many detainees unduly await trial because the docket has become so full. While any system of justice has administrative problems, some of the problems facing the ICTY and the ICTR could be easily remedied with a greater financial contribution from the international community. For example while the ICTY annual budget for the last two years was an excess of $250 million, the initial budget for 1993 was only $276,000. Indeed, it was not until after 1998 that the budget was increased to over $50 million. This is not to argue that simply providing more funds would alleviate all the problems surrounding these tribunals; however, more funds early in the process which could have been used to provide for more investigators, judges and chambers might have improved the current situation.[11] However, many of the issues discussed above do not lead to clear policy recommendations.

Another reason why these tribunals have not been more successful is because unlike Nuremburg and Tokyo, the ICTY and especially the ICTR have dealt with civil war conflict. The nature of the crimes committed in the former Yugoslavia and Rwanda are especially problematic for international humanitarian law. Roberts argues that "the atrocities of the 1980s and 1990s have been in conflicts with at least some element of civil war. Such wars are often more bitter than international wars. . [the] rules applicable to internal conflicts . . . are more limited than those for international armed conflicts" (1998b, pp. 138-9).[12]

The Use of Hybrids and Domestic Tribunals: A Better Option for the Delivery of Justice?

As discussed in Chapter 3 and 4, the SCSL, the ECC and the SCPET are hybrid tribunals that represent an attempt by the international community and host states to balance financial needs and the protection of state sovereignty with the need to prosecute individuals who are responsible for committing international crimes that would otherwise go unpunished. One of the main arguments in support of hybrid tribunals is that they can provide the basis for re-building the judicial system in post-conflict societies, provide training for local judicial officials and at the same time serve as an institution of justice. Fritz and Smith argue that "[k]nowledge gained, skills acquired, and personnel empowered may act as catalysts for the establishment of new institutions, structures, and cultures that will better safeguard the rule of law and outlive the existence of [hybrid courts]" (2001, p. 406).

The SCSL and the SCPET demonstrate that hybrid tribunals offer several advantages over purely international tribunals. Both have been much quicker to indict and bring suspects to trial than either the ICTY or the ICTR. In addition because the national legal system of both countries has been very involved in the process, these hybrid tribunals have provided greater educational and training benefits than international tribunals.[13] Moreover because the tribunal is located in the country and the prosecutorial team is composed of individuals selected by the government, there is a greater likelihood that this type of legal institution will bring a greater sense of reconciliation than international tribunals which are often viewed as too distant from the citizenry.

However, these advantages must be weighed against the shortcomings observed in the ECC and also the SCPET process. Fundamentally, it is difficult to establish mixed tribunals in countries without the necessary institutions and legal culture to support the rule of law. In the case of Cambodia, this disadvantage has been exacerbated because the ruling government is composed of former Khmer Rouge members. Because of the relationship of individuals such as Hun Sen to the Khmer Rouge, the government has attempted to limit the scope of suspects and the jurisdiction of the ECC (some would argue to even thwart its creation). In the case of East Timor, the problems of the SCPET reflect the pains of nation and state-building for a newly independent country.

Furthermore, even in the case of the SCSL, it is difficult to imagine that the Court could have fulfilled its mandate and prosecute those that bear the greatest responsibility for crimes committed in Sierra Leone without the arrest of Charles Taylor. Because the SCSL is not established based on Chapter VII authority, his arrest has been a political issue which was beyond the scope and jurisdiction of the SCSL.[14] In addition, for hybrid tribunals to create capacity-building, they must be fully funded. The financial problems that the SCSL has had since its inception are now beginning to have an adverse effect on the working of the Court, and the estimates for the ECC are also inadequate. A lack of commitment by the international community has stymied the process of providing justice.

The experiences of Sierra Leone, Cambodia and East Timor demonstrate that there is no one model that fits all situations. When deciding to cooperate in the creation of a hybrid tribunal, the international community would be wise to consider the legal culture and acceptance of the rule of law in the state as well as the sincerity of the government in creating a free and fair process. As seen in the case of Cambodia and East Timor, a flawed process cannot be considered superior to inaction. A flawed process does not serve the purpose of justice or reconciliation and can further alienate members of the society and call into question the commitment of the international community to genuine justice.

Some argue that the money spent on tribunals, whether international or hybrid would be better spent on re-building national judiciaries in post-conflict environments. Kritz (1996) argues that rather than establishing the ICTR, the donor community and Rwanda would have been better served by re-building the Rwandan legal system and educating a new generation of lawyers and judges to replace those that there killed or imprisoned. This would also seem to apply to Indonesia, as the country transitions towards democracy and rule of law after three decades of authoritarian rule.

In the case of Rwanda, the state requested the assistance of the international community in order to be able to provide justice to victims and reconciliation to society. However, what about situations such as the former Yugoslavia and to a lesser extent Cambodia and Indonesia in which the state is either completely opposed or very reluctant to embark on a process that would indict high-level officials and place burdens upon the judicial system? In these cases, simply providing funds to re-build the national legal system or train lawyers and judges misses the point.

The issue is how the international community can ensure that individuals who have committed war crimes, crimes against humanity and genocide are prosecuted in states in which there is no legal culture of accountability and judicial independence, or as in the case of Iraq, how to ensure that "victor's justice" is not applied. Indonesia escaped the ravages of civil war and was able to resist calls for an international or even a hybrid process. It was in a much stronger position to assert its sovereignty than the former Yugoslavia or Rwanda. However, we question whether it was realistic for the international community to deem Indonesia capable of holding the military accountable for human rights violations after decades of authoritarian rule.

If the IHCR process had led to prosecutions and sentences for those that were not transferred to Dili, then many might feel that justice within a national context was effectively rendered. Instead, the IHRC has been viewed by the Security Council, states and many Indonesian NGOs as a failure. Since the international community was not satisfied with the hybrid process in East Timor and especially the domestic process in Indonesia, the UN approved in February 2005 the creation of a Commission of Experts to evaluate the SCPET and the IHRC and to recommend further steps for achieving accountability. The report by the UN Commission suggested that an international tribunal may be necessary to ensure justice is done. However, the IHCR has served a broader purpose. The failures of the IHRC have focused important scrutiny on the Indonesian legal system as well as assisted NGOs in their calls for legal reforms. These reforms have assisted in codifying into Indonesian law important human rights principles.

On the broader issue of reconciliation and the establishment of a historical record of abuses, no tribunal model is totally effective. The ICTY has failed to serve as a vehicle for reconciliation among ethnic groups in the former Yugoslavia, and indeed some might argue that it has perpetuated ethnic resentment. The hybrid SCPET has been criticized by East Timor President Xanana Gusmão who has argued that the process undermined reconciliation between East Timor and Indonesia. At the same time, the purely domestic IHRC failed to provide a clear historical record of the abuses in East Timor and has been condemned by human rights organizations as well as most of the international community. For many, reconciliation should not be a goal of criminal tribunals. Instead, reconciliation is a social process which is best accomplished through mechanisms such as truth and reconciliation commissions (TRCs).

While TRCs vary in their structure, mandate and mode of data collection, TRCs as a group of human rights institutions can be characterized as non-judicial, official public sector organizations designed to investigate past wrongdoing. However for these institutions, defining the "truth" and "reconciliation" is a normative issue which limits the power of TRCs. While they can have several advantages compared to a tribunal, there are those who also argue that TRCs are fundamentally flawed institutions of justice. Synder and Vinjamuri (2003) suggest that TRCs may threaten powerful interests and lead to greater sectarian violence while others argue that compared to tribunals which can impose prison terms, TRCs are largely powerless institutions whose benefits have been greatly exaggerated (Mendeloff, 2004).

We note this debate over TRCs because it highlights the difficulty of all institutions of justice to provide a full range of benefits to society. Justice, reconciliation and security are broad goals which are difficult to achieve even under the best of circumstances. In post-conflict states which are in the process of re-building institutions and national identity, these goals become extremely difficult to accomplish. For some, no temporary process can ever achieve such long-term goals. Therefore, all of these considerations are important as the international community institutionalizes the International Criminal Court (ICC) and replaces *ad hoc* international justice with a permanent judicial body. As Goldstone and Bass argue, "the problems and delays inherent in setting up ad hoc tribunals in time of crisis are so daunting that they overwhelm the timely pursuit of justice" (2000, p. 58).

For this and other reasons, many scholars argue that one of the lasting contributions that these tribunals made was creating an international consensus which resulted in the establishment of the ICC in 2002. Perhaps, the greatest legacy of the tribunals is the fact that we may never again witness the creation of *ad hoc* justice. Once the ICTY and the ICTR fulfill their mandates, all future international prosecutions involving the criminality of individuals will be adjudicated by the ICC. The creation of these *ad hoc* tribunals represents an important moment in history in which international consensus ended the impunity of heads of state. While these tribunals have been criticized for not accomplishing their goals, they have provided important historical lessons which we can only hope that the international community, states and ultimately the ICC learn from. As the experience of theses tribunals has demonstrated, the creation of legal institutions is not a *panacea*. Undoubtedly, the ICC will suffer from many of the same state coordination problems that the *ad hoc* tribunals have endured. The assertion of sovereignty is a powerful right of the state which historically was used to deny justice to individuals. As institutions such as the ICC develop, perhaps the notion of sovereignty will also develop to include more consideration for the rights of individuals. In all states, the citizens should be regarded as the true sovereigns.

Notes

1. As noted in Chapter 6, a national court process has functioned alongside the international process in the former Yugoslavia and Rwanda; however until recently, the national courts in both cases have proven to be largely ineffective in conducting trials which met international standards of justice.
2. A number of authors have argued that the tribunals were established to deter future genocides. While the reports to the UN Secretary-General which eventually formed the basis of Resolution 827 and 955 lay out the need to deter future crimes, this rationale is not specifically mentioned in the authorizing resolutions.
3. General deterrence is defined as a concern with preventing the same crime in the future (Notes, 2001). So-called specific deterrence is concerned with preventing a specific individual from committing the same crime (recidivism).
4. A notable example is the massacre in Srebrenica in July 1995, almost two years after the creation of the ICTY as well as the violence in Kosovo in 1999.
5. Roberts (1998b) argues, however, that the presence of peacekeepers is no guarantee of peace-building efforts. He notes that UN peacekeepers were passive observers to the atrocities at Srebrenica in July 1995.
6. This includes a requirement to assist in the arrest of indicted individuals and their transfer to the Tribunal.
7. This practice was eliminated as individuals were increasingly arrested.
8. The refusal to transfer suspects is not specific to African countries. France and even the US have refused to surrender individuals to the ICTR. Moreover, there has been at least one case in which a country surrendered a suspect to the Rwandan national court rather than the ICTR (Morris, 1997).
9. She is serving an eleven-year sentence.
10. Several authors including Sarkin (1999) and Shinoda (2002) argue that the only means by which to foster national reconciliation is through the use of a truth and reconciliation commission. Sarkin argues that these commissions which have

been used in Chile, El Salvador, Argentina and most notably South Africa have been a successful vehicle for promoting reconciliation. The case of Sierra Leone demonstrates that these commissions can function along side a tribunal.

11. However, one could argue that as the needs of the ICTY grew, so did the funding.
12. However, these civil wars have contributed to the expansion of international humanitarian law to cover all forms of state conflict.
13. The creation of the Rules of the Road procedure as described in Chapter 6 has also provided this benefit.
14. As indicated in Chapter 3 at the time of this writing in May 2006, Charles Taylor had been apprehended attempting to flee Nigeria. The SCSL requested that he be tried at The Hague because of security concerns in Freetown. This request is being considered by the UN Security Council.

Appendix A

Structure, Jurisdiction and Composition of the Tribunals

	Yugoslavia	Rwanda
Conflict	1991-1995	1994
Parties	Serbia, Croatia, Bosnia	Internal: Hutus and Tutsis. Extends to surrounding nations.
Deaths	250,00 dead, 2.5 million displaced	1 million dead, 2 million displaced
Agreement Initiation	Security Council	Rwandan Government/ Security Council
Parties to Agreement	Security Council	Security Council
Tribunal Agreement	25 May 1993	November 1994
Beginning of Court	November 1993	July 1995
Location	The Hague, Netherlands	Arusha, Tanzania
Temporal Jurisdiction	Since 1 January 1991	1 January 1994 to 31 December 1994
Financing	United Nations General Budget, Article 17	United Nations General Budget, Article 17
Court Structure	Trial Chamber and Appeals Chamber	Trial Chamber and Appeals Chamber
Types of judges	International None from the same state	International None from the same state
Selection of Judges	By General Assembly, based on list vetted by the Security Council	By General Assembly, based on list vetted Security by the Council
Applicable Law	International Law	International Law
Working Language	English and French	English and French
Prosecutor	Nominated by the UN Secretary General, Approved by the Security Council	Shared with the ICTY (until recently)
Separate Domestic Court	Yes	Yes
Sentences	Fulfilled in other states: Denmark, Germany, Spain, France, Sweden, Austria, Norway, Finland, Italy	Fulfilled in other states: Mali, France, Swaziland

	Sierra Leone	Cambodia
Conflict	1991-2002	1975-1979
Parties	Revolutionary United Front (Liberian sponsored), the government and other factions	Khmer Rouge government and local population
Deaths	500,000 dead	2 million dead
Agreement Initiation	Sierra Leone Government/ Security Council	Cambodian Government
Parties to Agreement	Sierra Leone Government and UN Ratified by Legislature	Cambodian Government and UN. Ratified by Legislature
Tribunal Agreement	16 January 2002	17 March 2003
Beginning of Court	March 2003	Not Yet
Location	Freetown, Sierra Leone	Phnom Penh, Cambodia
Temporal Jurisdiction	Since 30 November 1996	17 April 1975 to 6 January 1979
Financing	Sierra Leone Government / UN Voluntary Contributions	Cambodia/ UN Voluntary Contributions
Court Structure	Trial Chamber and Appeals Chamber	Trial Chamber and Supreme Court
Types of Judges	International and Domestic (Mixed) Trial: 1 SL, 2 UN Appeals: 2 SL, 3 UN	International and Domestic (Mixed) Trial: 3 C, 2 UN Supreme: 4 C, 3 UN Super-majority vote
Selection of Judges	By UN Secretary General, upon nominations forwarded by States, and in particular the members of the Economic Community of West African States and the Commonwealth	Cambodian Supreme Council of Magistracy. International Judges list submitted by UN Secretary General
Applicable Law	Sierra Leone Law, International Law	Cambodian Law, International Law
Working Language	English	Khmer, English and French
Prosecutor	UN Secretary general consults with the Government of Sierra Leone	Two: one Cambodian, one International. Cambodian Supreme Council of Magistracy. International Judges list submitted by UN Secretary General
Separate Domestic Court	Yes	No
Sentences	Fulfilled in Sierra Leone, or ICTFR/ICTR locations	Cambodia

	East Timor	Indonesia
Conflict	1975-1999	1975-1999
Parties	Indonesian National Army, pro-Indonesia Timorese militias and local population	Indonesian National Army, pro-Indonesia Timorese militias and local population
Deaths	2,000 deaths and 500,000 displaced in 1999. Over 200,000 dead since 1975	2,000 deaths and 500,000 displaced in 1999. Over 200,000 dead since 1975
Agreement Initiation	UN Transitional Administration in East Timor.	Indonesian Government
Parties to the Agreement	UNTAET and transitional authority in East Timor.	Indonesian Government
Tribunal Agreement	6 March 2000	2000. Law 26
Beginning of Court	2001	March 2002
Location	Dili, East Timor	Jakarta, Indonesia
Temporal Jurisdiction	1 January 1999 to 25 October 1999	April and September 1999 Tanjung Priok Massacre in 1984
Financing	UN Transitional Administration in East Timor UN Voluntary Contributions	Indonesian Government
Court Structure	District Court and Courts of Appeals	District Court, High Court and Supreme Court
	East Timor	Indonesia
Types of Judges	International and Domestic (Mixed) Both Chambers: 2 International, 1 ET	Domestic All three 3 ad hoc, 2 permanent
Selection of Judges	Appointed by Special Representative of the Secretary General (Transitional Administrator), in Consultation with the President of the Court of Appeals, from nominations by Transitional Service Commission	Appointed and Dismissed by the President as Head of State, in consultation with the Supreme Court
Applicable Law	East Timor Law, International Law	Indonesian Law
Working Language	Tetum, Portuguese, Bahasa Indonesia, English (as appropriate)	Bahasa, Indonesia
Prosecutor	Recommended by the Transitional Service Commission created by the Transitional Administrator	From the Indonesian Attorney General's Office
Separate Domestic Court	No	Purely Domestic
Sentences	East Timor	Indonesia

Appendix B

Resolutions for the International Criminal Tribunal for the former Yugoslavia United Nations Security Council Resolutions 827, 1503 and 1534

RESOLUTION 827
ADOPTED 25 MAY 1993
S/RES/827

The Security Council,

Reaffirming its resolution 713 (1991) of 25 September 1991 and all subsequent relevant resolutions,

Having considered the report of the Secretary-General (S/25704 and Add.1) pursuant to paragraph 2 of resolution 808 (1993),

Expressing once again its grave alarm at continuing reports of widespread and flagrant violations of international humanitarian law occurring within the territory of the former Yugoslavia, and especially in the Republic of Bosnia and Herzegovina, including reports of mass killings, massive, organized and systematic detention and rape of women, and the continuance of the practice of ethnic cleansing, including for the acquisition and the holding of territory,

Determining that this situation continues to constitute a threat to international peace and security,

Determined to put an end to such crimes and to take effective measures to bring to justice the persons who are responsible for them,

Convinced that in the particular circumstances of the former Yugoslavia the establishment as an ad hoc measure by the Council of an international tribunal and the prosecution of persons responsible for serious violations of international humanitarian law would enable this aim to be achieved and would contribute to the restoration and maintenance of peace,

Believing that the establishment of an international tribunal and the prosecution of persons responsible for the above-mentioned violations of international humanitarian law will contribute to ensuring that such violations are halted and effectively redressed,

Noting in this regard the recommendation by the Co-Chairmen of the Steering Committee of the International Conference on the Former Yugoslavia for the establishment of such a tribunal (S/25221),

Reaffirming in this regard its decision in resolution 808 (1993) that an international tribunal shall be established for the prosecution of persons responsible for serious violations of international humanitarian law committed in the territory of the former Yugoslavia since 1991,

Considering that, pending the appointment of the Prosecutor of the International Tribunal, the Commission of Experts established pursuant to resolution 780 (1992) should continue on an urgent basis the collection of information relating to evidence of grave breaches of the Geneva Conventions and other violations of international humanitarian law as proposed in its interim report (S/25274),

Acting under Chapter VII of the Charter of the United Nations,

1. *Approves* the report of the Secretary-General;

2. *Decides* hereby to establish an international tribunal for the sole purpose of prosecuting persons responsible for serious violations of international humanitarian law committed in the territory of the former Yugoslavia between 1 January 1991 and a date to be determined by the Security Council upon the restoration of peace and to this end to adopt the Statute of the International Tribunal annexed to the above-mentioned report;

3. *Requests* the Secretary-General to submit to the judges of the International Tribunal, upon their election, any suggestions received from States for the rules of procedure and evidence called for in Article 15 of the Statute of the International Tribunal;

4. *Decides* that all States shall cooperate fully with the International Tribunal and its organs in accordance with the present resolution and the Statute of the International Tribunal and that consequently all States shall take any measures necessary under their domestic law to implement the provisions of the present resolution and the Statute, including the obligation of States to comply with requests for assistance or orders issued by a Trial Chamber under Article 29 of the Statute;

5. *Urges* States and intergovernmental and non-governmental organizations to contribute funds, equipment and services to the International Tribunal, including the offer of expert personnel;

6. *Decides* that the determination of the seat of the International Tribunal is subject to the conclusion of appropriate arrangements between the United Nations and the Netherlands acceptable to the Council, and that the International Tribunal may sit elsewhere when it considers it necessary for the efficient exercise of its functions;

7. *Decides also* that the work of the International Tribunal shall be carried out without prejudice to the right of the victims to seek, through appropriate means, compensation for damages incurred as a result of violations of international humanitarian law;

8. *Requests* the Secretary-General to implement urgently the present resolution and in particular to make practical arrangements for the effective functioning of the International Tribunal at the earliest time and to report periodically to the Council;

9. *Decides* to remain actively seized of the matter.

RESOLUTION 1503
ADOPTED ON 28 AUGUST 2003
S/RES/1503

The Security Council,

Recalling its resolutions 827 (1993) of 25 May 1993, 955 (1994) of 8 November 1994, 978 (1995) of 27 February 1995, 1165 (1998) of 30 April 1998, 1166 (1998) of 13 May 1998, 1329 (2000) of 30 November 2000, 1411 (2002) of 17 May 2002, 1431 (2002) of 14 August 2002, and 1481 (2003) of 19 May 2003,

Noting the letter from the Secretary-General to the President of the Security Council dated 28 July 2003 (S/2003/766),

Commending the important work of the International Criminal Tribunal for the Former Yugoslavia (ICTY) and the International Criminal Tribunal for Rwanda (ICTR) in contributing to lasting peace and security in the former Yugoslavia and Rwanda and the progress made since their inception,

Noting that an essential prerequisite to achieving the objectives of the ICTY and ICTR Completion Strategies is full cooperation by all States, especially in apprehending all remaining at-large persons indicted by the ICTY and the ICTR,

Welcoming steps taken by States in the Balkans and the Great Lakes region of Africa to improve cooperation and apprehend at-large persons indicted by the ICTY and ICTR, but noting with concern that certain States are still not offering full cooperation,

Urging Member States to consider imposing measures against individuals and groups or organizations assisting indictees at large to continue to evade justice, including measures designed to restrict the travel and freeze the assets of such individuals, groups, or organizations,

Recalling and *reaffirming* in the strongest terms the statement of 23 July 2002 made by the President of the Security Council (S/PRST/2002/21), which endorsed the ICTY's strategy for completing investigations by the end of 2004, all trial activities at first instance by the end of 2008, and all of its work in 2010 (ICTY Completion Strategy) (S/2002/678), by concentrating on the prosecution and trial of the most senior leaders suspected of being most responsible for crimes within the ICTY's jurisdiction and transferring cases involving those who may not bear this level of responsibility to competent national jurisdictions, as appropriate, as well as the strengthening of the capacity of such jurisdictions,

Urging the ICTR to formalize a detailed strategy, modelled on the ICTY Completion Strategy, to transfer cases involving intermediate- and lower-rank accused to competent national jurisdictions, as appropriate, including Rwanda, in order to allow the ICTR to achieve its objective of completing investigations by the end of 2004, all trial activities at first instance by the end of 2008, and all of its work in 2010 (ICTR Completion Strategy),

Noting that the above-mentioned Completion Strategies in no way alter the obligation of Rwanda and the countries of the former Yugoslavia to investigate those accused whose cases would not be tried by the ICTR or ICTY and take appropriate action with respect to indictment and prosecution, while bearing in mind the primacy of the ICTY and ICTR over national courts,

Noting that the strengthening of national judicial systems is crucially important to the rule of law in general and to the implementation of the ICTY and ICTR Completion Strategies in particular,

Noting that an essential prerequisite to achieving the objectives of the ICTY Completion Strategy is the expeditious establishment under the auspices of the High Representative and early functioning of a special chamber within the State Court of Bosnia and Herzegovina (the "War Crimes Chamber") and the subsequent referral by the ICTY of cases of lower- or intermediate-rank accused to the Chamber,

Convinced that the ICTY and the ICTR can most efficiently and expeditiously meet their respective responsibilities if each has its own Prosecutor,

Acting under Chapter VII of the Charter of the United Nations,

1. *Calls* on the international community to assist national jurisdictions, as part of the completion strategy, in improving their capacity to prosecute cases transferred from the ICTY and the ICTR and encourages the ICTY and ICTR Presidents, Prosecutors, and Registrars to develop and improve their outreach programmes;

2. *Calls* on all States, especially Serbia and Montenegro, Croatia, and Bosnia and Herzegovina, and on the Republika Srpska within Bosnia and Herzegovina, to intensify cooperation with and render all necessary assistance to the ICTY, particularly to bring Radovan Karadzic and Ratko Mladic, as well as Ante Gotovina and all other indictees to the ICTY and calls on these and all other at-large indictees of the ICTY to surrender to the ICTY;

3. *Calls* on all States, especially Rwanda, Kenya, the Democratic Republic of the Congo, and the Republic of the Congo, to intensify cooperation with and render all necessary assistance to the ICTR, including on investigations of the

Rwandan Patriotic Army and efforts to bring Felicien Kabuga and all other such indictees to the ICTR and calls on this and all other at-large indictees of the ICTR to surrender to the ICTR;

4. *Calls* on all States to cooperate with the International Criminal Police Organization (ICPO-Interpol) in apprehending and transferring persons indicted by the ICTY and the ICTR;

5. *Calls* on the donor community to support the work of the High Representative to Bosnia and Herzegovina in creating a special chamber, within the State Court of Bosnia and Herzegovina, to adjudicate allegations of serious violations of international humanitarian law;

6. *Requests* the Presidents of the ICTY and the ICTR and their Prosecutors, in their annual reports to the Council, to explain their plans to implement the ICTY and ICTR Completion Strategies;

7. *Calls* on the ICTY and the ICTR to take all possible measures to complete investigations by the end of 2004, to complete all trial activities at first instance by the end of 2008, and to complete all work in 2010 (the Completion Strategies);

8. *Decides* to amend Article 15 of the Statute of the International Tribunal for Rwanda and to replace that Article with the provision set out in Annex I to this resolution, and requests the Secretary-General to nominate a person to be the Prosecutor of the ICTR;

9. *Welcomes* the intention expressed by the Secretary-General in his letter dated 28 July 2003, to submit to the Security Council the name of Mrs. Carla Del Ponte as nominee for Prosecutor for the ICTY;

10. *Decides* to remain actively seized of the matter.

Annex I

Article 15

The Prosecutor

1. The Prosecutor shall be responsible for the investigation and prosecution of persons responsible for serious violations of international humanitarian law committed in the territory of Rwanda and Rwandan citizens responsible for such violations committed in the territory of neighbouring States, between 1 January 1994 and 31 December 1994.

2. The Prosecutor shall act independently as a separate organ of the International Tribunal for Rwanda. He or she shall not seek or receive instructions from any government or from any other source.

3. The Office of the Prosecutor shall be composed of a Prosecutor and such other qualified staff as may be required.

4. The Prosecutor shall be appointed by the Security Council on nomination by the Secretary-General. He or she shall be of high moral character and possess the highest level of competence and experience in the conduct of investigations and prosecutions of criminal cases. The Prosecutor shall serve for a four-year term and be eligible for reappointment. The terms and conditions of service of the Prosecutor shall be those of an Under-Secretary-General of the United Nations.

5. The staff of the Office of the Prosecutor shall be appointed by the Secretary-General on the recommendation of the Prosecutor.

Resolution 1534
Adopted on 26 March 2004
S/RES/1534

The Security Council,

Recalling its resolutions 827 (1993) of 25 May 1993, 955 (1994) of 8 November 1994, 978 (1995) of 27 February 1995, 1165 (1998) of 30 April 1998, 1166 (1998) of 13 May 1998, 1329 (2000) of 30 November 2000, 1411 (2002) of 17 May 2002, 1431 (2002) of 14 August 2002, and 1481 (2003) of 19 May 2003,

Recalling and *reaffirming* in the strongest terms the statement of 23 July 2002 made by the President of the Security Council (S/PRST/2002/21) endorsing the ICTY's completion strategy and its resolution 1503 (2003) of 28 August 2003,

Recalling that resolution 1503 (2003) called on the International Criminal Tribunal for the Former Yugoslavia (ICTY) and the International Criminal Tribunal for Rwanda (ICTR) to take all possible measures to complete investigations by the end of 2004, to complete all trial activities at first instance by the end of 2008, and to complete all work in 2010 (the Completion Strategies), and requested the President and Prosecutor of the ICTY and ICTR, in their annual reports to the Council, to explain their plans to implement the Completion Strategies,

Welcoming the presentations made by the ICTY and ICTR Presidents and Prosecutors to the Security Council on 9 October 2003,

Commending the important work of both Tribunals in contributing to lasting peace and security and national reconciliation and the progress made since their inception, commending them on their efforts so far to give effect to the Completion Strategies and calling on them to ensure effective and efficient use of their budgets, with accountability,

Reiterating its support for the ICTY and ICTR Prosecutors in their continuing efforts to bring at large indictees before the ICTY and the ICTR,

Noting with concern the problems highlighted in the presentations to the Security Council on 9 October 2003 in securing adequate regional cooperation,

Also noting with concern indications in the presentations made on 9 October, that it might not be possible to implement the Completion Strategies set out in resolution 1503 (2003),

Acting under Chapter VII of the Charter of the United Nations,

1. *Reaffirms* the necessity of trial of persons indicted by the ICTY and reiterates its call on all States, especially Serbia and Montenegro, Croatia and Bosnia and Herzegovina, and on the Republika Srpska within Bosnia and Herzegovina, to intensify cooperation with and render all necessary assistance to the ICTY, particularly to brig Radovan Karadzic and Ratko Mladic, as well as Ante Gotovina and all other indictees to the ICTY and calls on all at-large indictees of the ICTY to surrender to the ICTY;

2. *Reaffirms* the necessity of trial of persons indicted by the ICTR and reiterates its call on all States, especially Rwanda, Kenya, the Democratic Republic of the Congo and the Republic of the Congo to intensify cooperation with and render all necessary assistance to the ICTR, including on investigations of the Rwandan Patriotic Army and efforts to bring Felicien Kabuga and all other such indictees to the ICTR and calls on all at-large indictees of the ICTR to surrender to the ICTR;

3. *Emphasizes* the importance of fully implementing the Completion Strategies, as set out in paragraph 7 of resolution 1503 (2003), that calls on the ICTY and ICTR to take all possible measures to complete investigations by the end of 2004, to complete all trial activities at first instance by the end of 2008 and to complete all work in 2010, and urges each Tribunal to plan and act accordingly;

4. *Calls on* the ICTY and ICTR Prosecutors to review the case load of the ICTY and ICTR respectively in particular with a view to determining which cases should be proceeded with and which should be transferred to competent national jurisdictions, as well as the measures which will need to be taken to meet the Completion Strategy referred to in resolution 1503 (2003) and urges them to carry out this review as soon as possible and to include a progress report in the assessments to be provided to the Council under paragraph 6 of this resolution;

5. *Calls on* each Tribunal, in reviewing and confirming any new indictments, to ensure that any such indictments concentrate on the most senior leaders suspected of being most responsible for crimes within the jurisdiction of the relevant Tribunal as set out in resolution 1503 (2003);

6. *Requests* each Tribunal to provide to the Council, by 31 May 2004 and every six months thereafter, assessments by its President and Prosecutor, setting out in detail the progress made towards implementation of the Completion Strategy of the Tribunal, explaining what measures have been taken to implement the Completion Strategy and what measures remain to be taken, including the transfer of cases involving intermediate and lower rank accused to competent

national jurisdictions; and expresses the intention of the Council to meet with the President and Prosecutor of each Tribunal to discuss these assessments;

7. *Declares* the Council's determination to review the situation, and in the light of the assessments received under the foregoing paragraph to ensure that the time frames set out in the Completion Strategies and endorsed by resolution 1503 (2003) can be met;

8. *Commends* those States which have concluded agreements for the enforcement of sentences of persons convicted by the ICTY or the ICTR or have otherwise accepted such convicted persons to serve their sentences in their respective territories; encourages other States in a position to do so to act likewise; and invites the ICTY and the ICTR to continue and intensify their efforts to conclude further agreements for the enforcement of sentences or to obtain the cooperation of other States in this regard;

9. *Recalls* that the strengthening of competent national judicial systems is crucially important to the rule of law in general and to the implementation of the ICTY and ICTR Completion Strategies in particular;

10. *Welcomes* in particular the efforts of the Office of the High Representative, ICTY, and the donor community to create a war crimes chamber in Sarajevo; encourages all parties to continue efforts to establish the chamber expeditiously; and encourages the donor community to provide sufficient financial support to ensure the success of domestic prosecutions in Bosnia and Herzegovina and in the region;

11. *Decides* to remain actively seized of the matter.

Appendix C

Resolutions for the International Criminal Tribunal for Rwanda United Nations Security Council Resolution 955

RESOLUTION 955
ADOPTED 8 NOVEMBER 1994
S/RES/955

The Security Council,

Reaffirming all its previous resolutions on the situation in Rwanda,

Having considered the reports of the Secretary-General pursuant to paragraph 3 of resolution 935 (1994) of 1 July 1994 (S/1994/879 and S/1994/906), and *having taken note* of the reports of the Special Rapporteur for Rwanda of the United Nations Commission on Human Rights (S/1994/1157, annex I and annex II),

Expressing appreciation for the work of the Commission of Experts established pursuant to resolution 935 (1994), in particular its preliminary report on violations of international humanitarian law in Rwanda transmitted by the Secretary-General's letter of 1 October 1994 (S/1994/1125),

Expressing once again its grave concern at the reports indicating that genocide and other systematic, widespread and flagrant violations of international humanitarian law have been committed in Rwanda,

Determining that this situation continues to constitute a threat to international peace and security,

Determined to put an end to such crimes and to take effective measures to bring to justice the persons who are responsible for them,

Convinced that in the particular circumstances of Rwanda, the prosecution of persons responsible for serious violations of international humanitarian law would enable this aim to be achieved and would contribute to the process of national reconciliation and to the restoration and maintenance of peace,

Believing that the establishment of an international tribunal for the prosecution of persons responsible for genocide and the other above-mentioned violations of international humanitarian law will contribute to ensuring that such violations are halted and effectively redressed,

Stressing also the need for international cooperation to strengthen the courts and judicial system of Rwanda, having regard in particular to the necessity for those courts to deal with large numbers of suspects,

Considering that the Commission of Experts established pursuant to resolution 935 (1994) should continue on an urgent basis the collection of information relating to evidence of grave violations of international humanitarian law committed in the territory of Rwanda and should submit its final report to the Secretary-General by 30 November 1994,

Acting under Chapter VII of the Charter of the United Nations,

1. *Decides* hereby, having received the request of the Government of Rwanda (S/1994/1115), to establish an international tribunal for the sole purpose of prosecuting persons responsible for genocide and other serious violations of international humanitarian law committed in the territory of Rwanda and Rwandan citizens responsible for genocide and other such violations committed in the territory of neighbouring States, between 1 January 1994 and 31 December 1994 and to this end to adopt the Statute of the International Criminal Tribunal for Rwanda annexed hereto;

2. *Decides* that all States shall cooperate fully with the International Tribunal and its organs in accordance with the present resolution and the Statute of the International Tribunal and that consequently all States shall take any measures necessary under their domestic law to implement the provisions of the present resolution and the Statute, including the obligation of States to comply with requests for assistance or orders issued by a Trial Chamber under Article 28 of the Statute, and *requests* States to keep the Secretary-General informed of such measures;

3. *Considers* that the Government of Rwanda should be notified prior to the taking of decisions under articles 26 and 27 of the Statute;

4. *Urges* States and intergovernmental and non-governmental organizations to contribute funds, equipment and services to the International Tribunal, including the offer of expert personnel;

5. *Requests* the Secretary-General to implement this resolution urgently and in particular to make practical arrangements for the effective functioning of

the International Tribunal, including recommendations to the Council as to possible locations for the seat of the International Tribunal at the earliest time and to report periodically to the Council;

6. *Decides* that the seat of the International Tribunal shall be determined by the Council having regard to considerations of justice and fairness as well as administrative efficiency, including access to witnesses, and economy, and subject to the conclusion of appropriate arrangements between the United Nations and the State of the seat, acceptable to the Council, having regard to the fact that the International Tribunal may meet away from its seat when it considers it necessary for the efficient exercise of its functions; and *decides* that an office will be established and proceedings will be conducted in Rwanda, where feasible and appropriate, subject to the conclusion of similar appropriate arrangements;

7. *Decides* to consider increasing the number of judges and Trial Chambers of the International Tribunal if it becomes necessary;

8. *Decides* to remain actively seized of the matter.

Annex

Statute of the International Tribunal for Rwanda

Having been established by the Security Council acting under Chapter VII of the Charter of the United Nations, the International Criminal Tribunal for the Prosecution of Persons Responsible for Genocide and Other Serious Violations of International Humanitarian Law Committed in the Territory of Rwanda and Rwandan citizens responsible for genocide and other such violations committed in the territory of neighbouring States, between 1 January 1994 and 31 December 1994 (hereinafter referred to as "the International Tribunal for Rwanda") shall function in accordance with the provisions of the present Statute.

Article 1

Competence of the International Tribunal for Rwanda

The International Tribunal for Rwanda shall have the power to prosecute persons responsible for serious violations of international humanitarian law committed in the territory of Rwanda and Rwandan citizens responsible for such violations committed in the territory of neighbouring States, between 1 January 1994 and 31 December 1994, in accordance with the provisions of the present Statute.

Article 2

Genocide

1. The International Tribunal for Rwanda shall have the power to prosecute persons committing genocide as defined in paragraph 2 of this article or of committing any of the other acts enumerated in paragraph 3 of this article.

2. Genocide means any of the following acts committed with intent to destroy, in whole or in part, a national, ethnical, racial or religious group, as such:
   (a) Killing members of the group;
   (b) Causing serious bodily or mental harm to members of the group;
   (c) Deliberately inflicting on the group conditions of life calculated to bring about its physical destruction in whole or in part;
   (d) Imposing measures intended to prevent births within the group;
   (e) Forcibly transferring children of the group to another group.

3. The following acts shall be punishable:
   (a) Genocide;
   (b) Conspiracy to commit genocide;
   (c) Direct and public incitement to commit genocide;
   (d) Attempt to commit genocide;
   (e) Complicity in genocide.

Article 3

Crimes against humanity

The International Tribunal for Rwanda shall have the power to prosecute persons responsible for the following crimes when committed as part of a widespread or systematic attack against any civilian population on national, political, ethnic, racial or religious grounds:
   (a) Murder;
   (b) Extermination;
   (c) Enslavement;
   (d) Deportation;
   (e) Imprisonment;
   (f) Torture;
   (g) Rape;
   (h) Persecutions on political, racial and religious grounds;
   (i) Other inhumane acts.

Article 4

Violations of Article 3 common to the Geneva Conventions and of Additional Protocol II

The International Tribunal for Rwanda shall have the power to prosecute persons committing or ordering to be committed serious violations of Article 3 common to the Geneva Conventions of 12 August 1949 for the Protection of War Victims, and of Additional Protocol II thereto of 8 June 1977. These violations shall include, but shall not be limited to:

(a) Violence to life, health and physical or mental well-being of persons, in particular murder as well as cruel treatment such as torture, mutilation or any form of corporal punishment;
(b) Collective punishments;
(c) Taking of hostages;
(d) Acts of terrorism;
(e) Outrages upon personal dignity, in particular humiliating and degrading treatment, rape, enforced prostitution and any form of indecent assault;
(f) Pillage;
(g) The passing of sentences and the carrying out of executions without previous judgement pronounced by a regularly constituted court, affording all the judicial guarantees which are recognized as indispensable by civilized peoples;
(h) Threats to commit any of the foregoing acts.

Article 5

Personal jurisdiction

The International Tribunal for Rwanda shall have jurisdiction over natural persons pursuant to the provisions of the present Statute.

Article 6

Individual criminal responsibility

1. A person who planned, instigated, ordered, committed or otherwise aided and abetted in the planning, preparation or execution of a crime referred to in articles 2 to 4 of the present Statute, shall be individually responsible for the crime.

2. The official position of any accused person, whether as Head of State or Government or as a responsible Government official, shall not relieve such person of criminal responsibility nor mitigate punishment.

3. The fact that any of the acts referred to in articles 2 to 4 of the present Statute was committed by a subordinate does not relieve his or her superior of criminal responsibility if he or she knew or had reason to know that the subordinate was about to commit such acts or had done so and the superior failed to take the necessary and reasonable measures to prevent such acts or to punish the perpetrators thereof.

4. The fact that an accused person acted pursuant to an order of a Government or of a superior shall not relieve him or her of criminal responsibility, but may be considered in mitigation of punishment if the International Tribunal for Rwanda determines that justice so requires.

Article 7

Territorial and temporal jurisdiction

The territorial jurisdiction of the International Tribunal for Rwanda shall extend to the territory of Rwanda including its land surface and airspace as well as to the territory of neighbouring States in respect of serious violations of international humanitarian law committed by Rwandan citizens. The temporal jurisdiction of the International Tribunal for Rwanda shall extend to a period beginning on 1 January 1994 and ending on 31 December 1994.

Article 8

Concurrent jurisdiction

1. The International Tribunal for Rwanda and national courts shall have concurrent jurisdiction to prosecute persons for serious violations of international humanitarian law committed in the territory of Rwanda and Rwandan citizens for such violations committed in the territory of neighbouring States, between 1 January 1994 and 31 December 1994.

2. The International Tribunal for Rwanda shall have primacy over the national courts of all States. At any stage of the procedure, the International Tribunal for Rwanda may formally request national courts to defer to its competence in accordance with the present Statute and the Rules of Procedure and Evidence of the International Tribunal for Rwanda.

Article 9

Non bis in idem

1. No person shall be tried before a national court for acts constituting serious violations of international humanitarian law under the present Statute, for which he or she has already been tried by the International Tribunal for Rwanda.

2. A person who has been tried by a national court for acts constituting serious violations of international humanitarian law may be subsequently tried by the International Tribunal for Rwanda only if:
   (a) The act for which he or she was tried was characterized as an ordinary crime; or
   (b) The national court proceedings were not impartial or independent, were designed to shield the accused from international criminal responsibility, or the case was not diligently prosecuted.

3. In considering the penalty to be imposed on a person convicted of a crime under the present Statute, the International Tribunal for Rwanda shall take into account the extent to which any penalty imposed by a national court on the same person for the same act has already been served.

Article 10

Organization of the International Tribunal for Rwanda

The International Tribunal for Rwanda shall consist of the following organs:
   (a) The Chambers, comprising two Trial Chambers and an Appeals Chamber;
   (b) The Prosecutor; and
   (c) A Registry.

Article 11

Composition of the Chambers

The Chambers shall be composed of eleven independent judges, no two of whom may be nationals of the same State, who shall serve as follows:
   (a) Three judges shall serve in each of the Trial Chambers;
   (b) Five judges shall serve in the Appeals Chamber.

Article 12

Qualification and election of judges

1. The judges shall be persons of high moral character, impartiality and integrity who possess the qualifications required in their respective countries for appointment to the highest judicial offices. In the overall composition of the Chambers due account shall be taken of the experience of the judges in criminal law, international law, including international humanitarian law and human rights law.

2. The members of the Appeals Chamber of the International Tribunal for the Prosecution of Persons Responsible for Serious Violations of International Law Committed in the Territory of the Former Yugoslavia since 1991 (hereinafter referred to as "the International Tribunal for the Former Yugoslavia") shall also serve as the members of the Appeals Chamber of the International Tribunal for Rwanda.

3. The judges of the Trial Chambers of the International Tribunal for Rwanda shall be elected by the General Assembly from a list submitted by the Security Council, in the following manner:
   (a) The Secretary-General shall invite nominations for judges of the Trial Chambers from States Members of the United Nations and non-member States maintaining permanent observer missions at United Nations Headquarters;
   (b) Within thirty days of the date of the invitation of the Secretary-General, each State may nominate up to two candidates meeting the qualifications set out in paragraph 1 above, no two of whom shall be of the same nationality and neither of whom shall be of the same nationality as any judge on the Appeals Chamber;
   (c) The Secretary-General shall forward the nominations received to the Security Council. From the nominations received the Security Council shall establish a list of not less than twelve and not more than eighteen candidates, taking due account of adequate representation on the International Tribunal for Rwanda of the principal legal systems of the world;
   (d) The President of the Security Council shall transmit the list of candidates to the President of the General Assembly. From that list the General Assembly shall elect the six judges of the Trial Chambers. The candidates who receive an absolute majority of the votes of the States Members of the United Nations and of the non-Member States maintaining permanent observer missions at United Nations Headquarters, shall be declared elected. Should two candidates of the same nationality obtain the required majority vote,

the one who received the higher number of votes shall be considered elected.

4. In the event of a vacancy in the Trial Chambers, after consultation with the Presidents of the Security Council and of the General Assembly, the Secretary-General shall appoint a person meeting the qualifications of paragraph 1 above, for the remainder of the term of office concerned.

5. The judges of the Trial Chambers shall be elected for a term of four years. The terms and conditions of service shall be those of the judges of the International Tribunal for the Former Yugoslavia. They shall be eligible for re-election.

Article 13

Officers and members of the Chambers

1. The judges of the International Tribunal for Rwanda shall elect a President.

2. After consultation with the judges of the International Tribunal for Rwanda, the President shall assign the judges to the Trial Chambers. A judge shall serve only in the Chamber to which he or she was assigned.

3. The judges of each Trial Chamber shall elect a Presiding Judge, who shall conduct all of the proceedings of that Trial Chamber as a whole.

Article 14

Rules of procedure and evidence

The judges of the International Tribunal for Rwanda shall adopt, for the purpose of proceedings before the International Tribunal for Rwanda, the rules of procedure and evidence for the conduct of the pre-trial phase of the proceedings, trials and appeals, the admission of evidence, the protection of victims and witnesses and other appropriate matters of the International Tribunal for the Former Yugoslavia with such changes as they deem necessary.

Article 15

The Prosecutor

1. The Prosecutor shall be responsible for the investigation and prosecution of persons responsible for serious violations of international humanitarian law committed in the territory of Rwanda and Rwandan citizens responsible for such violations committed in the territory of neighbouring States, between 1 January 1994 and 31 December 1994.

2. The Prosecutor shall act independently as a separate organ of the International Tribunal for Rwanda. He or she shall not seek or receive instructions from any Government or from any other source.

3. The Prosecutor of the International Tribunal for the Former Yugoslavia shall also serve as the Prosecutor of the International Tribunal for Rwanda. He or she shall have additional staff, including an additional Deputy Prosecutor, to assist with prosecutions before the International Tribunal for Rwanda. Such staff shall be appointed by the Secretary-General on the recommendation of the Prosecutor.

Article 16

The Registry

1. The Registry shall be responsible for the administration and servicing of the International Tribunal for Rwanda.

2. The Registry shall consist of a Registrar and such other staff as may be required.

3. The Registrar shall be appointed by the Secretary-General after consultation with the President of the International Tribunal for Rwanda. He or she shall serve for a four- year term and be eligible for reappointment. The terms and conditions of service of the Registrar shall be those of an Assistant Secretary-General of the United Nations.

4. The staff of the Registry shall be appointed by the Secretary-General on the recommendation of the Registrar.

Article 17

Investigation and preparation of indictment

1. The Prosecutor shall initiate investigations ex-officio or on the basis of information obtained from any source, particularly from Governments, United Nations organs, intergovernmental and non-governmental organizations. The Prosecutor shall assess the information received or obtained and decide whether there is sufficient basis to proceed.

2. The Prosecutor shall have the power to question suspects, victims and witnesses, to collect evidence and to conduct on-site investigations. In carrying out these tasks, the Prosecutor may, as appropriate, seek the assistance of the State authorities concerned.

3. If questioned, the suspect shall be entitled to be assisted by counsel of his or her own choice, including the right to have legal assistance assigned to the suspect without payment by him or her in any such case if he or she does not have sufficient means to pay for it, as well as to necessary translation into and from a language he or she speaks and understands.

4. Upon a determination that a prima facie case exists, the Prosecutor shall prepare an indictment containing a concise statement of the facts and the crime or crimes with which the accused is charged under the Statute. The indictment shall be transmitted to a judge of the Trial Chamber.

Article 18

Review of the indictment

1. The judge of the Trial Chamber to whom the indictment has been transmitted shall review it. If satisfied that a prima facie case has been established by the Prosecutor, he or she shall confirm the indictment. If not so satisfied, the indictment shall be dismissed.

2. Upon confirmation of an indictment, the judge may, at the request of the Prosecutor, issue such orders and warrants for the arrest, detention, surrender or transfer of persons, and any other orders as may be required for the conduct of the trial.

Article 19

Commencement and conduct of trial proceedings

1. The Trial Chambers shall ensure that a trial is fair and expeditious and that proceedings are conducted in accordance with the rules of procedure and evidence, with full respect for the rights of the accused and due regard for the protection of victims and witnesses.

2. A person against whom an indictment has been confirmed shall, pursuant to an order or an arrest warrant of the International Tribunal for Rwanda, be taken into custody, immediately informed of the charges against him or her and transferred to the International Tribunal for Rwanda.

3. The Trial Chamber shall read the indictment, satisfy itself that the rights of the accused are respected, confirm that the accused understands the indictment, and instruct the accused to enter a plea. The Trial Chamber shall then set the date for trial.

4. The hearings shall be public unless the Trial Chamber decides to close the proceedings in accordance with its rules of procedure and evidence.

Article 20

Rights of the accused

1. All persons shall be equal before the International Tribunal for Rwanda.

2. In the determination of charges against him or her, the accused shall be entitled to a fair and public hearing, subject to article 21 of the Statute.

3. The accused shall be presumed innocent until proved guilty according to the provisions of the present Statute.

4. In the determination of any charge against the accused pursuant to the present Statute, the accused shall be entitled to the following minimum guarantees, in full equality:
   (a) To be informed promptly and in detail in a language which he or she understands of the nature and cause of the charge against him or her;
   (b) To have adequate time and facilities for the preparation of his or her defence and to communicate with counsel of his or her own choosing;
   (c) To be tried without undue delay;
   (d) To be tried in his or her presence, and to defend himself or herself in person or through legal assistance of his or her own choosing; to be informed, if he or she does not have legal assistance, of this right; and to have legal assistance assigned to him or her, in any case where the interests of justice so require, and without payment by him or her in any such case if he or she does not have sufficient means to pay for it;
   (e) To examine, or have examined, the witnesses against him or her and to obtain the attendance and examination of witnesses on his or her behalf under the same conditions as witnesses against him or her;
   (f) To have the free assistance of an interpreter if he or she cannot understand or speak the language used in the International Tribunal for Rwanda;
   (g) Not to be compelled to testify against himself or herself or to confess guilt.

Article 21

Protection of victims and witnesses

The International Tribunal for Rwanda shall provide in its rules of procedure and evidence for the protection of victims and witnesses. Such protection measures shall include, but shall not be limited to, the conduct of in camera proceedings and the protection of the victim's identity.

Article 22

Judgement

1. The Trial Chambers shall pronounce judgements and impose sentences and penalties on persons convicted of serious violations of international humanitarian law.

2. The judgement shall be rendered by a majority of the judges of the Trial Chamber, and shall be delivered by the Trial Chamber in public. It shall be accompanied by a reasoned opinion in writing, to which separate or dissenting opinions may be appended.

Article 23

Penalties

1. The penalty imposed by the Trial Chamber shall be limited to imprisonment. In determining the terms of imprisonment, the Trial Chambers shall have recourse to the general practice regarding prison sentences in the courts of Rwanda.

2. In imposing the sentences, the Trial Chambers should take into account such factors as the gravity of the offence and the individual circumstances of the convicted person.

3. In addition to imprisonment, the Trial Chambers may order the return of any property and proceeds acquired by criminal conduct, including by means of duress, to their rightful owners.

Article 24

Appellate proceedings

1. The Appeals Chamber shall hear appeals from persons convicted by the Trial Chambers or from the Prosecutor on the following grounds:
   (a) An error on a question of law invalidating the decision; or
   (b) An error of fact which has occasioned a miscarriage of justice.

2. The Appeals Chamber may affirm, reverse or revise the decisions taken by the Trial Chambers.

Article 25

Review proceedings

Where a new fact has been discovered which was not known at the time of the proceedings before the Trial Chambers or the Appeals Chamber and which could have been a decisive factor in reaching the decision, the convicted person or the Prosecutor may submit to the International Tribunal for Rwanda an application for review of the judgement.

Article 26

Enforcement of sentences

Imprisonment shall be served in Rwanda or any of the States on a list of States which have indicated to the Security Council their willingness to accept convicted persons, as designated by the International Tribunal for Rwanda. Such imprisonment shall be in accordance with the applicable law of the State concerned, subject to the supervision of the International Tribunal for Rwanda.

Article 27

Pardon or commutation of sentences

If, pursuant to the applicable law of the State in which the convicted person is imprisoned, he or she is eligible for pardon or commutation of sentence, the State concerned shall notify the International Tribunal for Rwanda accordingly. There shall only be pardon or commutation of sentence if the President of the International Tribunal for Rwanda, in consultation with the judges, so decides on the basis of the interests of justice and the general principles of law.

Article 28

Cooperation and judicial assistance

1. States shall cooperate with the International Tribunal for Rwanda in the investigation and prosecution of persons accused of committing serious violations of international humanitarian law.

2. States shall comply without undue delay with any request for assistance or an order issued by a Trial Chamber, including, but not limited to:
   (a) The identification and location of persons;
   (b) The taking of testimony and the production of evidence;

(c) The service of documents;
(d) The arrest or detention of persons;
(e) The surrender or the transfer of the accused to the International Tribunal for Rwanda.

Article 29

The status, privileges and immunities of the International Tribunal for Rwanda

1. The Convention on the Privileges and Immunities of the United Nations of 13 February 1946 shall apply to the International Tribunal for Rwanda, the judges, the Prosecutor and his or her staff, and the Registrar and his or her staff.

2. The judges, the Prosecutor and the Registrar shall enjoy the privileges and immunities, exemptions and facilities accorded to diplomatic envoys, in accordance with international law.

3. The staff of the Prosecutor and of the Registrar shall enjoy the privileges and immunities accorded to officials of the United Nations under articles V and VII of the Convention referred to in paragraph 1 of this article.

4. Other persons, including the accused, required at the seat or meeting place of the International Tribunal for Rwanda shall be accorded such treatment as is necessary for the proper functioning of the International Tribunal for Rwanda.

Article 30

Expenses of the International Tribunal for Rwanda

The expenses of the International Tribunal for Rwanda shall be expenses of the Organization in accordance with Article 17 of the Charter of the United Nations.

Article 31

Working languages

The working languages of the International Tribunal shall be English and French.

Article 32

Annual report

The President of the International Tribunal for Rwanda shall submit an annual report of the International Tribunal for Rwanda to the Security Council and to the General Assembly.

Appendix D

Resolutions for the Special Court for Sierra Leone United Nations Security Council Resolution 1315

RESOLUTION 1315
ADOPTED 14 AUGUST 2000
S/RES/1315

The Security Council:

Deeply concerned at the very serious crimes committed within the territory of Sierra Leone against the people of Sierra Leone and United Nations and associated personnel and at the prevailing situation of impunity,

Commending the efforts of the Government of Sierra Leone and the Economic Community of West African States (ECOWAS) to bring lasting peace to Sierra Leone,

Noting that the Heads of State and Government of ECOWAS agreed at the 23rd Summit of the Organization in Abuja on 28 and 29 May 2000 to dispatch a regional investigation of the resumption of hostilities,

Noting also the steps taken by the Government of Sierra Leone in creating a national truth and reconciliation process, as required by Article XXVI of the Lomé Peace Agreement (S/1999/777) to contribute to the promotion of the rule of law,

Recalling that the Special Representative of the Secretary-General appended to his signature of the Lomé Agreement a statement that the United Nations holds the understanding that the amnesty provisions of the Agreement shall not apply to international crimes of genocide, crimes against humanity, war crimes and other serious violations of international humanitarian law,

Reaffirming the importance of compliance with international humanitarian law, and *reaffirming further* that persons who commit or authorize serious violations of international humanitarian law are individually responsible and accountable for those violations and that the international community will exert every effort to bring those responsible to justice in accordance with international standards of justice, fairness and due process of law,

Recognizing that, in the particular circumstances of Sierra Leone, a credible system of justice and accountability for the very serious crimes committed there would end impunity and would contribute to the process of national reconciliation and to the restoration and maintenance of peace,

Taking note in this regard of the letter dated 12 June 2000 from the President of Sierra Leone to the Secretary-General and the Suggested Framework attached to it (S/2000/786, annex),

Recognizing further the desire of the Government of Sierra Leone for assistance from the United Nations in establishing a strong and credible court that will meet the objectives of bringing justice and ensuring lasting peace,

Noting the report of the Secretary-General of 31 July 2000 (S/2000/751) and, in particular, *taking note* with appreciation of the steps already taken by the Secretary-General in response to the request of the Government of Sierra Leone to assist it in establishing a special court,

Noting further the negative impact of the security situation on the administration of justice in Sierra Leone and the pressing need for international cooperation to assist in strengthening the judicial system of Sierra Leone,

Acknowledging the important contribution that can be made to this effort by qualified persons from West African States, the Commonwealth, other Member States of the United Nations and international organizations, to expedite the process of bringing justice and reconciliation to Sierra Leone and the region,

Reiterating that the situation in Sierra Leone continues to constitute a threat to international peace and security in the region,

1. *Requests* the Secretary-General to negotiate an agreement with the Government of Sierra Leone to create an independent special court consistent with this resolution, and *expresses* its readiness to take further steps expeditiously upon receiving and reviewing the report of the Secretary-General referred to in paragraph 6 below;

2. *Recommends* that the subject matter jurisdiction of the special court should include notably crimes against humanity, war crimes and other serious violations of international humanitarian law, as well as crimes under relevant Sierra Leonean law committed within the territory of Sierra Leone;

3. *Recommends further* that the special court should have personal jurisdiction over persons who bear the greatest responsibility for the commission of the crimes referred to in paragraph 2, including those leaders who, in committing such crimes, have threatened the establishment of and implementation of the peace process in Sierra Leone;

4. *Emphasizes* the importance of ensuring the impartiality, independence and credibility of the process, in particular with regard to the status of the judges and the prosecutors;

5. *Requests*, in this connection, that the Secretary-General, if necessary, send a team of experts to Sierra Leone as may be required to prepare the report referred to in paragraph 6 below;

6. *Requests* the Secretary-General to submit a report to the Security Council on the implementation of this resolution, in particular on his consultations and negotiations with the Government of Sierra Leone concerning the establishment of the special court, including recommendations, no later than 30 days from the date of this resolution;

7. *Requests* the Secretary-General to address in his report the questions of the temporal jurisdiction of the special court, an appeals process including the advisability, feasibility, and appropriateness of an appeals chamber in the special court or of sharing the Appeals Chamber of the International Criminal Tribunals for the Former Yugoslavia and Rwanda or other effective options, and a possible alternative host State, should it be necessary to convene the special court outside the seat of the court in Sierra Leone, if circumstances so require;

8. *Requests* the Secretary-General to include recommendations on the following:
   (a) any additional agreements that may be required for the provision of the international assistance which will be necessary for the establishment and functioning of the special court;
   (b) the level of participation, support and technical assistance of qualified persons from Member States of the United Nations, including in particular, member States of ECOWAS and the Commonwealth, and from the United Nations Mission in Sierra Leone that will be necessary for the efficient, independent and impartial functioning of the special court;
   (c) the amount of voluntary contributions, as appropriate, of funds, equipment and services to the special court, including through the offer of expert personnel that may be needed from States, intergovernmental organizations and nongovernmental organizations;

(d) whether the special court could receive, as necessary and feasible, expertise and advice from the International Criminal Tribunals for the Former Yugoslavia and Rwanda;

9. *Decides* to remain actively seized of the matter.

Appendix E

Resolutions for the Serious Crimes Panel for East Timor United Nations Security Council Resolution 1272 and UNTAET Regulation 2000/15

RESOLUTION 1272
Adopted on 25 October 1999
S/RES/1272

The Security Council,

Recalling its previous resolutions and the statements of its President on the situation in East Timor, in particular resolutions 384 (1975) of 22 December 1975, 389 (1976) of 22 April 1976, 1236 (1999) of 7 May 1999, 1246 (1999) of 11 June 1999, 1262 (1999) of 27 August 1999 and 1264 (1999) of 15 September 1999,

Recalling also the Agreement between Indonesia and Portugal on the question of East Timor of 5 May 1999 and the Agreements between the United Nations and the Governments of Indonesia and Portugal of the same date regarding the modalities for the popular consultation of the East Timorese through a direct ballot and security arrangements (S/1999/513, annexes I to III),

Reiterating its welcome for the successful conduct of the popular consultation of the East Timorese people of 30 August 1999, and taking note of its outcome through which the East Timorese people expressed their clear wish to begin a process of transition under the authority of the United Nations towards independence, which it regards as an accurate reflection of the views of the East Timorese people,

Welcoming the decision of the Indonesian People's Consultative Assembly on 19 October 1999 concerning East Timor,

Stressing the importance of reconciliation among the East Timorese people,

Commending the United Nations Mission in East Timor (UNAMET) for the admirable courage and determination shown in the implementation of its mandate,

Welcoming the deployment of a multinational force to East Timor pursuant to resolution 1264 (1999), and recognizing the importance of continued cooperation between the Government of Indonesia and the multinational force in this regard,

Noting the report of the Secretary-General of 4 October 1999 (S/1999/1024),

Noting with satisfaction the successful outcome of the trilateral meeting held on 28 September 1999, as outlined in the report of the Secretary-General,

Deeply concerned by the grave humanitarian situation resulting from violence in East Timor and the large-scale displacement and relocation of East Timorese civilians, including large numbers of women and children,

Reaffirming the need for all parties to ensure that the rights of refugees and displaced persons are protected, and that they are able to return voluntarily in safety and security to their homes,

Reaffirming respect for the sovereignty and territorial integrity of Indonesia,

Noting the importance of ensuring the security of the boundaries of East Timor, and noting in this regard the expressed intention of the Indonesian authorities to cooperate with the multinational force deployed pursuant to resolution 1264 (1999) and with the United Nations Transitional Administration in East Timor,

Expressing its concern at reports indicating that systematic, widespread and flagrant violations of international humanitarian and human rights law have been committed in East Timor, stressing that persons committing such violations bear individual responsibility, and calling on all parties to cooperate with investigations into these reports,

Recalling the relevant principles contained in the Convention on the Safety of United Nations and Associated Personnel adopted on 9 December 1994,

Determining that the continuing situation in East Timor constitutes a threat to peace and security,

Acting under Chapter VII of the Charter of the United Nations,

1. *Decides* to establish, in accordance with the report of the Secretary-General, a United Nations Transitional Administration in East Timor (UNTAET), which will be endowed with overall responsibility for the administration of East Timor and will be empowered to exercise all legislative and executive authority, including the administration of justice;

2. *Decides* also that the mandate of UNTAET shall consist of the following elements:
   (a) To provide security and maintain law and order throughout the territory of East Timor;
   (b) To establish an effective administration;
   (c) To assist in the development of civil and social services;
   (d) To ensure the coordination and delivery of humanitarian assistance, rehabilitation and development assistance;
   (e) To support capacity-building for self-government;
   (f) To assist in the establishment of conditions for sustainable development;

3. *Decides* further that UNTAET will have objectives and a structure along the lines set out in part IV of the report of the Secretary-General, and in particular that its main components will be:
   (a) A governance and public administration component, including an international police element with a strength of up to 1,640 officers;
   (b) A humanitarian assistance and emergency rehabilitation component;
   (c) A military component, with a strength of up to 8,950 troops and up to 200 military observers;

4. *Authorizes* UNTAET to take all necessary measures to fulfill its mandate;

5. *Recognizes* that, in developing and performing its functions under its mandate, UNTAET will need to draw on the expertise and capacity of Member States, United Nations agencies and other international organizations, including the international financial institutions;

6. *Welcomes* the intention of the Secretary-General to appoint a Special Representative who, as the Transitional Administrator, will be responsible for all aspects of the United Nations work in East Timor and will have the power to enact new laws and regulations and to amend, suspend or repeal existing ones;

7. *Stresses* the importance of cooperation between Indonesia, Portugal and UNTAET in the implementation of this resolution;

8. *Stresses* the need for UNTAET to consult and cooperate closely with the East Timorese people in order to carry out its mandate effectively with a view to the development of local democratic institutions, including an independent East Timorese human rights institution, and the transfer to these institutions of its administrative and public service functions;

9. *Requests* UNTAET and the multinational force deployed pursuant to resolution

1264 (1999) to cooperate closely with each other, with a view also to the replacement as soon as possible of the multinational force by the military component of UNTAET, as notified by the Secretary-General having consulted the leadership of the multinational force, taking into account conditions on the ground;

10. *Reiterates* the urgent need for coordinated humanitarian and reconstruction assistance, and calls upon all parties to cooperate with humanitarian and human rights organizations so as to ensure their safety, the protection of civilians, in particular children, the safe return of refugees and displaced persons and the effective delivery of humanitarian aid;

11. *Welcomes* the commitment of the Indonesian authorities to allow the refugees and displaced persons in West Timor and elsewhere in Indonesia to choose whether to return to East Timor, remain where they are or be resettled in other parts of Indonesia, and stresses the importance of allowing full, safe and unimpeded access by humanitarian organizations in carrying out their work;

12. *Stresses* that it is the responsibility of the Indonesian authorities to take immediate and effective measures to ensure the safe return of refugees in West Timor and other parts of Indonesia to East Timor, the security of refugees, and the civilian and humanitarian character of refugee camps and settlements, in particular by curbing the violent and intimidatory activities of the militias there;

13. *Welcomes* the intention of the Secretary-General to establish a Trust Fund available for, inter alia, the rehabilitation of essential infrastructure, including the building of basic institutions, the functioning of public services and utilities, and the salaries of local civil servants;

14. *Encourages* Member States and international agencies and organizations to provide personnel, equipment and other resources to UNTAET as requested by the Secretary-General, including for the building of basic institutions and capacity, and stresses the need for the closest possible coordination of these efforts;

15. *Underlines* the importance of including in UNTAET personnel with appropriate training in international humanitarian, human rights and refugee law, including child and gender-related provisions, negotiation and communication skills, cultural awareness and civilian-military coordination;

16. *Condemns* all violence and acts in support of violence in East Timor, calls for their immediate end, and demands that those responsible for such violence be brought to justice;

17. *Decides* to establish UNTAET for an initial period until 31 January 2001;

18. *Requests* the Secretary-General to keep the Council closely and regularly informed of progress towards the implementation of this resolution, including, in particular, with regard to the deployment of UNTAET and possible future reductions of its military component if the situation in East Timor improves, and to submit a report within three months of the date of adoption of this resolution and every six months thereafter;

19. *Decides* to remain actively seized of the matter.

UNTAET Regulation 2000/15
6 June 2000
UNTAET/REG/2000/15

ON THE ESTABLISHMENT OF PANELS WITH EXCLUSIVE JURISDICTION OVER SERIOUS CRIMINAL OFFENCES

The Special Representative of the Secretary-General (hereinafter: Transitional Administrator),

Pursuant to the authority given to him under United Nations Security Council resolution 1272 (1999) of 25 October 1999,

Taking into account United Nations Transitional Administration in East Timor (UNTAET) Regulation No.1999/1 of 27 November 1999 on the Authority of the Transitional Administration in East Timor (hereinafter: UNTAET Regulation No. 1999/1),

Taking into account UNTAET Regulation No. 2000/11 of 6 March 2000 on the Organisation of Courts in East Timor (hereinafter: UNTAET Regulation No. 2000/11) as amended by UNTAET Regulation No. 2000/14 of 10 May 2000 (hereinafter: UNTAET Regulation No. 2000/14),

Recalling the recommendations of the International Commission of Inquiry of East Timor in their report to the Secretary-General of January 2000,

After consultation in the National Consultative Council,

For the purpose of establishing panels with exclusive jurisdiction over serious criminal offences as referred to under Section 10.1 of UNTAET Regulation No. 2000/11,

Promulgates the following:

I. General

Section 1

Panels with Jurisdiction over Serious Criminal Offences

1.1 Pursuant to Section 10.3 of UNTAET Regulation No. 2000/11, there shall be established panels of judges (hereinafter: "panels") within the District Court in Dili with exclusive jurisdiction to deal with serious criminal offences.

1.2 Pursuant to Section 15.5 of UNTAET Regulation No. 2000/11 there shall be established panels within the Court of Appeal in Dili to hear and decide an appeal on a matter under Section 10 of UNTAET Regulation No. 2000/11, as specified in Sections 4 to 9 of the present regulation.

1.3 The panels established pursuant to Sections 10.3 and 15.5 of UNTAET Regulation No. 2000/11 and as specified under Section 1 of the present regulation, shall exercise jurisdiction in accordance with Section 10 of UNTAET Regulation No. 2000/11 and with the provisions of the present regulation with respect to the following serious criminal offences:

(a) Genocide;
(b) War Crimes;
(c) Crimes against Humanity;
(d) Murder;
(e) Sexual Offences; and
(f) Torture.

1.4 At any stage of the proceedings, in relation to cases of serious criminal offences listed under Section 10 (a) to (f) of UNTAET Regulation No. 2000/11, as specified in Sections 4 to 9 of the present regulation, a panel may have deferred to itself a case which is pending before another panel or court in East Timor.

Section 2

Jurisdiction

2.1 With regard to the serious criminal offences listed under Section 10.1 (a), (b), (c) and (f) of UNTAET Regulation No. 2000/11, as specified in Sections 4 to 7 of the present regulation, the panels shall have universal jurisdiction.

2.2 For the purposes of the present regulation, "universal jurisdiction" means jurisdiction irrespective of whether:

(a) the serious criminal offence at issue was committed within the territory of East Timor;
(b) the serious criminal offence was committed by an East Timorese citizen; or
(c) the victim of the serious criminal offence was an East Timorese citizen.

2.3 With regard to the serious criminal offences listed under Section 10.1(d) to (e) of UNTAET Regulation No. 2000/11 as specified in Sections 8 to 9 of the present regulation, the panels established within the District Court in Dili shall have exclusive jurisdiction only insofar as the offence was committed in the period between 1 January 1999 and 25 October 1999.

2.4 The panels shall have jurisdiction in respect of crimes committed in East Timor prior to 25 October 1999 only insofar as the law on which the serious criminal offence is based is consistent with Section 3.1 of UNTAET Regulation No. 1999/1 or any other UNTAET Regulation.

2.5 In accordance with Section 7.3 of UNTAET Regulation No. 2000/11, the panels established by the present regulation shall have jurisdiction (ratione loci) throughout the entire territory of East Timor.

Section 3

Applicable Law

3.1 In exercising their jurisdiction, the panels shall apply:
- (a) the law of East Timor as promulgated by Sections 2 and 3 of UNTAET Regulation No. 1999/1 and any subsequent UNTAET regulations and directives; and
- (b) where appropriate, applicable treaties and recognised principles and norms of international law, including the established principles of the international law of armed conflict.

3.2 In the event of a change in the law applicable to a given case prior to a final judgement, the law more favourable to the person being investigated, prosecuted or convicted shall apply.

II. Serious Criminal Offences

Section 4

Genocide

For the purposes of the present regulation, "genocide" means any of the following acts committed with intent to destroy, in whole or in part, a national, ethnical, racial or religious group, as such:

- (a) Killing members of the group;
- (b) Causing serious bodily or mental harm to members of the group;
- (c) Deliberately inflicting on the group conditions of life calculated to bring about its physical destruction in whole or in part;
- (d) Imposing measures intended to prevent births within the group;
- (e) Forcibly transferring children of the group to another group.

Section 5

Crimes Against Humanity

5.1 For the purposes of the present regulation, "crimes against humanity" means any of the following acts when committed as part of a widespread or systematic attack and directed against any civilian population, with knowledge of the attack:

(a) Murder;
(b) Extermination;
(c) Enslavement;
(d) Deportation or forcible transfer of population;
(e) Imprisonment or other severe deprivation of physical liberty in violation of fundamental rules of international law;
(f) Torture;
(g) Rape, sexual slavery, enforced prostitution, forced pregnancy, enforced sterilization, or any other form of sexual violence of comparable gravity;
(h) Persecution against any identifiable group or collectivity on political, racial, national, ethnic, cultural, religious, gender as defined in Section 5.3 of the present regulation, or other grounds that are universally recognized as impermissible under international law, in connection with any act referred to in this paragraph or any crime within the jurisdiction of the panels;
(i) Enforced disappearance of persons;
(j) The crime of apartheid;
(k) Other inhumane acts of a similar character intentionally causing great suffering, or serious injury to body or to mental or physical health.

5.2 For the purposes of Section 5.1 of the present regulation:

(a) "Extermination" includes the intentional infliction of conditions of life, inter alia the deprivation of access to food and medicine, calculated to bring about the destruction of part of a population;
(b) "Enslavement" means the exercise of any or all of the powers attaching to the right of ownership over a person and includes the exercise of such power in the course of trafficking in persons, in particular women and children;
(c) "Deportation or forcible transfer of population" means forced displacement of the persons concerned by expulsion or other coercive acts from the area in which they are lawfully present, without grounds permitted under international law;
(d) "Torture" means the intentional infliction of severe pain or suffering, whether physical or mental, upon a person in the custody or under the control of the accused; except that torture shall not include pain

or suffering arising only from, inherent in or incidental to, lawful sanctions;

(e) "Forced pregnancy" means the unlawful confinement of a woman forcibly made pregnant, with the intent of affecting the ethnic composition of any population or carrying out other grave violations of international law. This definition shall not in any way be interpreted as affecting national laws relating to pregnancy;

(f) "Persecution" means the intentional and severe deprivation of fundamental rights contrary to international law by reason of the identity of the group or collectivity;

(g) "The crime of apartheid" means inhumane acts of a character similar to those referred to in Section 5.1, committed in the context of an institutionalized regime of systematic oppression and domination by one racial group over any other racial group or groups and committed with the intention of maintaining that regime;

(h) "Enforced disappearance of persons" means the arrest, detention or abduction of persons by, or with the authorization, support or acquiescence of, a State or a political organization, followed by a refusal to acknowledge that deprivation of freedom or to give information on the fate or whereabouts of those persons, with the intention of removing them from the protection of the law for a prolonged period of time.

5.3 For the purpose of the present regulation, the term "gender" refers to the two sexes, male and female, within the context of society. The term "gender" does not indicate any meaning different from the above.

Section 6

War crimes

6.1 For the purposes of the present regulation, "war crimes" means:

(a) Grave breaches of the Geneva Conventions of 12 August 1949, namely, any of the following acts against persons or property protected under the provisions of the relevant Geneva Convention:

(i) Wilful killing;

(ii) Torture or inhuman treatment, including biological experiments;

(iii) Wilfully causing great suffering, or serious injury to body or health;

(iv) Extensive destruction and appropriation of property, not justified by military necessity and carried out unlawfully and wantonly;

(v) Compelling a prisoner of war or other protected person to serve in the forces of a hostile Power;

(vi) Wilfully depriving a prisoner of war or other protected person of the rights of fair and regular trial;

(vii) Unlawful deportation or transfer or unlawful confinement;
(viii) Taking of hostages.

(b) Other serious violations of the laws and customs applicable in international armed conflict, within the established framework of international law, namely, any of the following acts:

(i) Intentionally directing attacks against the civilian population as such or against individual civilians not taking direct part in hostilities;
(ii) Intentionally directing attacks against civilian objects, that is, objects which are not military objectives;
(iii) Intentionally directing attacks against personnel, installations, material, units or vehicles involved in a humanitarian assistance or peacekeeping mission in accordance with the Charter of the United Nations, as long as they are entitled to the protection given to civilians or civilian objects under the international law of armed conflict;
(iv) Intentionally launching an attack in the knowledge that such attack will cause incidental loss of life or injury to civilians or damage to civilian objects or widespread, long-term and severe damage to the natural environment which would be clearly excessive in relation to the concrete and direct overall military advantage anticipated;
(v) Attacking or bombarding, by whatever means, towns, villages, dwellings or buildings which are undefended and which are not military objectives;
(vi) Killing or wounding a combatant who, having laid down his arms or having no longer means of defence, has surrendered at discretion;
(vii) Making improper use of a flag of truce, of the flag or of the military insignia and uniform of the enemy or of the United Nations, as well as of the distinctive emblems of the Geneva Conventions, resulting in death or serious personal injury;
(viii) The transfer, directly or indirectly, by the Occupying Power of parts of its own civilian population into the territory it occupies, or the deportation or transfer of all or parts of the population of the occupied territory within or outside this territory;
(ix) Intentionally directing attacks against buildings dedicated to religion, education, art, science or charitable purposes, historic monuments, hospitals and places where the sick and wounded are collected, provided they are not military objectives;
(x) Subjecting persons who are in the power of an adverse party to physical mutilation or to medical or scientific experiments of any kind which are neither justified by the medical, dental or hospital treatment of the person concerned nor carried out in his or her interest, and which cause death to or seriously endanger the health of such person or persons;

(xi) Killing or wounding treacherously individuals belonging to the hostile nation or army;

(xii) Declaring that no quarter will be given;

(xiii) Destroying or seizing the enemy's property unless such destruction or seizure be imperatively demanded by the necessities of war;

(xiv) Declaring abolished, suspended or inadmissible in a court of law the rights and actions of the nationals of the hostile party;

(xv) Compelling the nationals of the hostile party to take part in the operations of war directed against their own country, even if they were in the belligerent's service before the commencement of the war;

(xvi) Pillaging a town or place, even when taken by assault;

(xvii) Employing poison or poisoned weapons;

(xviii) Employing asphyxiating, poisonous or other gases, and all analogous liquids, materials or devices;

(xix) Employing bullets which expand or flatten easily in the human body, such as bullets with a hard envelope which does not entirely cover the core or is pierced with incisions;

(xx) Employing weapons, projectiles and material and methods of warfare which are of a nature to cause superfluous injury or unnecessary suffering or which are inherently indiscriminate in violation of the international law of armed conflict;

(xxi) Committing outrages upon personal dignity, in particular humiliating and degrading treatment;

(xxii) Committing rape, sexual slavery, enforced prostitution, forced pregnancy, as defined in Section 5.2 (e) of the present regulation, enforced sterilization, or any other form of sexual violence also constituting a grave breach of the Geneva Conventions;

(xxiii) Utilizing the presence of a civilian or other protected person to render certain points, areas or military forces immune from military operations;

(xxiv) Intentionally directing attacks against buildings, material, medical units and transport, and personnel using the distinctive emblems of the Geneva Conventions in conformity with international law;

(xxv) Intentionally using starvation of civilians as a method of warfare by depriving them of objects indispensable to their survival, including wilfully impeding relief supplies as provided for under the Geneva Conventions;

(xxvi) Conscripting or enlisting children under the age of fifteen years into the national armed forces or using them to participate actively in hostilities.

(c) In the case of an armed conflict not of an international character, serious violations of Article 3 common to the four Geneva Conventions of 12 August 1949, namely, any of the following acts committed against persons taking no active part in the hostilities, including members of armed forces who have laid down their arms and those placed hors de combat by sickness, wounds, detention or any other cause:

(i) Violence to life and person, in particular murder of all kinds, mutilation, cruel treatment and torture;

(ii) Committing outrages upon personal dignity, in particular humiliating and degrading treatment;

(iii) Taking of hostages;

(iv) The passing of sentences and the carrying out of executions without previous judgement pronounced by a regularly constituted court, affording all judicial guarantees which are generally recognized as indispensable.

(d) Section 6.1 (c) of the present regulation applies to armed conflicts not of an international character and thus does not apply to situations of internal disturbances and tensions, such as riots, isolated and sporadic acts of violence or other acts of a similar nature.

(e) Other serious violations of the laws and customs applicable in armed conflicts not of an international character, within the established framework of international law, namely, any of the following acts:

(i) Intentionally directing attacks against the civilian population as such or against individual civilians not taking direct part in hostilities;

(ii) Intentionally directing attacks against buildings, material, medical units and transport, and personnel using the distinctive emblems of the Geneva Conventions in conformity with international law;

(iii) Intentionally directing attacks against personnel, installations, material, units or vehicles involved in a humanitarian assistance or peacekeeping mission in accordance with the Charter of the United Nations, as long as they are entitled to the protection given to civilians or civilian objects under the international law of armed conflict;

(iv) Intentionally directing attacks against buildings dedicated to religion, education, art, science or charitable purposes, historic monuments, hospitals and places where the sick and wounded are collected, provided they are not military objectives;

(v) Pillaging a town or place, even when taken by assault;

(vi) Committing rape, sexual slavery, enforced prostitution, forced pregnancy, as defined in Section 5.2 (e) of the present regulation, enforced sterilization, and any other form of sexual violence also constituting a serious violation of Article 3 common to the four Geneva Conventions;

(vii) Conscripting or enlisting children under the age of fifteen years into armed forces or groups or using them to participate actively in hostilities;

(viii) Ordering the displacement of the civilian population for reasons related to the conflict, unless the security of the civilians involved or imperative military reasons so demand;
(ix) Killing or wounding treacherously a combatant adversary;
(x) Declaring that no quarter will be given;
(xi) Subjecting persons who are in the power of another party to the conflict to physical mutilation or to medical or scientific experiments of any kind which are neither justified by the medical, dental or hospital treatment of the person concerned nor carried out in his or her interest, and which cause death to or seriously endanger the health of such person or persons;
(xii) Destroying or seizing the property of an adversary unless such destruction or seizure be imperatively demanded by the necessities of the conflict;

(f) Section 6.1 (e) of the present regulation applies to armed conflicts not of an international character and thus does not apply to situations of internal disturbances and tensions, such as riots, isolated and sporadic acts of violence or other acts of a similar nature. It applies to armed conflicts that take place in the territory of a State when there is protracted armed conflict between governmental authorities and organized armed groups or between such groups.

6.2 Nothing in Section 6.1 (c) and (e) of the present regulation shall affect the responsibility of a Government to maintain or re-establish law and order in the State or to defend the unity and territorial integrity of the State, by all legitimate means.

Section 7

Torture

7.1 For the purposes of the present regulation, torture means any act by which severe pain or suffering, whether physical or mental, is intentionally inflicted on a person for such purposes as obtaining from him/her or a third person information or a confession, punishing him/her for an act he/she or a third person has committed or is suspected of having committed, or humiliating, intimidating or coercing him/her or a third person, or for any reason based on discrimination of any kind. It does not include pain or suffering arising only from, inherent in or incidental to lawful sanctions.

7.2 This Section is without prejudice to any international instrument or national legislation which does or may contain provisions of wider application.

7.3 No exceptional circumstances whatsoever, whether a state of war or a threat of war, internal political instability or any other public emergency, may be invoked as a justification of torture.

Section 8

Murder

For the purposes of the present regulation, the provisions of the applicable Penal Code in East Timor shall, as appropriate, apply.

Section 9

Sexual Offences

For the purposes of the present regulation, the provisions of the applicable Penal Code in East Timor shall, as appropriate, apply.

Section 10

Penalties

10.1 A panel may impose one of the following penalties on a person convicted of a crime specified under Sections 4 to 7 of the present regulation:

(a) Imprisonment for a specified number of years, which may not exceed a maximum of 25 years. In determining the terms of imprisonment for the crimes referred to in Sections 4 to 7 of the present regulation, the panel shall have recourse to the general practice regarding prison sentences in the courts of East Timor and under international tribunals; for the crimes referred to in Sections 8 and 9 of the present regulation, the penalties prescribed in the respective provisions of the applicable Penal Code in East Timor, shall apply.

(b) A fine up to a maximum of US$ 500,000.

(c) A forfeiture of proceeds, property and assets derived directly or indirectly from the crime, without prejudice to the rights of bona fide third parties.

10.2 In imposing the sentences, the panel shall take into account such factors as the gravity of the offence and the individual circumstances of the convicted person.

10.3 In imposing a sentence of imprisonment, the panel shall deduct the time, if any, previously spent in detention due to an order of the panel or any other court in East Timor (for the same criminal conduct). The panel may deduct any time otherwise spent in detention in connection with the conduct (underlying the crime).

III. General Principles of Criminal Law

Section 11

Ne bis in idem

11.1 No person shall be tried before a panel established by the present regulation with respect to conduct (which formed the basis of crimes) for which the person has been convicted or acquitted by a panel.

11.2 No person shall be tried by another court (in East Timor) for a crime referred to in Sections 4 to 9 of the present regulation for which that person has already been convicted or acquitted by a panel.

11.3 No person who has been tried by another court for conduct also proscribed under Sections 4 to 9 of the present regulation shall be tried by a panel with respect to the same conduct unless the proceedings in the other court:
   (a) Were for the purpose of shielding the person concerned from criminal responsibility for crimes within the jurisdiction of the panel; or
   (b) Otherwise were not conducted independently or impartially in accordance with the norms of due process recognized by international law and were conducted in a manner which, in the circumstances, was inconsistent with an intent to bring the person concerned to justice.

Section 12

Nullum crimen sine lege

12.1 A person shall not be criminally responsible under the present regulation unless the conduct in question constitutes, at the time it takes place, a crime under international law or the laws of East Timor.

12.2 The definition of a crime shall be strictly construed and shall not be extended by analogy. In case of ambiguity, the definition shall be interpreted in favour of the person being investigated, prosecuted or convicted.

12.3 The present Section shall not affect the characterization of any conduct as criminal under principles and rules of international law independently of the present regulation.

Section 13

Nulla poena sine lege

A person convicted by a panel may be punished only in accordance with the present regulation.

Section 14

Individual criminal responsibility

14.1 The panels shall have jurisdiction over natural persons pursuant to the present regulation.

14.2 A person who commits a crime within the jurisdiction of the panels shall be individually responsible and liable for punishment in accordance with the present regulation.

14.3 In accordance with the present regulation, a person shall be criminally responsible and liable for punishment for a crime within the jurisdiction of the panels if that person:

(a) commits such a crime, whether as an individual, jointly with another or through another person, regardless of whether that other person is criminally responsible;

(b) orders, solicits or induces the commission of such a crime which in fact occurs or is attempted;

(c) for the purpose of facilitating the commission of such a crime, aids, abets or otherwise assists in its commission or its attempted commission, including providing the means for its commission;

(d) in any other way contributes to the commission or attempted commission of such a crime by a group of persons acting with a common purpose. Such contribution shall be intentional and shall either:

(i) be made with the aim of furthering the criminal activity or criminal purpose of the group, where such activity or purpose involves the commission of a crime within the jurisdiction of the panels; or

(ii) be made in the knowledge of the intention of the group to commit the crime;

(e) in respect of the crime of genocide, directly and publicly incites others to commit genocide;

(f) attempts to commit such a crime by taking action that commences its execution by means of a substantial step, but the crime does not occur because of circumstances independent of the person's intentions. However, a person who abandons the effort to commit the crime or otherwise prevents the completion of the crime shall not be liable for punishment under the present regulation for the attempt to commit that crime if that person completely and voluntarily gave up the criminal purpose.

Section 15

Irrelevance of official capacity

15.1 The present regulation shall apply equally to all persons without any distinction based on official capacity. In particular, official capacity as a Head of State or Government, a member of a Government or parliament, an elected representative or a government official shall in no case exempt a person from criminal responsibility under the present regulation, nor shall it, in and of itself, constitute a ground for reduction of sentence.

15.2 Immunities or special procedural rules which may attach to the official capacity of a person, whether under national or international law, shall not bar the panels from exercising its jurisdiction over such a person.

Section 16

Responsibility of commanders and other superiors

In addition to other grounds of criminal responsibility under the present regulation for serious criminal offences referred to in Sections 4 to 7 of the present regulation, the fact that any of the acts referred to in the said Sections 4 to 7 was committed by a subordinate does not relieve his superior of criminal responsibility if he knew or had reason to know that the subordinate was about to commit such acts or had done so and the superior failed to take the necessary and reasonable measures to prevent such acts or to punish the perpetrators thereof.

Section 17

Statute of limitations

17.1 The serious criminal offences under Section 10.1 (a), (b), (c) and (f) of UNTAET Regulation No. 2000/11 and under Sections 4 to 7 of the present regulation shall not be subject to any statute of limitations.

17.2 The serious criminal offences under Section 10.1 (d) to (e) of UNTAET Regulation No. 2000/11 and under Sections 8 to 9 of the present regulation shall be subject to applicable law.

Section 18

Mental element

18.1 A person shall be criminally responsible and liable for punishment for a crime within the jurisdiction of the panels only if the material elements are committed with intent and knowledge.

18.2 For the purposes of the present Section, a person has "intent" where:
- (a) In relation to conduct, that person means to engage in the conduct;
- (b) In relation to a consequence, that person means to cause that consequence or is aware that it will occur in the ordinary course of events.

18.3 For the purposes of the present Section, "knowledge" means awareness that a circumstance exists or a consequence will occur in the ordinary course of events. "Know" and "knowingly" shall be construed accordingly.

Section 19

Grounds for excluding criminal responsibility

19.1 A person shall not be criminally responsible if, at the time of that person's conduct:
- (a) the person suffers from a mental disease or defect that destroys that person's capacity to appreciate the unlawfulness or nature of his or her conduct, or capacity to control his or her conduct to conform to the requirements of law;
- (b) the person is in a state of intoxication that destroys that person's capacity to appreciate the unlawfulness or nature of his or her conduct, or capacity to control his or her conduct to conform to the requirements of law, unless the person has become voluntarily intoxicated under such circumstances that the person knew, or disregarded the risk, that, as a result of the intoxication, he or she was likely to engage in conduct constituting a crime within the jurisdiction of the panels;
- (c) the person acts reasonably to defend himself or herself or another person or, in the case of war crimes, property which is essential for the survival of the person or another person or property which is essential for accomplishing a military mission, against an imminent and unlawful use of force in a manner proportionate to the degree of danger to the person or the other person or property protected. The fact that the person was involved in a defensive operation conducted by forces shall not in itself constitute a ground for excluding criminal responsibility under this subparagraph;
- (d) the conduct which is alleged to constitute a crime within the jurisdiction of the panels has been caused by duress resulting from a threat of imminent death or of continuing or imminent serious bodily harm against that person or another person, and the person acts necessarily and reasonably to avoid this threat, provided that the person does not intend to cause a greater harm than the one sought to be avoided. Such a threat may either be:
  - (i) made by other persons; or
  - (ii) onstituted by other circumstances beyond that person's control.

19.2 The panel shall determine the applicability of the grounds for excluding criminal responsibility provided for in the present regulation to the case before it.

19.3 At trial, the panel may consider a ground for excluding criminal responsibility other than those referred to in Section 19.1 of the present regulation where such a ground is derived from applicable law. The procedures relating to the consideration of such a ground shall be provided for in an UNTAET directive.

Section 20

Mistake of fact or mistake of law

20.1 A mistake of fact shall be a ground for excluding criminal responsibility only if it negates the mental element required by the crime.

20.2 A mistake of law as to whether a particular type of conduct is a crime within the jurisdiction of the panels shall not be a ground for excluding criminal responsibility. A mistake of law may, however, be a ground for excluding criminal responsibility if it negates the mental element required by such a crime, or as provided for in Section 21 of the present regulation.

Section 21

Superior orders and prescription of law

The fact that an accused person acted pursuant to an order of a Government or of a superior shall not relieve him of criminal responsibility, but may be considered in mitigation of punishment if a panel determines that justice so requires.

IV. Composition of the Panels and Procedure

Section 22

Composition of the Panels

22.1 In accordance with Sections 9 and 10.3 of UNTAET Regulation No. 2000/11 the panels in the District Court of Dili shall be composed of two international judges and one East Timorese judge.

22.2 In accordance with Section 15 of UNTAET Regulation No. 2000/11 the panels in the Court of Appeal in Dili shall be composed of two international judges and one East Timorese judge. In cases of special importance or gravity a panel of five judges composed of three international and two East Timorese judges may be established.

Section 23

Qualifications of Judges

23.1 The judges of the panels established within the District Court in Dili and the Court of Appeal in Dili shall be selected and appointed in accordance with UNTAET Regulation No. 1999/3, Section 10.3 of UNTAET Regulation No. 2000/11 and Sections 22 and 23 of the present regulation.

23.2 The judges shall be persons of high moral character, impartiality and integrity who possess the qualifications required in their respective countries for appointment to judicial offices. In the overall composition of the panels due account shall be taken of the experience of the judges in criminal law, international law, including international humanitarian law and human rights law.

V. Other Matters

Section 24

Witness Protection

24.1 The panels shall take appropriate measures to protect the safety, physical and psychological well-being, dignity and privacy of victims and witnesses. In so doing, the panels shall have regard to all relevant factors, including age, gender, health and the nature of the crime, in particular, but not limited to, where the crime involves sexual or gender violence or violence against children.

24.2 Procedures regarding the protection of witnesses shall be elaborated in an UNTAET directive.

Section 25

Trust Fund

25.1 A Trust Fund may be established by decision of the Transitional Administrator in consultation with the National Consultative Council for the benefit of victims of crimes within the jurisdiction of the panels, and of the families of such victims.

25.2 The panels may order money and other property collected through fines, forfeiture, foreign donors or other means to be transferred to the Trust Fund.

25.3 The Trust Fund shall be managed according to criteria to be determined by an UNTAET directive.

Section 26

Entry into force

The present regulation shall enter into force on 6 June 2000.

Sergio Vieira de Mello, Transitional Administrator

Appendix F

Resolutions for the Extraordinary Chambers for Cambodia United Nations General Assembly Resolutions GA 52/135 and GA 57/228B

RESOLUTION ADOPTED BY THE GENERAL ASSEMBLY [ON THE REPORT OF THE THIRD COMMITTEE (A/52/644/ADD.2)] 27 FEBRUARY 1998

A/RES/52/135

52/135. Situation of human rights in Cambodia

The General Assembly,

Guided by the purposes and principles embodied in the Charter of the United Nations, the Universal Declaration of Human Rights Resolution 217 A (III). and the International Covenants on Human Rights, Resolution 2200 A (XXI), annex.

Recalling the Agreement on a Comprehensive Political Settlement of the Cambodia Conflict, signed in Paris on 23 October 1991, A/46/608-S/23177, annex; see *Official Records of the Security Council, Forty-sixth Year, Supplement for October, November and December 1991*, document S/23177. including part III thereof, relating to human rights,

Taking note of Commission on Human Rights resolution 1997/49 of 11 April 1997, See *Official Records of the Economic and Social Council, 1997, Supplement No. 3* (E/1997/23), chap. II, sect. A. and recalling General Assembly resolution 51/98 of 12 December 1996 and previous relevant resolutions, including Commission on Human Rights resolution 1993/6 of 19 February 1993, Ibid., 1993, *Supplement No. 3* (E/1993/23), chap. II, sect. A. in which the Commission recommended the appointment of a special representative for human rights in Cambodia, and the subsequent appointment by the Secretary-General of a special representative,

Recognizing that the tragic history of Cambodia requires special measures to assure the promotion and protection of the human rights of all people in Cambodia and the non-return to the policies and practices of the past, as stipulated in the Agreement signed in Paris on 23 October 1991,

Desiring that the United Nations respond positively to assist efforts to investigate Cambodia's tragic history, including responsibility for past international crimes, such as acts of genocide and crimes against humanity,

Welcoming the continuing role of the United Nations High Commissioner for Human Rights in the promotion and protection of human rights in Cambodia,

1. *Requests* the Secretary-General, through his Special Representative for human rights in Cambodia, in collaboration with the office in Cambodia of the United Nations High Commissioner for Human Rights, to assist the Government of Cambodia in ensuring the protection of the human rights of all people in Cambodia, to ensure adequate resources for the enhanced functioning of the operational presence in Cambodia of the Office of the High Commissioner and to enable the Special Representative to continue to fulfil his tasks expeditiously;

2. *Welcomes* the report of the Secretary-General on the situation of human rights in Cambodia, A/52/489. in particular the section concerning the role of the Office of the United Nations High Commissioner for Human Rights in assisting the Government and the people of Cambodia in the promotion and protection of human rights, and encourages the Government of Cambodia to continue to cooperate with the Office;

3. *Takes note with appreciation* of the report of the Special Representative on the situation of human rights in Cambodia, E/CN.4/1997/85. in particular his concerns for a legislative framework for the forthcoming national elections and his concerns about the problem of impunity, the independence of the judiciary and the establishment of the rule of law, the use of torture, the administration of prisons and the ill-treatment of prisoners and child prostitution and trafficking;

4. *Notes with concern* the lack of response by the Government of Cambodia to several of the recommendations contained in the previous reports of the Special Representative, and urges that it respond as soon as possible;

5. *Expresses grave concern* about numerous instances of violations of human rights, including extrajudicial executions, torture, including rape, illegal arrest and detention, as detailed in the reports of the Special Representative and his predecessor, and calls upon the Government of Cambodia to prosecute, in

accordance with due process of the law and international standards relating to human rights, all those who have perpetrated human rights violations;

6. *Also expresses grave concern* about the serious violations of human rights committed during the armed violence of early July 1997 and in its aftermath, as reported by the Special Representative and by the office in Cambodia of the United Nations High Commissioner for Human Rights in its memorandum on summary executions, torture and missing persons, and urges the Government of Cambodia as a high priority to investigate thoroughly and impartially and to bring to justice those responsible for such serious crimes;

7. *Notes* that the perpetrators of the violence in Phnom Penh, on 30 March 1997, against a peaceful and lawful opposition rally exercising its democratic rights which resulted in numerous deaths and injuries have not been identified and brought to justice, and urges the Government of Cambodia to take action;

8. *Notes with serious concern* the comments of the Special Representative concerning corrupt practices within the judicial system and in the prison administration, and strongly urges the Government of Cambodia to address the problem of corrupt practices and to increase its efforts to create a functioning and impartial system of justice, including convening the Supreme Council of Magistracy, to institute a system to guarantee the essential sustenance of prisoners and to continue its efforts to improve the physical environment of prisons;

9. *Stresses* that addressing the continuing problem of impunity, as detailed by the Special Representative, including the repeal of article 51 of the law on civil servants of 1994 and bringing to justice those responsible for human rights violations, together with ensuring security of persons and rights of association, assembly and expression, is a matter of critical and urgent priority and essential to the creation of an atmosphere conducive to the holding of free, fair and credible elections;

10. *Notes* that national elections are scheduled to be held in May 1998, and strongly urges the Government of Cambodia to promote and uphold the effective functioning of multi-party democracy, including the right to form political parties, to stand for election, to take part freely in a representative Government, as well as the right to freedom of expression and the right to information, in accordance with the principles set out in paragraphs 2 and 4 of annex 5 to the Agreement signed in Paris on 23 October 1991;

11. *Expresses* support for the Secretary-General's efforts in Cambodia, including the role of United Nations offices in monitoring the return of political leaders currently outside the country and their unfettered resumption of political

activity, and requests the Secretary-General to continue to consider any request from the Government of Cambodia for assistance with the holding of the elections, including coordination and monitoring;

12. *Welcomes* the proposed measures outlined by the Government of Cambodia in its comments A/51/453/Add.1. on the report of the Secretary-General to the General Assembly at its fifty-first session A/51/453. to ensure that the forthcoming national elections are free and fair and the assurances given by the Cambodian leaders to the Secretary-General stating their commitment to holding elections and to guaranteeing the security and safety of all returning political leaders, as well as their full resumption of political activities, and expresses the hope that this will facilitate the return of political leaders from abroad;

13. *Emphasizes* the need for the legislative framework for the elections, in accordance with established international standards, to be agreed upon and adopted by the National Assembly, for the security forces to remain neutral during the election campaign, for free and equal access to the electronic and print media, for the individual vote to be confidential, for full cooperation to be given to local and international observers and for all parties to act in a constructive manner and to accept the outcome of the elections;

14. *Strongly encourages* the Government of Cambodia to establish an independent body to supervise the holding of the elections, to ensure that the elections are free, fair and credible and to ensure that the Constitutional Council will be convened in order to resolve election disputes;

15. *Endorses* the comments of the Special Representative that the most serious human rights violations in Cambodia in recent history have been committed by the Khmer Rouge and that their crimes, including the taking and killing of hostages, have continued to the present, and notes with concern that no Khmer Rouge leader has been brought to account for his crimes;

16. *Requests* the Secretary-General to examine the request by the Cambodian authorities for assistance in responding to past serious violations of Cambodian and international law, including the possibility of the appointment, by the Secretary-General, of a group of experts to evaluate the existing evidence and propose further measures, as a means of bringing about national reconciliation, strengthening democracy and addressing the issue of individual accountability;

17. *Urges* the Government of Cambodia to take concrete action to combat child prostitution and trafficking and, in this connection, to work with the office in Cambodia of the United Nations High Commissioner for Human Rights,

the United Nations Children's Fund and non-governmental organizations to develop an action plan;

18. *Welcomes* the signature in May 1997 of a memorandum of understanding between the International Labour Organization and the Government of Cambodia to formalize areas of cooperation in the field of child labour;

19. *Encourages* the Government of Cambodia to include Cambodian non-governmental organizations active in the field of human rights in the rehabilitation and reconstruction of Cambodia, and recommends that their skills be drawn upon to assist in ensuring that forthcoming elections are free, fair and credible;

20. *Also encourages* the Government of Cambodia to request the Office of the United Nations High Commissioner for Human Rights to provide advice and technical assistance with respect to the creation of an independent national institution for the promotion and protection of human rights, and looks forward to the establishment of such an institution;

21. *Notes with appreciation* the use by the Secretary-General of the United Nations Trust Fund for a Human Rights Education Programme in Cambodia to finance the programme of activities of the office in Cambodia of the United Nations High Commissioner for Human Rights, as defined in resolutions of the General Assembly and the Commission on Human Rights, and invites Governments, intergovernmental and non-governmental organizations, foundations and individuals to consider contributing funds to the Trust Fund;

22. *Expresses grave concern* about the devastating consequences and destabilizing effects of the use of anti-personnel landmines on Cambodian society, encourages the Government of Cambodia to continue its support and efforts for the removal of these mines, and urges the Government of Cambodia to give priority to banning all anti-personnel landmines;

23. *Requests* the Secretary-General to report to the General Assembly at its fifty-third session on the role of the Office of the United Nations High Commissioner for Human Rights in assisting the Government and the people of Cambodia in the promotion and protection of human rights and on the recommendations made by the Special Representative on matters within his mandate;

24. *Decides* to continue its consideration of the situation of human rights in Cambodia at its fifty-third session.

70th plenary meeting
12 December 1997

RESOLUTION ADOPTED BY THE GENERAL ASSEMBLY [ON THE REPORT OF THE THIRD COMMITTEE (A/57/806)] 22 MAY 2003 A/RES/57/228 B

57/228. Khmer Rouge trials

B[1]

The General Assembly,

Recalling its resolution 57/228 of 18 December 2002,

Welcoming the efforts of the Secretary-General and the Royal Government of Cambodia to conclude the negotiation of the draft Agreement between the United Nations and the Royal Government of Cambodia concerning the Prosecution under Cambodian Law of Crimes Committed during the Period of Democratic Kampuchea contained in the annex to the present resolution,

Taking note of the report of the Secretary-General,2

1. *Approves* the draft Agreement between the United Nations and the Royal Government of Cambodia concerning the Prosecution under Cambodian Law of Crimes Committed during the Period of Democratic Kampuchea contained in the annex to the present resolution;

2. *Urges* the Secretary-General and the Royal Government of Cambodia to take all the measures necessary to allow the draft Agreement referred to in paragraph 1 to enter into force, and to implement it fully after its entry into force;

3. *Decides* that the expenses of the Extraordinary Chambers to be defrayed by the United Nations in accordance with the relevant provisions of the draft Agreement shall be borne by voluntary contributions from the international community as indicated in paragraph 9 of resolution 57/228, and appeals to the international community to provide assistance, including financial and personnel support to the Extraordinary Chambers;

4. *Requests* the Secretary-General to report to the General Assembly at its fifty-eighth session on the implementation of the present resolution.

85th plenary meeting 13 May 2003

Notes:

1 Consequently, resolution 57/228, in section V of the *Official Records of the General Assembly, Fifty-seventh Session, Supplement No. 49* and corrigendum (A/57/49 and A/57/49 (Vol. I)/Corr.1), vol. I, becomes resolution 57/228 A.
2 A/57/769.

Annex

Draft Agreement between the United Nations and the Royal Government of Cambodia concerning the Prosecution under Cambodian Law of Crimes Committed during the Period of Democratic Kampuchea

Whereas the General Assembly of the United Nations, in its resolution 57/228 of 18 December 2002, recalled that the serious violations of Cambodian and international humanitarian law during the period of Democratic Kampuchea from 1975 to 1979 continue to be matters of vitally important concern to the international community as a whole,

Whereas in the same resolution the General Assembly recognized the legitimate concern of the Government and the people of Cambodia in the pursuit of justice and national reconciliation, stability, peace and security,

Whereas the Cambodian authorities have requested assistance from the United Nations in bringing to trial senior leaders of Democratic Kampuchea and those who were most responsible for the crimes and serious violations of Cambodian penal law, international humanitarian law and custom, and international conventions recognized by Cambodia, that were committed during the period from 17 April 1975 to 6 January 1979,

Whereas prior to the negotiation of the present Agreement substantial progress had been made by the Secretary-General of the United Nations (hereinafter, "the Secretary-General") and the Royal Government of Cambodia towards the establishment, with international assistance, of Extraordinary Chambers within the existing court structure of Cambodia for the prosecution of crimes committed during the period of Democratic Kampuchea,

Whereas by its resolution 57/228, the General Assembly welcomed the promulgation of the Law on the Establishment of the Extraordinary Chambers in the Courts of Cambodia for the Prosecution of Crimes Committed during the Period of Democratic Kampuchea and requested the Secretary-General to resume negotiations, without delay, to conclude an agreement with the Government, based on previous negotiations on the establishment of the Extraordinary Chambers consistent with the provisions of the said resolution, so that the Extraordinary Chambers may begin to function promptly,

Whereas the Secretary-General and the Royal Government of Cambodia have held negotiations on the establishment of the Extraordinary Chambers,

Now therefore the United Nations and the Royal Government of Cambodia have agreed as follows:

Article 1

Purpose

The purpose of the present Agreement is to regulate the cooperation between the United Nations and the Royal Government of Cambodia in bringing to trial senior leaders of Democratic Kampuchea and those who were most responsible for the crimes and serious violations of Cambodian penal law, international humanitarian law and custom, and international conventions recognized by Cambodia, that were committed during the period from 17 April 1975 to 6 January 1979. The Agreement provides, inter alia, the legal basis and the principles and modalities for such cooperation.

Article 2

The Law on the Establishment of Extraordinary Chambers

1. The present Agreement recognizes that the Extraordinary Chambers have subject-matter jurisdiction consistent with that set forth in "the Law on the Establishment of the Extraordinary Chambers in the Courts of Cambodia for the Prosecution of Crimes Committed During the Period of Democratic Kampuchea" (hereinafter: "the Law on the Establishment of the Extraordinary Chambers"), as adopted and amended by the Cambodian Legislature under the Constitution of Cambodia. The present Agreement further recognizes that the Extraordinary Chambers have personal jurisdiction over senior leaders of Democratic Kampuchea and those who were most responsible for the crimes referred to in Article 1 of the Agreement.

2. The present Agreement shall be implemented in Cambodia through the Law on the Establishment of the Extraordinary Chambers as adopted and amended. The Vienna Convention on the Law of Treaties, and in particular its Articles 26 and 27, applies to the Agreement.

3. In case amendments to the Law on the Establishment of the Extraordinary Chambers are deemed necessary, such amendments shall always be preceded by consultations between the parties.

Article 3

Judges

1. Cambodian judges, on the one hand, and judges appointed by the Supreme Council of the Magistracy upon nomination by the Secretary-General of the United Nations (hereinafter: "international judges"), on the other hand, shall serve in each of the two Extraordinary Chambers.

2. The composition of the Chambers shall be as follows:
   (a) The Trial Chamber: three Cambodian judges and two international judges;
   (b) The Supreme Court Chamber, which shall serve as both appellate chamber and final instance: four Cambodian judges and three international judges.

3. The judges shall be persons of high moral character, impartiality and integrity who possess the qualifications required in their respective countries for appointment to judicial offices. They shall be independent in the performance of their functions and shall not accept or seek instructions from any Government or any other source.

4. In the overall composition of the Chambers due account should be taken of the experience of the judges in criminal law, international law, including international humanitarian law and human rights law.

5. The Secretary-General of the United Nations undertakes to forward a list of not less than seven nominees for international judges from which the Supreme Council of the Magistracy shall appoint five to serve as judges in the two Chambers. Appointment of international judges by the Supreme Council of the Magistracy shall be made only from the list submitted by the Secretary-General.

6. In the event of a vacancy of an international judge, the Supreme Council of the Magistracy shall appoint another international judge from the same list.

7. The judges shall be appointed for the duration of the proceedings.

8. In addition to the international judges sitting in the Chambers and present at every stage of the proceedings, the President of a Chamber may, on a case-

by-case basis, designate from the list of nominees submitted by the Secretary-General, one or more alternate judges to be present at each stage of the proceedings, and to replace an international judge if that judge is unable to continue sitting.

Article 4

Decision-making

1. The judges shall attempt to achieve unanimity in their decisions. If this is not possible, the following shall apply:
   (a) A decision by the Trial Chamber shall require the affirmative vote of at least four judges;
   (b) A decision by the Supreme Court Chamber shall require the affirmative vote of at least five judges.

2. When there is no unanimity, the decision of the Chamber shall contain the views of the majority and the minority.

Article 5

Investigating judges

1. There shall be one Cambodian and one international investigating judge serving as co-investigating judges. They shall be responsible for the conduct of investigations.

2. The co-investigating judges shall be persons of high moral character, impartiality and integrity who possess the qualifications required in their respective countries for appointment to such a judicial office.

3. The co-investigating judges shall be independent in the performance of their functions and shall not accept or seek instructions from any Government or any other source. It is understood, however, that the scope of the investigation is limited to senior leaders of Democratic Kampuchea and those who were most responsible for the crimes and serious violations of Cambodian penal law, international humanitarian law and custom, and international conventions recognized by Cambodia, that were committed during the period from 17 April 1975 to 6 January 1979.

4. The co-investigating judges shall cooperate with a view to arriving at a common approach to the investigation. In case the co-investigating judges are unable to agree whether to proceed with an investigation, the investigation shall proceed unless the judges or one of them requests within thirty days that the difference shall be settled in accordance with Article 7.

5. In addition to the list of nominees provided for in Article 3, paragraph 5, the Secretary-General shall submit a list of two nominees from which the Supreme Council of the Magistracy shall appoint one to serve as an international co-investigating judge, and one as a reserve international co-investigating judge.

6. In case there is a vacancy or a need to fill the post of the international co-investigating judge, the person appointed to fill this post must be the reserve international co-investigating judge.

7. The co-investigating judges shall be appointed for the duration of the proceedings.

Article 6

Prosecutors

1. There shall be one Cambodian prosecutor and one international prosecutor competent to appear in both Chambers, serving as co-prosecutors. They shall be responsible for the conduct of the prosecutions.

2. The co-prosecutors shall be of high moral character, and possess a high level of professional competence and extensive experience in the conduct of investigations and prosecutions of criminal cases.

3. The co-prosecutors shall be independent in the performance of their functions and shall not accept or seek instructions from any Government or any other source. It is understood, however, that the scope of the prosecution is limited to senior leaders of Democratic Kampuchea and those who were most responsible for the crimes and serious violations of Cambodian penal law, international humanitarian law and custom, and international conventions recognized by Cambodia, that were committed during the period from 17 April 1975 to 6 January 1979.

4. The co-prosecutors shall cooperate with a view to arriving at a common approach to the prosecution. In case the prosecutors are unable to agree whether to proceed with a prosecution, the prosecution shall proceed unless the prosecutors or one of them requests within thirty days that the difference shall be settled in accordance with Article 7.

5. The Secretary-General undertakes to forward a list of two nominees from which the Supreme Council of the Magistracy shall select one international co-prosecutor and one reserve international co-prosecutor.

6. In case there is a vacancy or a need to fill the post of the international co-prosecutor, the person appointed to fill this post must be the reserve international co-prosecutor.

7. The co-prosecutors shall be appointed for the duration of the proceedings.

8. Each co-prosecutor shall have one or more deputy prosecutors to assist him or her with prosecutions before the Chambers. Deputy international prosecutors shall be appointed by the international co-prosecutor from a list provided by the Secretary-General.

Article 7

Settlement of differences between the co-investigating judges or the co-prosecutors

1. In case the co-investigating judges or the co-prosecutors have made a request in accordance with Article 5, paragraph 4, or Article 6, paragraph 4, as the case may be, they shall submit written statements of facts and the reasons for their different positions to the Director of the Office of Administration.

2. The difference shall be settled forthwith by a Pre-Trial Chamber of five judges, three appointed by the Supreme Council of the Magistracy, with one as President, and two appointed by the Supreme Council of the Magistracy upon nomination by the Secretary-General. Article 3, paragraph 3, shall apply to the judges.

3. Upon receipt of the statements referred to in paragraph 1, the Director of the Office of Administration shall immediately convene the Pre-Trial Chamber and communicate the statements to its members.

4. A decision of the Pre-Trial Chamber, against which there is no appeal, requires the affirmative vote of at least four judges. The decision shall be communicated to the Director of the Office of Administration, who shall publish it and communicate it to the co-investigating judges or the co-prosecutors. They shall immediately proceed in accordance with the decision of the Chamber. If there is no majority, as required for a decision, the investigation or prosecution shall proceed.

Article 8

Office of Administration

1. There shall be an Office of Administration to service the Extraordinary Chambers, the Pre-Trial Chamber, the co-investigating judges and the Prosecutors' Office.

2. There shall be a Cambodian Director of this Office, who shall be appointed by the Royal Government of Cambodia. The Director shall be responsible for the overall management of the Office of Administration, except in matters that are subject to United Nations rules and procedures.

3. There shall be an international Deputy Director of the Office of Administration, who shall be appointed by the Secretary-General. The Deputy Director shall be responsible for the recruitment of all international staff and all administration of the international components of the Extraordinary Chambers, the Pre-Trial Chamber, the co-investigating judges, the Prosecutors' Office and the Office of Administration. The United Nations and the Royal Government of Cambodia agree that, when an international Deputy Director has been appointed by the Secretary-General, the assignment of that person to that position by the Royal Government of Cambodia shall take place forthwith.

4. The Director and the Deputy Director shall cooperate in order to ensure an effective and efficient functioning of the administration.

Article 9

Crimes falling within the jurisdiction of the Extraordinary Chambers

The subject-matter jurisdiction of the Extraordinary Chambers shall be the crime of genocide as defined in the 1948 Convention on the Prevention and Punishment of the Crime of Genocide, crimes against humanity as defined in the 1998 Rome Statute of the International Criminal Court and grave breaches of the 1949 Geneva Conventions and such other crimes as defined in Chapter II of the Law on the Establishment of the Extraordinary Chambers as promulgated on 10 August 2001.

Article 10

Penalties

The maximum penalty for conviction for crimes falling within the jurisdiction of the Extraordinary Chambers shall be life imprisonment.

Article 11

Amnesty

1. The Royal Government of Cambodia shall not request an amnesty or pardon for any persons who may be investigated for or convicted of crimes referred to in the present Agreement.

2. This provision is based upon a declaration by the Royal Government of Cambodia that until now, with regard to matters covered in the law, there has been only one case, dated 14 September 1996, when a pardon was granted to only one person with regard to a 1979 conviction on the charge of genocide. The United Nations and the Royal Government of Cambodia agree that the scope of this pardon is a matter to be decided by the Extraordinary Chambers.

Article 12

Procedure

1. The procedure shall be in accordance with Cambodian law. Where Cambodian law does not deal with a particular matter, or where there is uncertainty regarding the interpretation or application of a relevant rule of Cambodian law, or where there is a question regarding the consistency of such a rule with international standards, guidance may also be sought in procedural rules established at the international level.

2. The Extraordinary Chambers shall exercise their jurisdiction in accordance with international standards of justice, fairness and due process of law, as set out in Articles 14 and 15 of the 1966 International Covenant on Civil and Political Rights, to which Cambodia is a party. In the interest of securing a fair and public hearing and credibility of the procedure, it is understood that representatives of Member States of the United Nations, of the Secretary-General, of the media and of national and international non-governmental organizations will at all times have access to the proceedings before the Extraordinary Chambers. Any exclusion from such proceedings in accordance with the provisions of Article 14 of the Covenant shall only be to the extent strictly necessary in the opinion of the Chamber concerned and where publicity would prejudice the interests of justice.

Article 13

Rights of the accused

1. The rights of the accused enshrined in Articles 14 and 15 of the 1966 International Covenant on Civil and Political Rights shall be respected throughout the trial process. Such rights shall, in particular, include the right: to a fair and public hearing; to be presumed innocent until proved guilty; to engage a counsel of his or her choice; to have adequate time and facilities for the preparation of his or her defence; to have counsel provided if he or she does not have sufficient means to pay for it; and to examine or have examined the witnesses against him or her.

2. The United Nations and the Royal Government of Cambodia agree that the provisions on the right to defence counsel in the Law on the Establishment of Extraordinary Chambers mean that the accused has the right to engage counsel of his or her own choosing as guaranteed by the International Covenant on Civil and Political Rights.

Article 14

Premises

The Royal Government of Cambodia shall provide at its expense the premises for the co-investigating judges, the Prosecutors' Office, the Extraordinary Chambers, the Pre-Trial Chamber and the Office of Administration. It shall also provide for such utilities, facilities and other services necessary for their operation that may be mutually agreed upon by separate agreement between the United Nations and the Government.

Article 15

Cambodian personnel

Salaries and emoluments of Cambodian judges and other Cambodian personnel shall be defrayed by the Royal Government of Cambodia.

Article 16

International personnel

Salaries and emoluments of international judges, the international co-investigating judge, the international co-prosecutor and other personnel recruited by the United Nations shall be defrayed by the United Nations.

Article 17

Financial and other assistance of the United Nations

The United Nations shall be responsible for the following:

(a) Remuneration of the international judges, the international co-investigating judge, the international co-prosecutor, the Deputy Director of the Office of Administration and other international personnel;
(b) Costs for utilities and services as agreed separately between the United Nations and the Royal Government of Cambodia;
(c) Remuneration of defence counsel;
(d) Witnesses' travel from within Cambodia and from abroad;
(e) Safety and security arrangements as agreed separately between the United Nations and the Government;
(f) Such other limited assistance as may be necessary to ensure the smooth functioning of the investigation, the prosecution and the Extraordinary Chambers.

Article 18

Inviolability of archives and documents

The archives of the co-investigating judges, the co-prosecutors, the Extraordinary Chambers, the Pre-Trial Chamber and the Office of Administration, and in general all documents and materials made available, belonging to or used by them, wherever located in Cambodia and by whomsoever held, shall be inviolable for the duration of the proceedings.

Article 19

Privileges and immunities of international judges, the international co-investigating judge, the international co-prosecutor and the Deputy Director of the Office of Administration

1. The international judges, the international co-investigating judge, the international co-prosecutor and the Deputy Director of the Office of Administration, together with their families forming part of their household, shall enjoy the privileges and immunities, exemptions and facilities accorded to diplomatic agents in accordance with the 1961 Vienna Convention on Diplomatic Relations. They shall, in particular, enjoy:
   (a) Personal inviolability, including immunity from arrest or detention;
   (b) Immunity from criminal, civil and administrative jurisdiction in conformity with the Vienna Convention;
   (c) Inviolability for all papers and documents;

(d) Exemption from immigration restrictions and alien registration;

(e) The same immunities and facilities in respect of their personal baggage as are accorded to diplomatic agents.

2. The international judges, the international co-investigating judge, the international co-prosecutor and the Deputy Director of the Office of Administration shall enjoy exemption from taxation in Cambodia on their salaries, emoluments and allowances.

Article 20

Privileges and immunities of Cambodian and international personnel

1. Cambodian judges, the Cambodian co-investigating judge, the Cambodian co-prosecutor and other Cambodian personnel shall be accorded immunity from legal process in respect of words spoken or written and all acts performed by them in their official capacity under the present Agreement. Such immunity shall continue to be accorded after termination of employment with the co-investigating judges, the co-prosecutors, the Extraordinary Chambers, the Pre-Trial Chamber and the Office of Administration.

2. International personnel shall be accorded:
(a) Immunity from legal process in respect of words spoken or written and all acts performed by them in their official capacity under the present Agreement. Such immunity shall continue to be accorded after termination of employment with the co-investigating judges, the co-prosecutors, the Extraordinary Chambers, the Pre-Trial Chamber and the Office of Administration;
(b) Immunity from taxation on salaries, allowances and emoluments paid to them by the United Nations;
(c) Immunity from immigration restrictions;
(d) The right to import free of duties and taxes, except for payment for services, their furniture and effects at the time of first taking up their official duties in Cambodia.

3. The United Nations and the Royal Government of Cambodia agree that the immunity granted by the Law on the Establishment of the Extraordinary Chambers in respect of words spoken or written and all acts performed by them in their official capacity under the present Agreement will apply also after the persons have left the service of the co-investigating judges, the co-prosecutors, the Extraordinary Chambers, the Pre-Trial Chamber and the Office of Administration.

Article 21

Counsel

1. The counsel of a suspect or an accused who has been admitted as such by the Extraordinary Chambers shall not be subjected by the Royal Government of Cambodia to any measure which may affect the free and independent exercise of his or her functions under the present Agreement.

2. In particular, the counsel shall be accorded:
   (a) Immunity from personal arrest or detention and from seizure of personal baggage;
   (b) Inviolability of all documents relating to the exercise of his or her functions as a counsel of a suspect or accused;
   (c) Immunity from criminal or civil jurisdiction in respect of words spoken or written and acts performed by them in their official capacity as counsel. Such immunity shall continue to be accorded to them after termination of their functions as a counsel of a suspect or accused.

3. Any counsel, whether of Cambodian or non-Cambodian nationality, engaged by or assigned to a suspect or an accused shall, in the defence of his or her client, act in accordance with the present Agreement, the Cambodian Law on the Statutes of the Bar and recognized standards and ethics of the legal profession.

Article 22

Witnesses and experts

Witnesses and experts appearing on a summons or a request of the judges, the co-investigating judges, or the co-prosecutors shall not be prosecuted, detained or subjected to any other restriction on their liberty by the Cambodian authorities. They shall not be subjected by the authorities to any measure which may affect the free and independent exercise of their functions.

Article 23

Protection of victims and witnesses

The co-investigating judges, the co-prosecutors and the Extraordinary Chambers shall provide for the protection of victims and witnesses. Such protection measures shall include, but shall not be limited to, the conduct of in camera proceedings and the protection of the identity of a victim or witness.

Article 24

Security, safety and protection of persons referred to in the present Agreement

The Royal Government of Cambodia shall take all effective and adequate actions which may be required to ensure the security, safety and protection of persons referred to in the present Agreement. The United Nations and the Government agree that the Government is responsible for the security of all accused, irrespective of whether they appear voluntarily before the Extraordinary Chambers or whether they are under arrest.

Article 25

Obligation to assist the co-investigating judges, the co-prosecutors and the Extraordinary Chambers

The Royal Government of Cambodia shall comply without undue delay with any request for assistance by the co-investigating judges, the co-prosecutors and the Extraordinary Chambers or an order issued by any of them, including, but not limited to:
(a) Identification and location of persons;
(b) Service of documents;
(c) Arrest or detention of persons;
(d) Transfer of an indictee to the Extraordinary Chambers.

Article 26

Languages

1. The official language of the Extraordinary Chambers and the Pre-Trial Chamber is Khmer.

2. The official working languages of the Extraordinary Chambers and the Pre-Trial Chamber shall be Khmer, English and French.

3. Translations of public documents and interpretation at public hearings into Russian may be provided by the Royal Government of Cambodia at its discretion and expense on condition that such services do not hinder the proceedings before the Extraordinary Chambers.

Article 27

Practical arrangements

1. With a view to achieving efficiency and cost-effectiveness in the operation of the Extraordinary Chambers, a phased-in approach shall be adopted for their establishment in accordance with the chronological order of the legal process.

2. In the first phase of the operation of the Extraordinary Chambers, the judges, the co-investigating judges and the co-prosecutors will be appointed along with investigative and prosecutorial staff, and the process of investigations and prosecutions shall be initiated.

3. The trial process of those already in custody shall proceed simultaneously with the investigation of other persons responsible for crimes falling within the jurisdiction of the Extraordinary Chambers.

4. With the completion of the investigation of persons suspected of having committed the crimes falling within the jurisdiction of the Extraordinary Chambers, arrest warrants shall be issued and submitted to the Royal Government of Cambodia to effectuate the arrest.

5. With the arrest by the Royal Government of Cambodia of indicted persons situated in its territory, the Extraordinary Chambers shall be fully operational, provided that the judges of the Supreme Court Chamber shall serve when seized with a matter. The judges of the Pre-Trial Chamber shall serve only if and when their services are needed.

Article 28

Withdrawal of cooperation

Should the Royal Government of Cambodia change the structure or organization of the Extraordinary Chambers or otherwise cause them to function in a manner that does not conform with the terms of the present Agreement, the United Nations reserves the right to cease to provide assistance, financial or otherwise, pursuant to the present Agreement.

Article 29

Settlement of disputes

Any dispute between the Parties concerning the interpretation or application of the present Agreement shall be settled by negotiation, or by any other mutually agreed upon mode of settlement.

Article 30

Approval

To be binding on the parties, the present Agreement must be approved by the General Assembly of the United Nations and ratified by Cambodia. The Royal Government of Cambodia will make its best endeavours to obtain this ratification by the earliest possible date.

Article 31

Application within Cambodia

The present Agreement shall apply as law within the Kingdom of Cambodia following its ratification in accordance with the relevant provisions of the internal law of the Kingdom of Cambodia regarding competence to conclude treaties.

Article 32

Entry into force

The present Agreement shall enter into force on the day after both parties have notified each other in writing that the legal requirements for entry into force have been complied with.
Done at [place] on [day, month] 2003 in two copies in the English language.

For the United Nations

For the Royal Government of Cambodia

Bibliography

Akhavan, Payam (1996), 'The Yugoslav Tribunal at a Crossroads: The Dayton Peace Agreement and Beyond,' *Human Rights Quarterly*, vol.18, pp.259-285.

Akhavan, Payam (1998), 'Justice in the Hague, Peace in the Former Yugoslavia? A Commentary on the United Nations War Crimes Tribunal,' *Human Rights Quarterly*, vol.20, pp.737-816.

Akhavan, Payam (2001), 'Beyond Impunity: Can International Criminal Justice Prevent Future Atrocities?' *American Journal of International Law,* vol. 95, pp. 7-31.

Alesina, Alberto and David Dollar (2000), 'Who Gives Foreign Aid to Whom and Why?' *Journal of Economic Growth,* vol. 5, pp. 33-63.

Amann, Diane Marie (2001), 'Calling Children to Account: The Proposal for a Juvenile Chamber in the Special Court for Sierra Leone,' *Pepperdine Law Review,* vol. 29, pp.167-185.

Amnesty International (1998), 'Major Step Back for Human Rights as Rwanda Stages 22 Executions,' AI Index: AFR 47/14/98.

Amnesty International (2001), 'Amnesty International's Comments on the Law on Human Rights Courts (Law No.26/2000),' ASA 21/005/2001. Amnesty International (2002), '*Gacaca*: A Question of Justice,' AI Index: AFR 47/007/2002.

Baehr, Peter R (2001), *Human Rights: Universality in Practice*, New York, Palgrave.

Bald, Stephanie (2002), 'Searching for a Lost Childhood: Will the Special Court of Sierra Leone Find Justice for Its Children?' *American University International Law Review,* vol.18, pp. 537-583.

Bass, Gary Jonathan (2000), *Stay the Hand of Vengeance: The Politics of War Crimes Tribunals*, Princeton, Princeton University Press.

Bassiouni, M. Cherif (1996), 'The Commission of Experts Established Pursuant to Security Council Resolution 780: Investigating Violations of Humanitarian Law in the Former Yugoslavia,' In Roger S. Clark and Madeleine Sann (eds.) *The Prosecution of International Crimes*, New Brunswick, Transaction Publishers.

BBC News (2005), 'Cambodia Says KR Tribunal at Risk,' (available at news.bbc.co.uk/2/hi/asia-pacific/4152668.stm).

Beigbeder, Yves (1999), *Judging War Criminals: The Politics of International Justice*, New York, St. Martin's Press.

Blakesley, Christopher L. (1998), 'Obstacles to the Creation of a Permanent War Crimes Tribunal' In Charlotte Ku and Paul F. Fiehl (eds.) *International LawClassic and Contemporary Readings*, Boulder, Lynne Rienner Publishers.

Bohlander, Michael (2004), 'The Transfer of Cases from International Tribunals to

National Courts,' Paper presented at the Colloquium of Prosecutors of International Criminal Tribunals.

Boulding, Carew Elizabeth (2004), 'The Foreign Aid Puzzle: Bilateral versus Multilateral Development Assistance," Presented at the Annual Meeting of the American Political Science Association.

Brackman, Arnold C. (1987), *The Other Nuremberg: The Untold Story of the Tokyo War Crimes Trials*, New York, William Morrow and Company, Inc.

Burns, Peter (1996), 'An International Tribunal: The Difficult Union of Principle and Politics,' In Roger S. Clark and Madeleine Sann (eds.) *The Prosecution of International Crimes*, New Brunswick, Transaction Publishers.

Cassen, Robert (1994), *Does Aid Work? Report to an Intergovernmental Task Force*, Oxford, Clarendon Press.

Cerone, John (2002), 'The Special Court for Sierra Leone: Establishing a New Approach to International Criminal Justice,' *ILSA: The Journal of International & Comparative Law,* vol. 8, pp. 379-387.

Chandler, David (1992), *A History of Cambodia*, 2nd Edition, Boulder, Westview Press.

Chopra, Jarat and Thomas G. Weiss (1998), 'Sovereignty is No Longer Sacrosanct: Codifying Humanitarian Intervention' In Charlotte Ku and Paul F. Fiehl (eds.) *International Law: Classic and Contemporary Readings*, Boulder, Lynne Rienner Publishers.

Cingranelli David L. and Thomas E. Pasquarello (1985), 'Human Rights Practices and the Distribution of US Foreign Aid to Latin American Countries,' *American Journal of Political Science,* vol. 29, pp. 539-563.

Cohen, David (2002), 'Seeking Justice on the Cheap: Is the East Timor Tribunal Really a Model for the Future?,' *Asia Pacific Issues*, vol. 61, pp. 1-8.

Cohen, David (2003), 'Intended to Fail: The Trials Before the Ad Hoc Human Rights Court in Jakarta,' International Center for Transitional Justice.

Cook, Susan E. (2001), 'Prosecuting Genocide in Cambodia: The Winding Path towards Justice,' (available at www.crimesofwar.org/tribun-mag/cambodia_print.html).

Corey, Allison and Sandra F. Joireman (2004), 'Retributive Justice: The *Gacaca* Courts in Rwanda,' *African Affairs,* vol.103, pp. 73-89.

Cryer, Robert (2001), 'A 'Special Court' for Sierra Leone?' *The International and Comparative Law Quarterly,* vol. 50, pp. 435-446.

Daly, Erin (2002), 'Between Punitive and Reconstructive Justice: The *Gacaca* Courts in Rwanda,' *Journal of International Law,* vol. 34, pp. 355-396.

de Bertodano, Sylvia (2003), 'Current Developments in Internationalized Courts,' *Journal of International Criminal Law*, vol. 1, pp. 226-244.

De Nike, Howard J., John Quigley and Kenneth J. Robinson, eds. (2000), *Genocide in Cambodia: Documents from the Trial of Pol Pot and Ieng Sary*, Philadelphia, University of Pennsylvania Press.

Degnbol-Martinusen, John and Poul Engberg-Pedersen (2003), *Aid: Understanding International Development Cooperation*, London, Zed Books.

Drumbl, Mark A. (2000), "Punishment, Postgenocide: From Guilt to Shame to Civis in Rwanda,' *New York University Law Review,* vol. 75, pp. 1221-1326.

Duffield, Mark (2001), *Global Governance and the New Wars: The Merger of Development and Security*, London, Zed Books.

Fierens, Jacques (2005), '*Gacaca* Courts: Between Fantasy and Reality,' *Journal of International Criminal Justice,* vol. 3, pp. 896-919.

Fritz, Nicole, and Alison Smith (2001), 'Current Apathy for Coming Anarchy: Building the Special Court for Sierra Leone,' *Fordham International Law Journal,* vol. 25, pp. 391-430.

Gallagher, Karen (2000), 'No Justice, No Peace: The Legalities and Realities of Amnesty in Sierra Leone,' *Thomas Jefferson Law Review,* vol. 23, pp. 149-198.

Goldstone, Richard J. and Gary Jonathan Bass (2000), 'Lessons from the International Criminal Tribunals,' In Sarah B. Sewall and Carl Kaysen (eds.) *The United States and the International Criminal Court*, Lanham, MD, Rowman and Littlefield.

Grant, Richard and Jan Nijman (1997), 'Historical Changes in U.S. and Japanese Foreign Aid to the Asia-Pacific Region,' *Annals of the Association of American Geographers,* vol. 87, pp. 32-51.

Haile-Mariam, Yacob (1999), 'The Quest for Justice and Reconciliation: The International Criminal Tribunal for Rwanda and the Ethiopian High Court,' *Hastings International and Comparative Law Review,* vol. 22, pp. 668-725.

Heder, Stephen and Brian D. Tittemore (2001), *Seven Candidates for Prosecution: Accountability for the Crimes of the Khmer Rouge*, Washington, DC, War Crimes Research Office, American University.

Hirsch, John L. (2001), *Sierra Leone: Diamonds and the Struggle for Democracy*, Boulder, Lynne Rienner Publishers.

Hosoya, C., N. Ando, Y. Onuma and R. Minear, eds. (1986), *The Tokyo War Crimes Trial: An International Symposium*, New York, Harper & Row.

Howland, Todd and William Calathes (1998), 'The U.N.'s International Criminal Tribunal: Is It Justice or Jingoism for Rwanda? A Call for Transformation,' *Virginia Journal of International Law,* vol. 39, pp. 135-167.

Huxley, Tim (2002), *Disintegrating Indonesia? Implications for Regional Security*, Oxford, International Institute for Strategic Studies.

ICG (2002a), 'Indonesia: Implications of the Timor Trials,' ICG Briefing Paper, 8 May.

ICG (2002b), 'Sierra Leone's Truth and Reconciliation Commission: A Fresh Start?,' 20 December.

Ishay, Micheline R. (2004), *The History of Human Rights: From Ancient Times to the Globalization Era*, Berkeley, University of California Press.

Jarvis, Helen (2002), 'Trials and Tribulations: The Latest Twist in the Long Quest for Justice for the Cambodian Genocide,' *Critical Asian Studies,* vol. 34, pp. 607-624.

Jolliffe, Jill (1978), *East Timor: Nationalism and Colonialism,* Brisbane, University of Queensland Press.

Jones G. (2001), 'Social Policy Issues in East Timor,' In Hal Hilla and João M.

Saldanha (eds.) *East Timor: Development Challenges for the World's Newest Nation*, Singapore, Institute of Southeast Asian Studies.

Kamm, Henry (1998), *Cambodia: Reports from a Stricken Land*, New York, Arcade Publishing.

Katzenstein, Suzanne (2003), 'Hybrid Tribunals: Searching for Justice in East Timor,' *Harvard Human Rights Journal*, vol.16, pp. 245-278.

Kiernan, Ben (1996), *The Pol Pot Regime: Race, Power, and Genocide in Cambodia Under the Khmer Rouge, 1975-1979*, New Haven, Yale University Press.

Kiernan, Ben (2002), 'Introduction: Conflict in Cambodia, 1945-2002,' *Critical Asian Studies,* vol. 34, pp. 483-495.

Kritz, Neil J. (1996), 'Coming to Terms with Atrocities: A Review of Accountability Mechanisms for Mass Violations of Human Rights,' *Law & Contemporary Problems,* vol. 59, pp. 127-131.

Kuperman, Alan J. (2000), 'Rwanda in Retrospect,' *Foreign Affairs,* vol. 79, pp. 94-118.

Leigh, Monroe (1996), 'The Yugoslav Tribunal: Use of Unnamed Witnessed Against Accused,' *American Journal of International Law,* vol. 90, pp. 235-238.

Li, Peter (2003), 'Hirohito's War Crimes Responsibility: The Unrepentant Emperor,' *Human Rights Review,* pp. 3-10.

Linton, Suzannah (2001), 'Cambodia, East Timor and Sierra Leone: Experiments in International Justice,' *Criminal Law Forum,* vol. 12, pp. 185-246.

Linton, Suzannah (2002), 'New Approaches to International Justice in Cambodia and East Timor,' *IRRC*, vol. 84, pp. 93-119.

Macaluso, Daniel J. (2001), 'Absolute and Free Pardon: The Effect of the Amnesty Provision in the Lomé Peace Agreement on the Jurisdiction of the Special Court for Sierra Leone,' *Brooklyn Journal of International Law,* vol. 27, pp. 347-381.

Magnarella, Paul J. (2000), *Justice in Africa: Rwanda's Genocide, Its Courts, and the UN Criminal Tribunal*, Aldershot, Ashgate Publishing.

Mayerfeld, Jamie (2003), 'Who Shall Be Judge?: The United States, the International Criminal Court, and the Global Enforcement of Human Rights,' *Human Rights Quarterly*, vol. 25, pp. 93–129.

Mayall, James (1996), *The New Interventionism 1991-1994: United Nations Experience in Cambodia, former Yugoslavia and Somali,* Cambridge, Cambridge University Press.

McDonald, Avril (2002), 'Sierra Leone's Shoestring Special Court,' *International Review of the Red Cross,* vol. 84, pp. 121-142.

Meltzer, Bernard D. (2002), 'The Nuremberg Trial: A Prosecutor's Perspective,' *Journal of Genocide Research,* vol. 4, pp 561-568.

Mendeloff, David (2004), 'Truth-Seeking, Truth-Telling and Post-Conflict Peacebuilding: Curb the Enthusiasm?,' *International Studies Review*, vol. 6, pp. 355-80.

Mendeloff, David (2004), 'Truth-Seeking, Truth-Telling and Post-Conflict Peacebuilding: Curb the Enthusiasm?,' *International Studies Review, vol.* 6, pp. 355-380.

Meron, Theodor (1997), 'Answering for War Crimes: Lessons from the Balkans,' *Foreign Affairs,* vol. 76, pp. 2-8.

Meron, Theodor (2005), 'Statement by Judge Theodor Meron, President, International Criminal Tribunal for the Former Yugoslavia, to the Security Council,' TM/MOW/976e.

Minear, Richard H. (1971), *Victor's Justice: The Tokyo War Crimes Trials*, Princeton, Princeton University Press.

Mingst, Karen A. and Margaret P. Karns (2000), *The United Nations in the Post-Cold Wart Era*, Bolder, Westview Press.

Minikes, Stephan M. (2003), 'Statement on the International Criminal Tribunal for the Former Yugoslavia,' OSCE, 4 November.

Morgenthau, Hans (1962), 'A Political Theory of Foreign Aid,' *American Political Science Review,* vol. 56, pp. 301-309.

Morris, Madeline H. (1997), 'The Trials of Concurrent Jurisdiction: The Case of Rwanda,' *Duke Journal of Comparative & International Law,* vol. 7, pp. 349-374.

Møse, Erik (2005), 'Completion Strategy of the International Criminal Tribunal for Rwanda,' UN Doc. S/2005/336.

Mundis, Daryl A. (2000), 'Current Developments: Improving the Operation and Functioning of the International Criminal Tribunals,' *American Journal of International Law,* vol. 94, pp. 759-773.

Murphy, Sean D. (1999), 'Progress and Jurisprudence of the International Criminal Tribunal for the Former Yugoslavia,' *American Journal of International Law,* vol. 93, pp. 57-97.

Neier, Aryeh (1998), *War Crimes: Brutality, Genocide, Terror and the Struggle for Justice*, New York, Random House.

Notes (2001), 'Development in the Law: International Criminal Law,' *Harvard Law Review,* vol. 114, pp. 1943-1073.

O'Brien, James C. (1993), 'The International Tribunal for Violations of International Humanitarian Law in the Former Yugoslavia,' *American Journal of International Law,* vol. 87, pp. 639-659.

Office of High Representative (2004), 'War Crimes Chamber Project: Project Implementation Plan Registry Progress Report.'

Opello, Walter C. (1991), *Portugal: From Monarchy to Pluralist Democracy*, Boulder, CO, Westview Press.

Orr, Robert M. (1988), 'The Aid Factor in U.S.-Japan Relations,' *Asian Survey,* vol. 28, p. 740-756.

OSCE (2005a), 'Background Report on National War Crime Prosecutions, Transfer of ICTY Proceedings and Missing Persons.'

OSCE (2005b), 'War Crimes Trials before National Courts of Bosnia and Herzegovina: Progress and Obstacles.'

Piccigallo, Philip R. (1979), *The Japanese on Trial: Allied War Crimes Operation in the East, 1945-1951*, Austin, University of Texas Press.

Pomeroy, Jacqueline (2001), 'Coffee and the Economy in East Timor,' In Hal Hilla and João M. Saldanha (eds.) *East Timor: Development Challenges for the World's Newest Nation*, Singapore, Institute of Southeast Asian Studies.

Pringle, John (2004), 'Meanwhile: The Quiet Retirement of Pol Pot's Cronies,' 17 April, *International Herald Tribune*.

Prunier, Gérard (1995), *The Rwanda Crisis: History of a Genocide*, New York, Columbia University Press.

Rae, James (2003), 'War Crimes Accountability: Justice and Reconciliation in Cambodia and East Timor?,' *Global Change, Peace and Security*, vol. 15, pp. 156-178.

Ratner, Steven R. and Jason S. Abrams (2001), *Accountability for Human Rights Atrocities in International Law: Beyond the Nuremberg Legacy*, Oxford, Oxford University Press.

Roberts, Adam (1998a), 'Implementation of the Laws of War in Late 20th-Century Conflicts Part II,' *Security Dialogue*, vol. 29, pp. 265-280.

Roberts, Adam (1998b), 'Implementation of the Laws of War in Late 20th-Century Conflicts Part I,' *Security Dialogue*, vol. 29, pp. 137-150.

Robertson, Geoffrey (1999), *Crimes Against Humanity: The Struggle for Global Justice*, New York, NY, The New Press.

Rudolph, Christopher (2001), 'Constructing an Atrocities Regime: The Politics of War Crimes Tribunals,' *International Organization*, vol. 55, pp. 655-693.

Sarkin, Jeremy (1999), 'The Necessity and Challenges of Establishing a Truth and Reconciliation Commission in Rwanda,' *Human Rights Quarterly*, vol. 21, pp. 767-823.

Scarf, Michael P. (2004), 'Trading Justice for Efficiency,' *Journal of International Criminal Justice*, vol. 2, pp. 1070-1081.

Schabas, William A. (2005), 'Genocide Trials and *Gacaca* Courts,' *Journal of International Criminal Justice*, vol. 3, pp. 879-895.

Schindler, Dietrich (2003), 'International Humanitarian Law: Its Remarkable Development and its Persistent Violation,' *Journal of the History of International Law*, vol. 5, pp. 165-188.

Schrader, Peter J., Steven W. Hook and Bruce Taylor (1998), 'Clarifying the Foreign Aid Puzzle: A Comparison of American, Japanese, French, and Swedish Aid Flows,' *World Politics*, vol. 50, pp. 294-323.

Shinoda, Hideaki (2002), 'Peace-Building by the Rule of Law: An Examination of Intervention in the Form of International Tribunals,' *International Journal of Peace Studies*, vol. 7, pp. 41-58.

Shraga, Daphna and Ralph Zacklin (1996), 'The International Criminal Tribunal for Rwanda,' *European Journal of International Law*, vol. 7, pp. 501-518.

Smith, Anthony L. (2004), 'East Timor: Elections in the World's Newest Nation,' *Journal of Democracy*, vol. 15, pp. 145-161.

Synder, Jack and Leslie Vinjamuri, (2003), 'Trials and Errors: Principle and Pragmatism in Strategies of International Justice,' *International Security*, vol. 28, pp. 5-44.

Taylor, Telford (1992), *The Anatomy of the Nuremberg Trials*, New York, Alfred A. Knopf.

Tisch, Sarah J. and Michael B. Wallace (1994), *Dilemmas of Development Assistance: The What, Why, and How of Foreign Aid*, Boulder, CO, Westview Press.

Tusa, Ann and John Tusa (1984), *The Nuremberg Trial*, New York, Atheneum.

United Nations Doc. (2000), *Report of the Secretary-General on the Establishment of a Special Court for Sierra Leone*. UN SCOR. 52nd Sess., Doc. S/2000/915.

United Nations Doc. (2002a), *Seventh Annual Report of the International Criminal Tribunal for the Prosecution of Persons Responsible for Genocide and Other Serious Violations of International Humanitarian Law Committed in the Territory of Rwanda and Rwandan Citizens Responsible for Genocide and Other Such Violations Committed in the Territory of Neighbouring States between 1 January and 31 December 1994*, A/57/163-S/2002/733.

United Nations Doc. (2002b), *Report of the International Tribunal for the Prosecution of Persons Responsible for Serious Violations of International Humanitarian Law Committed in the Territory of the Former Yugoslavia since 1991*, A/57/379–S/2002/985

United Nations High Commission for Refugees (2003), 'The Balkans,' (available at www.unhcr.ch/cgi-bin/texis/vtx/Balkans).

United Nations Legal Council (2002), *Negotiations between the UN and Cambodia Regarding the Establishment of the Court to Try Khmer Rouge Leaders: Statement by UN Legal Counsel Hans Corell*.

Vassall-Adams, Guy (1994), *Rwanda: An Agenda for International Action*, Oxford, Oxfam Publishing.

Wasserstrom, Richard (1974), 'The relevance of Nuremberg' in *War and Moral Responsibility: A Philosophy and Public Affairs Reader*, Marshall Cohen, etal, eds. Princeton, NJ, Princeton University Press.

Wang, T.Y. (1999), 'U.S. Foreign Aid and UN Voting: An Analysis of Important Issues,' *International Studies Quarterly*, vol. 43, pp. 199-210.

Wells, Donald A. (1991), *War Crimes and Laws of War*, New York, NY, University Press of America.

Vinjamuri, Leslie and Jack Snyder (2004), 'Advocacy and Scholarship in the Study of International War Crimes Tribunals and Transitional Justice,' *Annual Reviews of Political Science*, vol.7, pp. 345-362.

Yacoubian, George S., Jr. (1998), 'Sanctioning Alternatives in International Criminal Law: Recommendations for the International Criminal Tribunals for Rwanda and Yugoslavia,' *World Affairs*, vol. 161, pp. 48-55.

Zoglin, Katie (2005), 'The Future of War Crimes Prosecutions in the Former Yugoslavia: Accountability or Junk Justice?,' *Human Rights Quarterly*, vol. 27, pp. 41-77.

Index

www.ingramcontent.com/pod-product-compliance
Lightning Source LLC
LaVergne TN
LVHW011132300926
849160LV00008B/612

* 9 7 8 1 1 3 8 6 1 9 3 3 3 *